Paula Deen
LOVE AND BEST DISHES

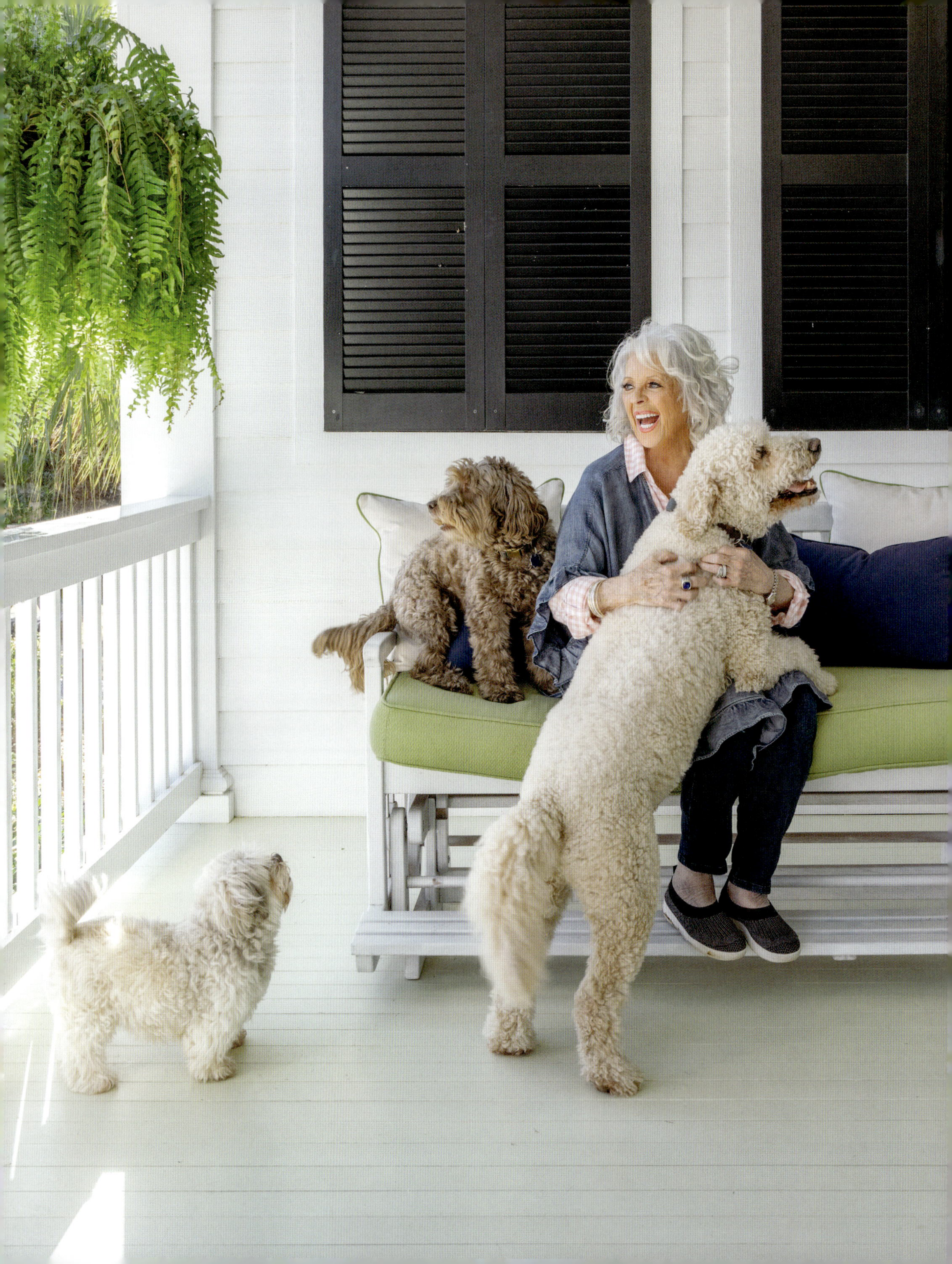

Paula Deen
LOVE AND BEST DISHES

*A Collection of Recipes, Stories,
and Letters from the Heart*

83 press

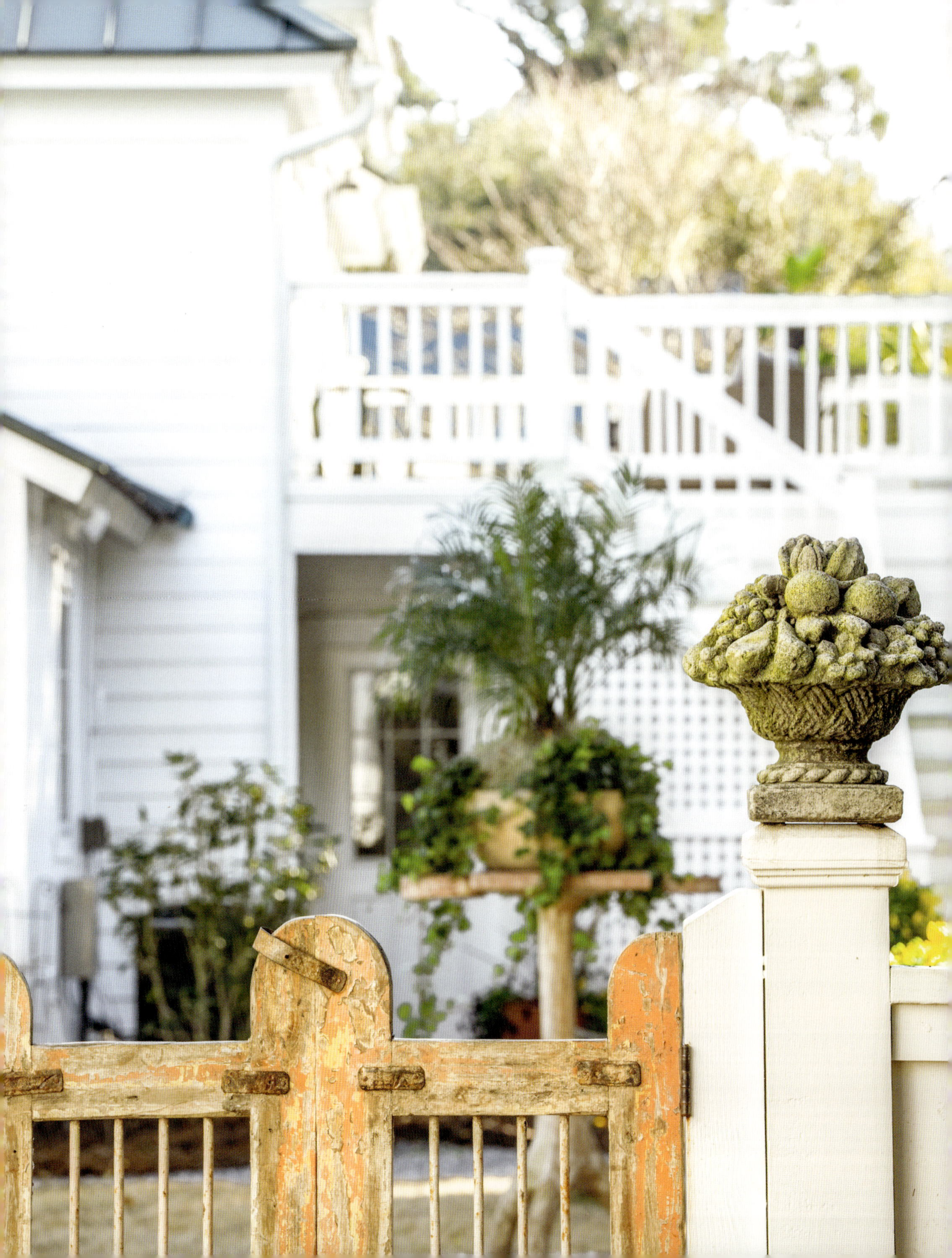

ALSO BY *Paula Deen*

The Lady & Sons Savannah Country Cookbook

The Lady & Sons, Too! A Whole New Batch of Recipes from Savannah

The Lady & Sons Just Desserts

Paula Deen & Friends: Living It Up, Southern Style

Paula Deen's Kitchen Classics

Paula Deen Celebrates!

Paula Deen: It Ain't All About the Cookin'

Christmas with Paula Deen

Paula Deen's Kitchen Wisdom and Recipe Journal

Paula Deen's My First Cookbook

Paula Deen's The Deen Family Cookbook

Paula Deen's Cookbook for the Lunch-Box Set

Paula Deen's Savannah Style

Paula Deen's Southern Cooking Bible

Paula Deen Cuts the Fat

Paula Deen's Air Fryer Cookbook

Favorite Recipes of the Lady & Her Friends

At the Southern Table with Paula Deen

Paula Deen's Southern Baking

83 press

Copyright © 2023 by 83 Press

All rights reserved. No part of this book may be reproduced or transmitted in any form or by any means, electronic or mechanical, including photocopying, or by any information storage and retrieval system, without permission in writing from 83 Press. Reviewers may quote brief passages for specific inclusion in a magazine or newspaper.

83 Press
2323 2nd Avenue North
Birmingham, Alabama 35203
83press.com

ISBN: 979-8-9874820-0-1
Printed in China

CONTENTS

INTRODUCTION	8
DEDICATION	10
FOREWORD	12
TRIBUTES	14

CHAPTER ONE
Albany Roots 16
Take a trip down memory lane with Paula as she shares stories from her childhood at River Bend.

CHAPTER TWO
Passed Down 42
Learn more about Paula's early life and the heritage recipes she still cherishes.

CHAPTER THREE
Becoming a Momma 70
Paula tells stories from her early years of motherhood and her favorite recipes that remind her of raising her boys—Jamie and Bobby.

CHAPTER FOUR
Settling into Savannah 90
In a tribute to her beautiful city, Paula talks about her first experiences in Savannah and shares all the flavors and flair it has to offer.

CHAPTER FIVE
The Lady & Sons 112
From running The Bag Lady out of her home to her very first location in downtown Savannah, dive into recipes from Paula's original restaurant.

CHAPTER SIX
Taking Flight 140
Small-town living turns to stardom! What seemed like overnight success came from years of hard work and perseverance.

CHAPTER SEVEN
Family Matters 156
Paula talks about meeting her husband Michael and gives her best advice for blending families.

CHAPTER EIGHT
Life's Lessons 188
Paula reflects on the past, shares her hopes for the future, and shows her gratitude to her fans and supporters.

CHAPTER NINE
Guinny and Her Loves 204
Grandbabies galore! Paula, a.k.a. Guinny, dotes on her precious grandchildren and reveals the recipes they love most.

CHAPTER TEN
Staying Present 220
Paula talks about what life looks like today and what keeps her busy and brings her the most joy.

TO MY GRANDCHILDREN	250
RECIPE INDEX & CREDITS	252
ACKNOWLEDGEMENTS	254

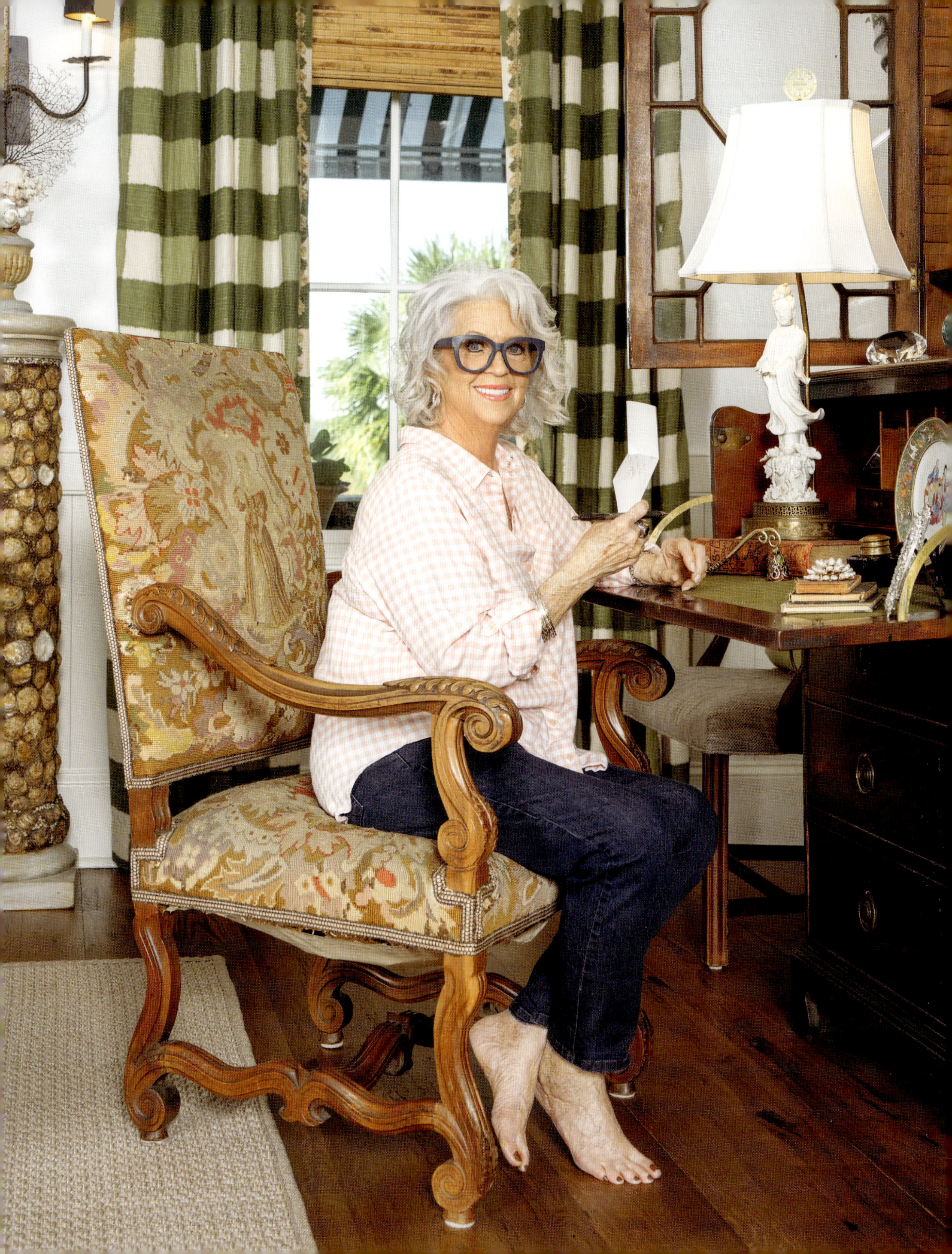

INTRODUCTION

I so vividly remember the day my very first cookbook was printed. I had taken all my recipes from running The Bag Lady and The Lady & Sons and turned them into a book for my customers at the restaurant. I figured that if they loved our food, they might want to have some of the recipes for themselves.

There was a print shop down the street from the restaurant. I told them, "I want 5,000 copies!" Everybody thought I was crazy for buying that many, but once I knew the more I ordered, the cheaper they'd be, I wanted 5,000.

The print shop called me once a few copies were ready for me to look at. I grabbed Jamie and Bobby, and we all walked down the street together from the restaurant.

Jamie stopped suddenly and said, "Momma, you're going to cry when you see this book." I said, "Oh no, I'm not! I'm just so happy it's done. I might laugh but I definitely won't cry."

We walked a few more steps and he put out his hand and said, "I bet you $100 this book makes you cry." I said, "You're on, big boy!"

When we got to the print shop, the printer handed us each a copy. Jamie told me to turn to a certain page, and sure enough, I started to cry. Jamie and Bobby had secretly written a dedication to me and given it to the printer to include. It was so sweet and touching. I definitely lost that bet! We went on to sell out that first cookbook and make many more together.

Now, I am so blessed and thrilled to be sharing this new cookbook with my readers. I hope you will find some happy tears of your own along with new favorite recipes to make for your loved ones.

Love and Best Dishes, Y'all!

Top photo, back row, from left to right: Bobby, Linton, Claudia, Sandy, Aunt Peggy, Bubbles, Phil, John, Michelle, Henry, Daniel, Madison, Ashley, Anthony, Eddie, Jack, and Jamie. **Top photo, front row, from left to right:** Olivia, Amelia, Michael, Bennett, me, Corrie, Davis, Brooke, and Matthew. Not pictured: Brian and Sullivan. **Left photo:** Aunt Peggy, me, and Eddie.

10 LOVE AND BEST DISHES | DEDICATION

Dedicated TO MY FANS AND SUPPORTERS

When I decided to write this cookbook, I knew right away that I wanted it to be a love letter of sorts to my fans. They have loved me, supported me, and seen me through the hardest times in my life. The process of writing this book and reflecting on old recipes and memories was an experience I will never forget.

Thank you for walking down memory lane with me, and thank you for being a part of my story.

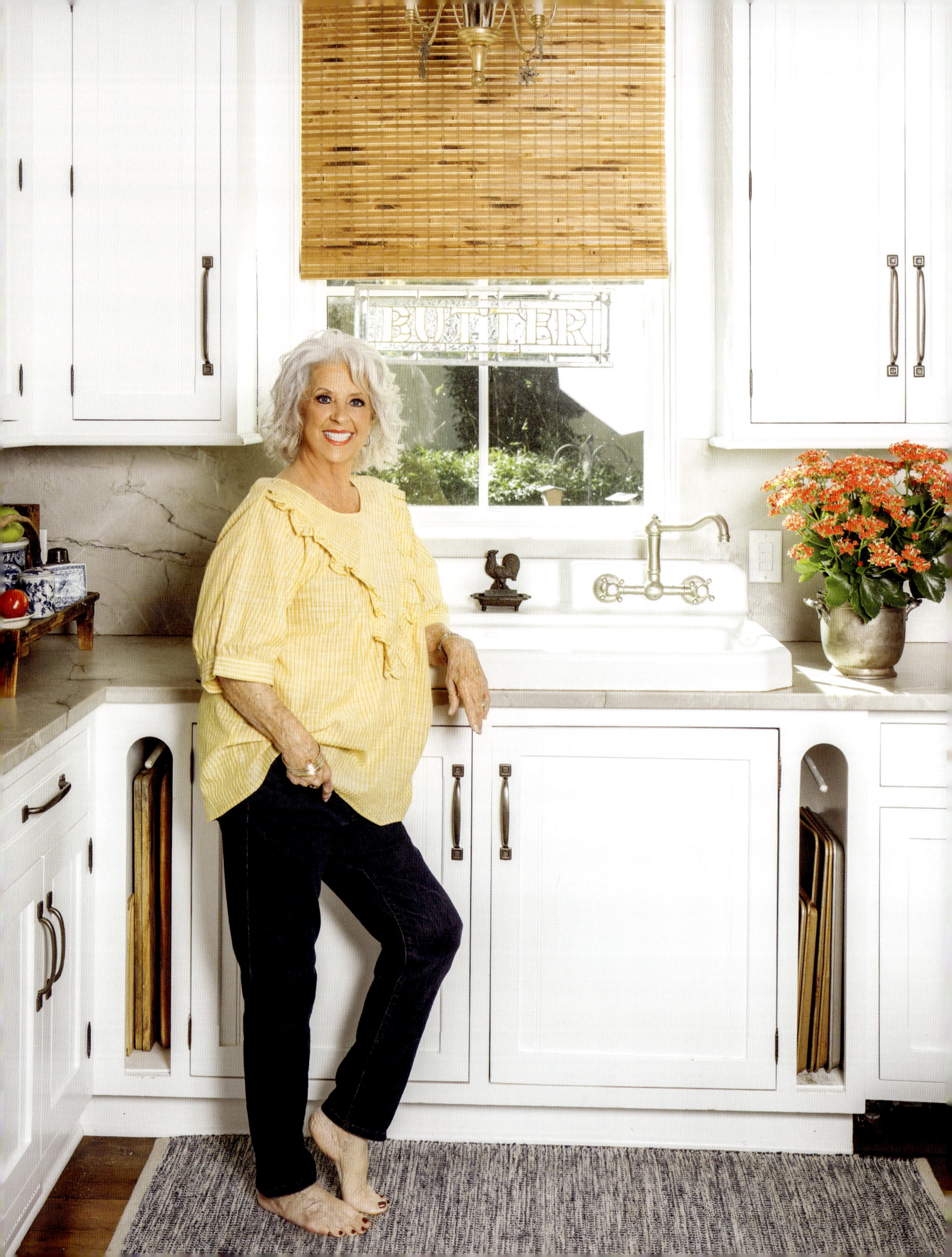
BUTTER

FOREWORD

To know her is to love her.

Years ago, we met Paula Deen while we were on location at Kim's Miss Mississippi USA pageant. Like millions of other people, we felt as if we already knew Paula. After all, she had spent considerable time in our home—through our TV. We quickly found that her sweet smile and infectious laugh were as warm in person as you'd imagine they would be, and she makes you feel as though she has known you your whole life. An enduring friendship was born.

Not long after that, Paula and Michael invited us to their Savannah home, where we shared stories, laughs, and some of the best food ever to meet a plate. It was that night that we first learned about her deep love for our country and devotion to those who serve in our military. Lee invited Paula to join us at an event honoring wounded veterans, and we watched as she loved on America's bravest and their spouses with tears in those sparkling blue eyes. Paula shows up in a really big way for our wounded veterans and cares for them from the deepest place in that big heart of hers.

Paula made her own path to success during a time when so many opportunities were not available to women. As she achieved success through her own hard work and determination, she became a beacon of light, warmth, and goodness to so many! Paula is the real deal—she is smart, savvy, and full of Southern grit and determination while also remaining compassionate, kind, and generous with her time. Over the years, we have shared many adventures and heartfelt moments with Paula, her family, and her team. From her insistence that our children promise to call her Aunt Paula to the many events honoring our military and their families to her hosting the tribute event honoring 40-plus years of Lee's career and music.

We consider it such an honor to write these few words introducing Paula's newest cookbook. We are all so lucky to be able to learn from more of Paula's down-to-earth wisdom, life lessons, and cooking! Thank you, Paula for being the strong woman of faith that you are and for your unwavering love for this great country (and butter). We are looking forward to more nights in your kitchen as well as Paula Deen's Family Kitchens and continued fun times. God bless you, Paula Deen, and your beautiful family—you're an American treasure, and we are so very blessed by your friendship.

With love,
Lee and Kim Greenwood

Tributes TO PAULA

Few things in life are more satisfying and heartwarming than sitting down to a home-cooked meal that Mom made just for you.

Just the aroma of her offerings can bring back memories of years gone by. All mothers have this power, and it's best not to take it for granted. Now, if your mom is Paula Deen, those food memories are amplified.

In good times and bad, our family has spent many a morning, noon, and night around Momma's kitchen table solving all the world's problems over a meal. She's been THE best mom, and now grandmother to my triplets. She feeds our bodies and souls with her food and is providing my children with lifelong memories of their grandmother's exceptional cooking.

They're too young yet to know how lucky they are. Thank heavens we've got an amazing collection of recipes and scores of cookbooks from "Guinny" that will always be in our kitchen. I'm happy that this latest book is not only filled with recipes that, until now, have been unpublished but also stories not yet shared.

With this book, you have access to stories and recipes handed down over time by my mother, Paula, and some of her closest friends and family. She truly is "the queen of Southern cuisine." Enjoy this latest offering from my mom and find out what I know so well—the lady can cook.

We love you, Momma!

Bobby, Claudia, Amelia, Olivia, and Linton

I've always said that I was the luckiest man in television because of Paula Deen. In the summer of 2000, I went to her small family-run restaurant in Savannah after I was told her cooking actually made people cry from the sweet memories it brought back to them. I walked into her 60-seat gem of a restaurant and immediately discovered a woman, a family, a story, and a love for food that was busting to be shared.

TV was made for people like Paula and her boys, Bobby and Jamie—warm, authentic, and funny as a fart (that's a Paula-ism by the way). I spent the next dozen or so years laughing, listening, and eating with Paula and her family while we happened to create more than 600 wonderful episodes of her shows. I never worked less in my life. She's a force, a gift, and a great woman. I bless the day she let me come on the ride she was destined to have.

Gordon Elliott

(Producer of *Paula's Home Cooking, Paula's Best Dishes,* and *Paula's Party* on Food Network)

Dear Paula,

I remember when you were named Southern Lady of the Year for *Southern Lady* magazine in 2004. You and your family attended the Southern Lady Celebration, and we spent a weekend in Destin, Florida, together. We had a wonderful time, and the ladies who attended the celebration loved you! At the end of the final day, I presented you with a mock cover and content sheet for a new magazine, *Cooking with Paula Deen*. You laughed in your very Southern way and said, "No one wants to read about me." But we knew they would! We printed 1,000,000 copies of issue 4. Yes, Paula, your readers love you!

Congratulations, Momma!

Looking back on our 34 years of business as a family is always a reason to celebrate. To succeed in this industry is a great achievement. To succeed as an untrained family on the brink of destruction? Unheard of. Were we lucky at times? Certainly. Did we sacrifice every day to do better? To serve with a sense of gratitude? Yes! Every day, we did.

How do we measure our success? The awards, the recognition, the money? While those are all tangible measures of success, I believe that the three of us sticking together as a family and as a business may be our greatest accomplishment.

You were always quick to share how proud of me you are, and looking back over the years, it turns out that's the thing that matters the most to me. I love you, Mom, and congratulations on your new book. I can't wait to see what we do together next.

Love,

Jamie, Brooke, Jack, Matthew, and Davis

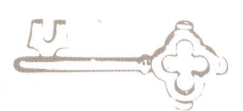

Love,

Phyllis Hoffman DePiano

Phyllis Hoffman DePiano
(Chairman of the Board of Hoffman Media, publisher of *Cooking with Paula Deen*)

TRIBUTES | LOVE AND BEST DISHES   15

CHAPTER ONE

ALBANY ROOTS

You could probably say I had an unusual childhood. My Grandmother and Grandfather Paul owned a place in Albany, Georgia, called River Bend. It was like a little resort in that it had a restaurant, skating rink, swimming pool, a motel, and cabins. It sat right on US 19 and was like our town's little theme park, but a lot of northern folks who were headed to Florida—the snowbirds—would stop and stay a lot, too.

River Bend had the only swimming pool that Albany folks had access to. So, on Saturdays, the churches would bring busloads of children out there. Oh man, I thought they were all coming to play with me! I couldn't wait for them to get there. They'd pack great picnic lunches, and one family would bring their ice cream maker. I just thought, "Well, they must want me there, too!" So, I would join them in the evenings for ice cream.

It was like I had my very own playground that came with friends. My Aunt Trina was only three and a half years older than me, so we were like sisters rather than aunt and niece. We didn't make a move without the other, but she would also get me in a lot of trouble.

My parents ended up buying the service station across the street from River Bend, and my brother Bubba and I lived there with them. We sold everything from blankets and lamps to groceries—it was like a general store. We had our little living quarters in the back of the station, but the only bathrooms we had were the outdoor ladies' and men's rooms. The men's room had the only shower, and that was what we had to use to get clean.

So, Trina and I had the swimming pool, skating rink, and restaurant all at our disposal. I think I had a wonderful childhood, but as I grew up and tried to talk to my mother about those days, she said, "Paula, I'm sorry. I can't talk about that, it's just too painful." Looking back, my mother was changing oil, pumping gas, and selling groceries out of the service station all while trying to raise her children.

It was also way out away from the rest of town, so it was deserted at night. My mother said some nights she would get so scared because she'd see men walking around out there and Daddy would be out, probably playing cards with his buddies, but she didn't let me see any of that fear.

Momma was a waitress at the River Bend restaurant before we bought the service station, and my Aunt Peggy was a lifeguard at the pool. Everybody in the family worked there and supported the business. My grandmother was a cook, and she had a wonderful kitchen and made the most delicious Southern foods—fried chicken, fresh green beans—it was heaven! When you went out the back door of the kitchen, there were picnic tables under a tin roof. When I would start bothering her too much, my grandmother would get a watermelon and slice it up and send Trina and me outside to eat it and get out of her hair.

There was also a jukebox in the River Bend dining room, and I always thought it would be a good idea to get out my hula skirt and do the hula for our guests. I just know they loved this little brat running around dancing for them while they were trying to eat!

Opposite page, left to right: My momma when she was about 15 and Aunt Peggy—these two were only two years apart but look at the height difference! Little me with a Momma-given bowl haircut. Me in Daddy's arms in front of the sign for River Bend. **This page, top to bottom:** The menu from the River Bend Restaurant. Aunt Trina and me. The River Bend swimming pool. My beautiful Grandma Paul.

OLD-FASHIONED TEA CAKES

This classic Southern recipe will quickly become one of your new favorites. I bet you can't eat just one!

Makes about 75

- 1 cup salted butter, softened
- 2 cups sugar
- 2 large eggs
- ½ cup whole buttermilk
- 4 cups all-purpose flour
- 2 teaspoons baking powder
- 1 teaspoon baking soda

1. Preheat oven to 350°. Line several large rimmed baking sheets with parchment paper.

2. In a large bowl, beat butter and sugar with a mixer at medium speed until fluffy, 2 to 3 minutes, stopping to scrape sides of bowl. Add eggs, one at a time, beating well after each addition. Beat in buttermilk until combined.

3. In a medium bowl, stir together flour, baking powder, and baking soda. Gradually add flour mixture to butter mixture, beating at low speed until combined and stopping to scrape sides of bowl. (Dough will be soft.)

4. Turn out dough onto a heavily floured surface, and roll to ¼-inch thickness. Using a 2-inch round cutter dipped in flour, cut dough, rerolling scraps as needed. Place 1 inch apart on prepared pans.

5. Bake until tops are dry and edges are golden brown, 10 to 12 minutes. Let cool on pans for 2 minutes. Remove from pans, and let cool completely on wire racks.

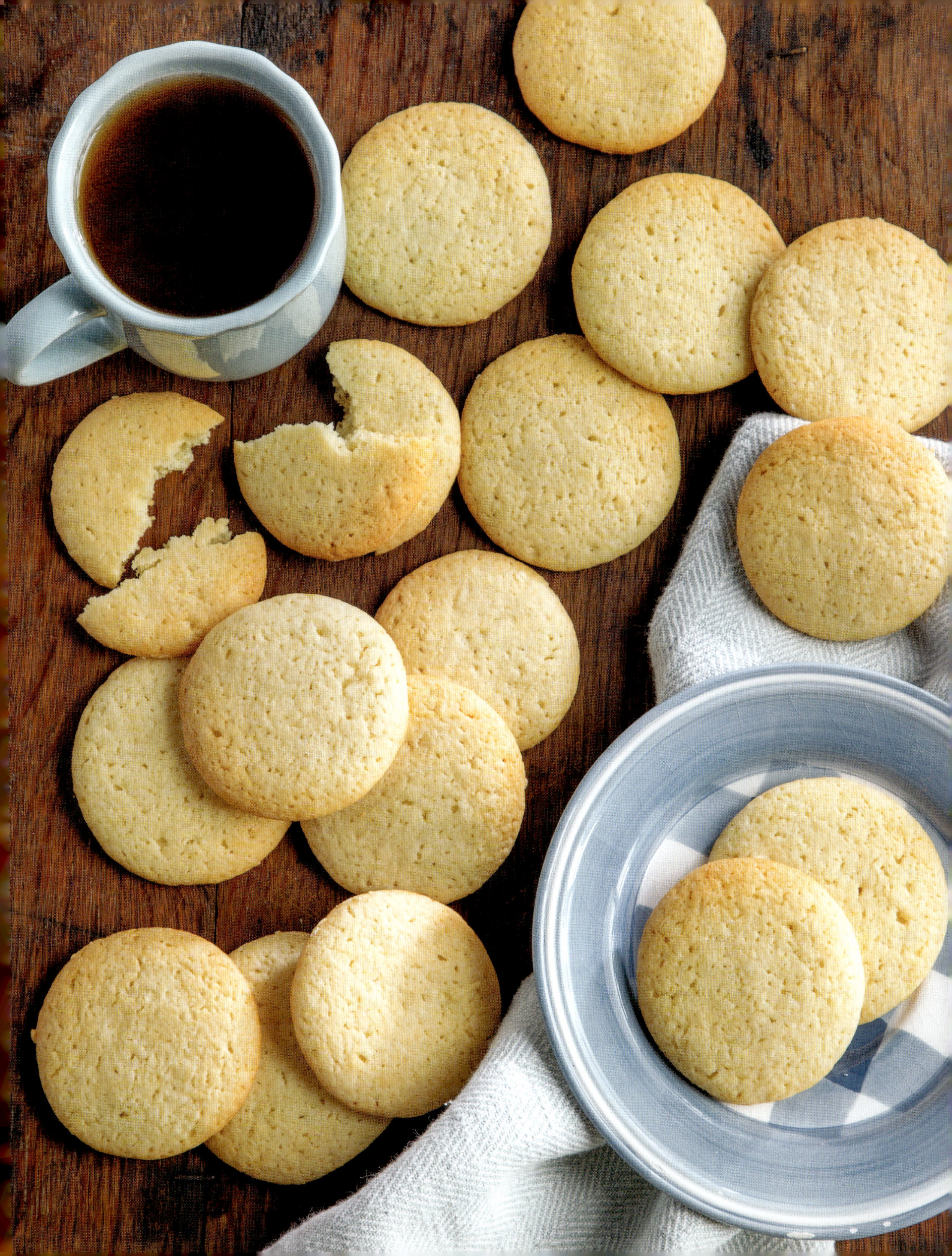

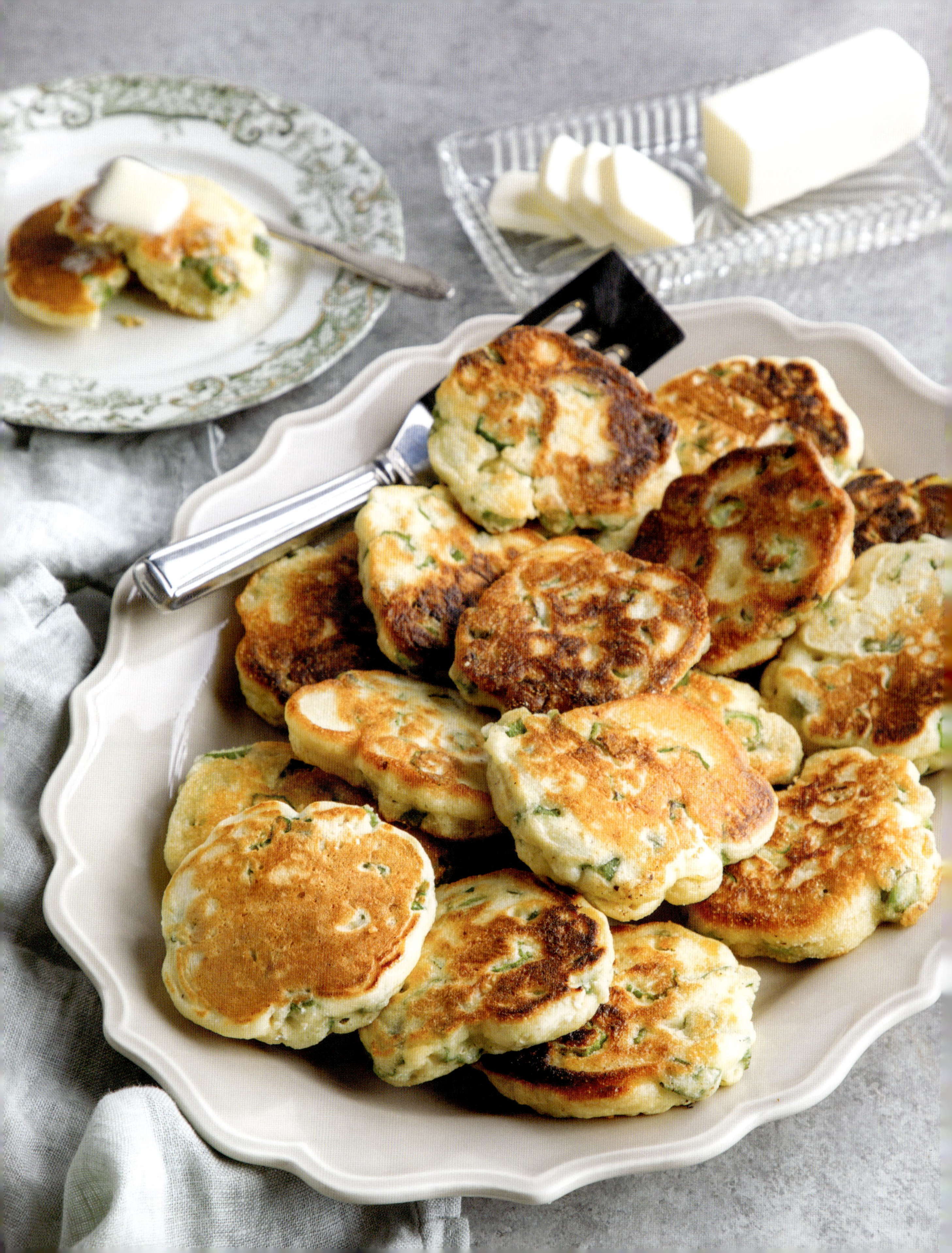

OKRA HOECAKES

These hoecakes are crispy on the outside but fluffy on the inside and take everyone's favorite fried vegetable to the next level. I love mine slathered with butter!

Makes 18 to 20

- 1 cup self-rising flour
- 1 cup self-rising buttermilk cornmeal mix
- ¾ cup whole buttermilk
- ⅓ cup water
- 2 large eggs
- 1 tablespoon sugar
- 1 (16-ounce) bag frozen whole okra, sliced ⅛ inch thick
- Vegetable oil, for frying
- Butter, to serve

1. In a large bowl, stir together flour, cornmeal, buttermilk, ⅓ cup water, eggs, and sugar until combined. Fold in okra.

2. In a large cast-iron skillet, pour oil to a depth of ¼ inch, and heat over medium heat. Drop batter by 3 tablespoonfuls 1 inch apart into hot oil. Cook until browned and crisp, about 2 minutes per side. Remove from skillet, and let drain on paper towels. Repeat with remaining batter. Serve with butter.

My parents, Bubba, and me on Easter Sunday.

Recipe Tip

Slice your okra while it's still frozen. This will make it easier to get very thin slices.

ALBANY ROOTS | LOVE AND BEST DISHES

BARBECUE SAUCES

My daddy's (Earl) barbecue sauce was famous in my family for a reason! A little tangy, with tons of flavor—it's perfect served with chicken. Uncle George's sauce is just as delicious but a more classic take.

EARL'S BARBECUE SAUCE

Makes 4 cups

1½ cups apple cider vinegar
1 stick salted butter
Juice of 2 lemons
2 tablespoons chili powder
2 tablespoons celery seed
1 to 2 tablespoons Worcestershire sauce
1 teaspoon salt
1 teaspoon ground black pepper

1. In a medium saucepan, combine all ingredients, and bring to a boil over medium heat. Reduce heat, and simmer for 20 minutes.

UNCLE GEORGE'S BARBECUE SAUCE

Makes 4 cups

---

1 cup apple cider vinegar
⅓ cup Worcestershire sauce
⅓ cup peanut butter
1 stick salted butter
Juice of 2 lemons
2 tablespoons chili powder
2 tablespoons celery seed
1 teaspoon salt
1 teaspoon ground black pepper

1. In a medium saucepan, bring all ingredients to boil over medium heat, and cook, stirring frequently, until peanut butter is melted.

UNCLE GEORGE'S BARBECUE SAUCE

EARL'S BARBECUE SAUCE

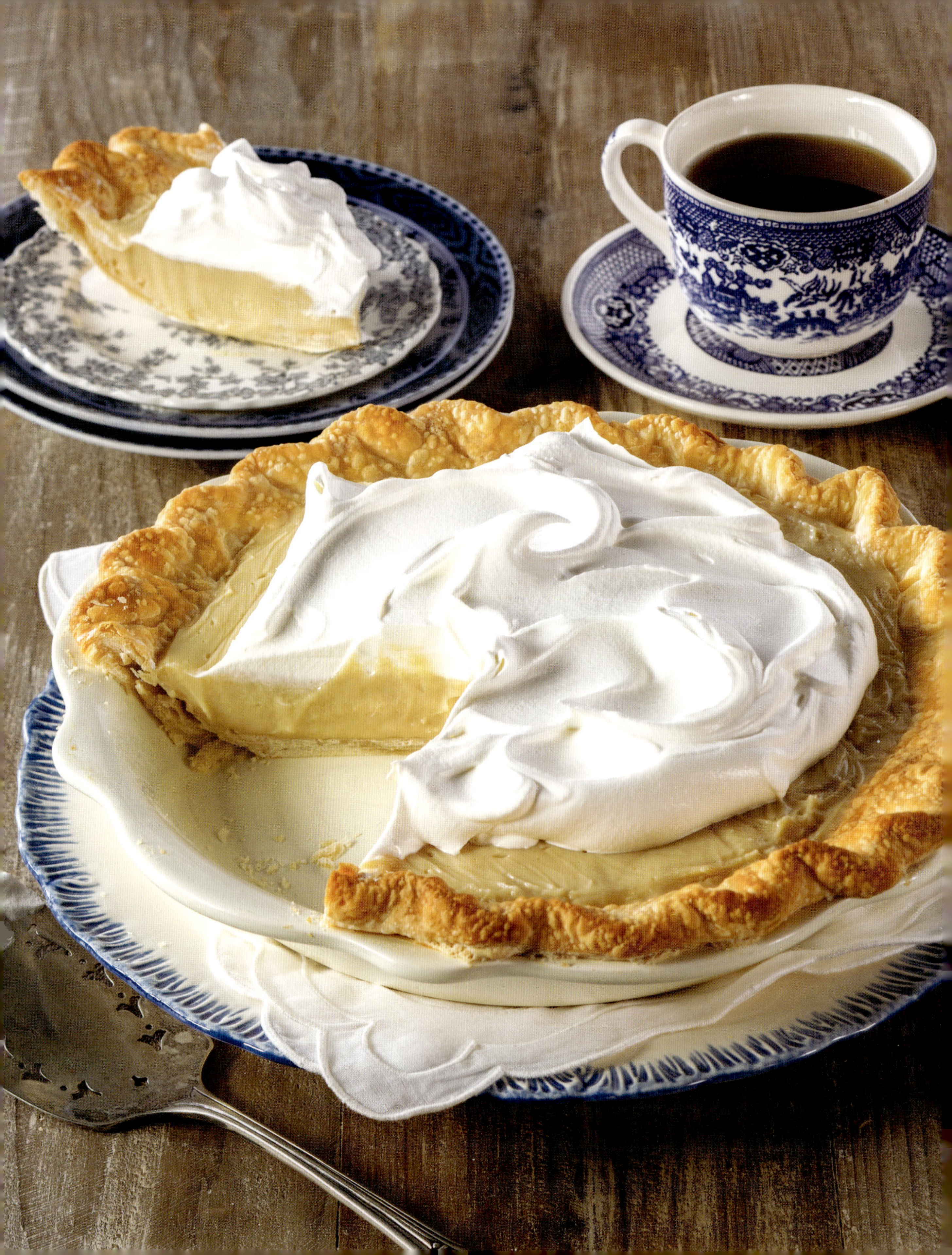

RICH BUTTERSCOTCH PIE

This creamy and delicious pie calls for basic pantry items so you can whip it up anytime!

Makes 1 (9-inch) pie

- ½ (1.14-ounce) package refrigerated piecrust
- 2½ cups whole milk
- 6 tablespoons salted butter, divided
- ½ cup all-purpose flour
- ¾ cup firmly packed light brown sugar
- ¼ cup granulated sugar
- 3 large egg yolks, lightly beaten
- 1 teaspoon vanilla extract
- 2 cups sweetened whipped cream

1. Bake piecrust in a 9-inch pie plate according to package directions.

2. In a small saucepan, heat milk over medium heat just until bubbles form around sides of pan. (Do not boil.) Remove from heat.

3. In a medium saucepan, melt 5 tablespoons butter over medium heat. Stir in flour, forming a smooth paste. Stir in sugars. Cook, stirring constantly, until sugars are melted and mixture is smooth. Gradually add hot milk.

4. In a small bowl, whisk egg yolks. Slowly add ½ cup hot milk mixture, whisking constantly. Add egg yolk mixture to remaining hot milk mixture, and bring to a boil, whisking constantly; cook for 3 minutes, whisking constantly. Whisk in vanilla and remaining 1 tablespoon butter. Pour into prepared crust. Cover with a piece of plastic wrap, pressing wrap directly onto surface of filling, and refrigerate.

5. Just before serving, spread whipped cream onto filling, swirling as desired.

My sweet momma
and my brother, Bubba

BUTTER NUT CAKE

My Grandmother Hiers was known for this perfectly frosted butter nut cake! Every time we went to Winterhaven, Florida, to visit Grandmother and Granddaddy Hiers, this cake was surely on her sideboard.

Makes 1 (8-inch) cake

- 1 cup all-vegetable shortening
- 2 cups sugar
- 4 large eggs
- 1 tablespoon butter nut flavoring
- 2 cups self-rising flour
- 1 cup whole milk

FROSTING

- 1 cup salted butter, softened
- 1 (2-pound) package confectioners' sugar
- 2 tablespoons whole milk
- 1 tablespoon butter nut flavoring
- 1 cup chopped pecans

1. Preheat oven to 350°. Spray 3 (8-inch) round cake pans with baking spray with flour.

2. For cake: In a large bowl, beat shortening and sugar with a mixer at medium speed until fluffy, 3 to 4 minutes, stopping to scrape sides of bowl. Add eggs and butter nut flavoring, and beat well. Gradually add flour alternately with milk, beginning and ending with flour, beating at low speed until combined after each addition. Spread batter into prepared pans.

3. Bake until a wooden pick inserted in center comes out clean, 25 to 30 minutes. Let cool in pans for 10 minutes. Remove from pans, and let cool completely on wire racks.

4. For frosting: In a large bowl, beat butter with a mixer at medium speed until creamy. Gradually add confectioners' sugar and milk, beating at low speed until combined. Beat in flavoring. Stir in pecans. Spread frosting between layers and on top and sides of cake.

Recipe Tip

I find my butter nut flavoring online. It is easy to find on Amazon!

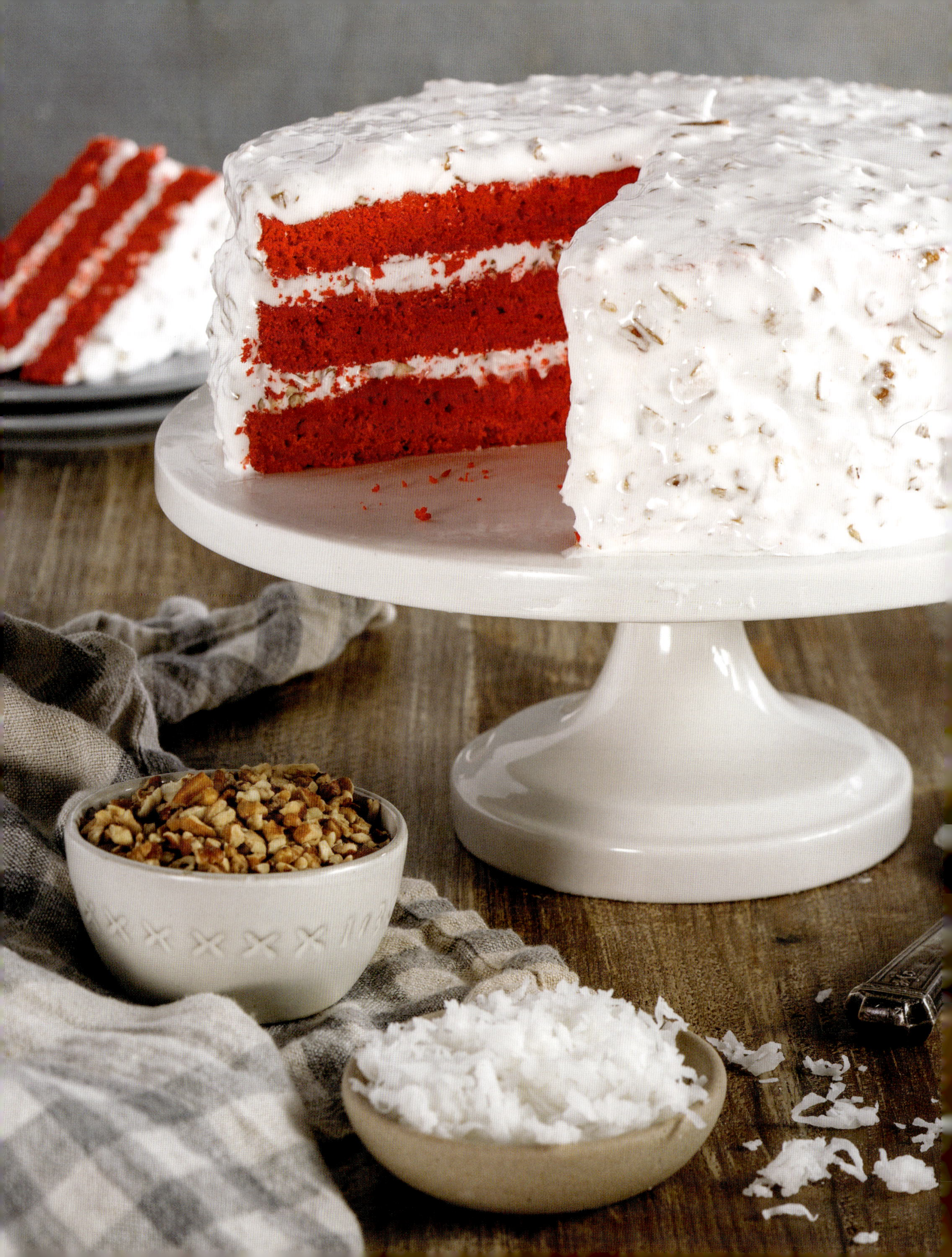

RED VELVET CAKE

My Grandmother Paul used to make this perfect red velvet cake.

Makes 1 (9-inch) cake

- 2 large eggs
- 2 cups sugar
- 1 tablespoon unsweetened cocoa powder
- 2 (1-ounce) bottles red food coloring
- 1 cup salted butter, softened
- 1 teaspoon vanilla extract
- 2½ cups cake flour
- 1 teaspoon salt
- 1 cup whole buttermilk
- 1 tablespoon vinegar
- ½ teaspoon baking soda

ICING

- 1½ cups sugar
- 2 large egg whites
- 5 tablespoons cold water
- 2 tablespoons light corn syrup
- 1 cup mini marshmallows
- 1 cup shredded sweetened coconut
- 1 cup chopped pecans

1. Preheat oven to 350°. Spray 3 (9-inch) round cake pans with baking spray with flour.

2. For cake: In a medium bowl, whisk eggs; whisk in sugar.

3. In the bowl of a stand mixer, stir together cocoa and food coloring. Add egg mixture, butter, and vanilla; using the paddle attachment, beat at medium speed until smooth.

4. In another medium bowl, sift together flour and salt. With mixer on medium-low speed, add flour mixture to cocoa mixture alternately with buttermilk.

5. In a small bowl, combine vinegar and baking soda, and stir into batter. Divide batter among prepared pans.

6. Bake until a wooden pick inserted in center comes out clean, 20 to 25 minutes. Let cool in pans for 10 minutes. Remove from pans, and let cool completely on wire racks.

7. For icing: In the top of a double boiler, combine sugar, egg whites, 5 tablespoons cold water, and corn syrup. Cook over simmering water, beating with a mixer at medium speed, until smooth. Add marshmallows, and beat at high speed until mixture is thick and glossy, about 7 minutes. Remove from heat. Spread icing between layers and on top and sides of cake.

BUBBA'S BEER BISCUITS

Most of my brother's cooking was usually confined to his charcoal grill, but he always made an appearance in the kitchen to whip up these biscuits. I love you lots, brother.

Makes 12

- 4 cups all-purpose baking mix*
- 1 (12-ounce) can pale ale
- 2 tablespoons to ¼ cup sugar
- 2 tablespoons salted butter, melted
- Honey butter, to serve

1. Preheat oven to 400°. Spray a 12-cup muffin pan with baking spray with flour.

2. In a large bowl, stir together baking mix, beer, sugar, and melted butter until dry ingredients are moistened. Divide batter among prepared muffins cups.

3. Bake until wooden pick inserted in the center comes out clean, 15 to 20 minutes. Serve with honey butter.

After my grandparents sold River Bend, my family and I moved into town. I started fifth grade at Magnolia Elementary School. My first years of school were spent in a tiny country elementary school that was so small, two grades at a time would share a classroom.

A sweet older man named Les worked with Momma at the service station, and he also helped take care of Bubba. If there was a day Les couldn't come in, I told Momma I could take Bubba to school with me. So, there I was, a 9-year-old bringing my 2-year-old brother on the school bus with me. He was so good. He'd sit on my lap with me at my desk and then run and play at recess and have lunch with me. Things were so different then—families just did what they could to survive and take care of each other.

Daddy died when I was 19 and Bubba was only 12. Daddy died early in the morning, and that afternoon, Bubba had a baseball game. There was nothing Daddy loved more than watching his son play baseball, so Momma told him he should go on and play in the game. I like to think he hit a homerun for Daddy that day.

Recipe Tip

*I used Paula Deen Original Recipes Mix. You can order this online or you can use Bisquick.

SKILLET BLACK-EYED PEAS

My Aunt Trina gave me this recipe! It is full of flavor and perfect for pairing with your favorite cornbread.

Makes about 4 servings

- ½ pound smoked sausage, diced
- 1 (15.8-ounce) can black-eyed peas, drained
- 1 (10.5-ounce) can French onion soup
- 1 cup water
- ½ cup long-grain rice
- 1 tablespoon salted butter
- Garnish: chopped green onion

1. In a large skillet, cook sausage over high heat, stirring occassionally, until browned. Add peas, soup, 1 cup water, rice and butter, and bring to a boil. Cover, reduce heat, and simmer for 25 minutes, adding additional water as needed. Garnish with green onion, if desired.

My dear family,

No words can express what you mean to me, but I hope that reading this book will give you as much joy as writing it has given me. Spending time looking at old photos, reading handwritten recipes, and sharing stories from my life has filled my cup. I am so, so blessed. Thank you for your love and support. This collection is a celebration for us all!

Much Love,
Paula

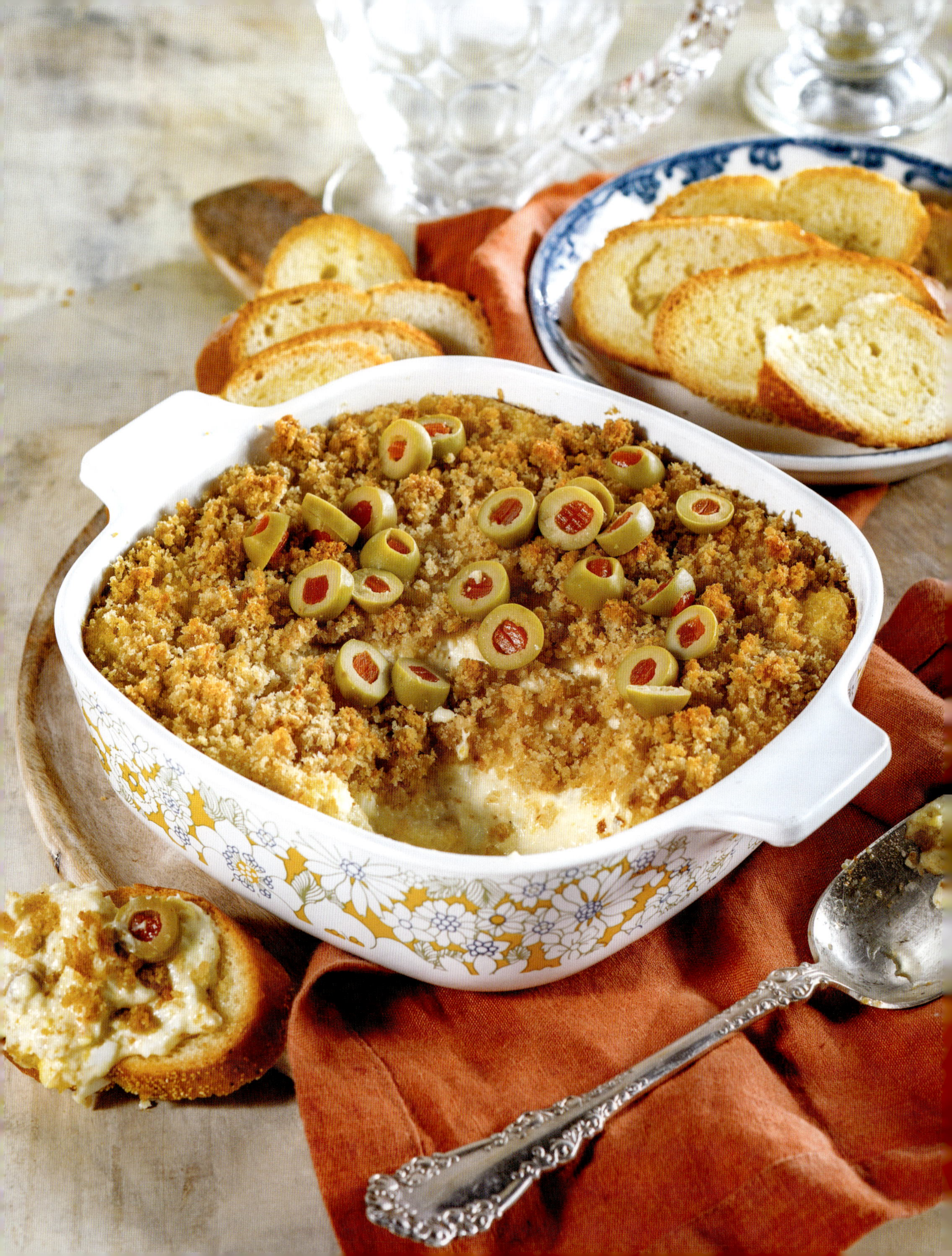

LUNCHEON SEAFOOD BAKE

Whether you're serving your best girlfriends a tasty lunch or carrying a dish to a party, this seafood bake is quick, creamy, and wonderful served with crusty bread.

Makes 6 servings

- 1 (6.5-ounce) can crabmeat, drained and picked free of shell
- 1 cup soft bread crumbs, divided
- 1 cup mayonnaise
- ¾ cup whole milk
- 6 hard-cooked eggs, peeled and finely chopped
- ⅓ cup chopped onion
- ¾ teaspoon salt
- 2 tablespoons butter, melted
- ¼ cup sliced stuffed green olives

1. Preheat oven to 350°.

2. Break crabmeat into chunks. In a large bowl, stir together crab, ½ cup bread crumbs, mayonnaise, milk, eggs, onion, and salt.

3. In a small bowl, stir together melted butter and remaining ½ cup bread crumbs.

4. Pour crab mixture into a 1-quart baking dish, and top with bread crumb mixture.

5. Bake until browned and bubbly, 20 to 25 minutes. Top with olives. Serve with crusty bread.

Left: Me as a little girl standing on US 19.
Right: My daddy's car lot, Earl Hiers Motors. I can't count how many times I drove there to beg my daddy for a quarter for some gas.

ALBANY ROOTS | LOVE AND BEST DISHES

HOMESTYLE BANANA PUDDING

My momma would have this delicious dessert sitting up on the counter for when Bubba and I would run in from school. She would time it just right so it would still be warm, and it was our absolute favorite.

Makes 8 to 10 servings

- 1 cup plus 3 tablespoons sugar, divided
- ⅓ cup all-purpose flour
- ¼ teaspoon salt
- 2½ cups whole milk
- 4 large eggs, separated and room temperature
- 1 tablespoon salted butter
- 1 teaspoon vanilla extract
- 5 cups vanilla wafers
- 4 medium bananas, sliced ¼ inch thick

1. In a medium saucepan, combine 1 cup sugar, flour, and salt.

2. In a medium bowl, whisk together milk and egg yolks until combined. Add milk mixture to sugar mixture, whisking until smooth. Cook over medium heat, whisking constantly, until mixture is very thick, 10 to 12 minutes. Remove from heat, and whisk in butter and vanilla.

3. In a 2½-quart baking dish, layer half of vanilla wafers, half of bananas, and half of custard. Repeat layers.

4. Preheat oven to 350°.

5. In a large bowl, beat egg whites with a mixer at medium-high speed until soft peaks form. Gradually add remaining 3 tablespoons sugar, beating until stiff peaks form. Spread meringue over custard.

6. Bake until golden brown, 12 to 15 minutes. Serve warm, or cover and refrigerate.

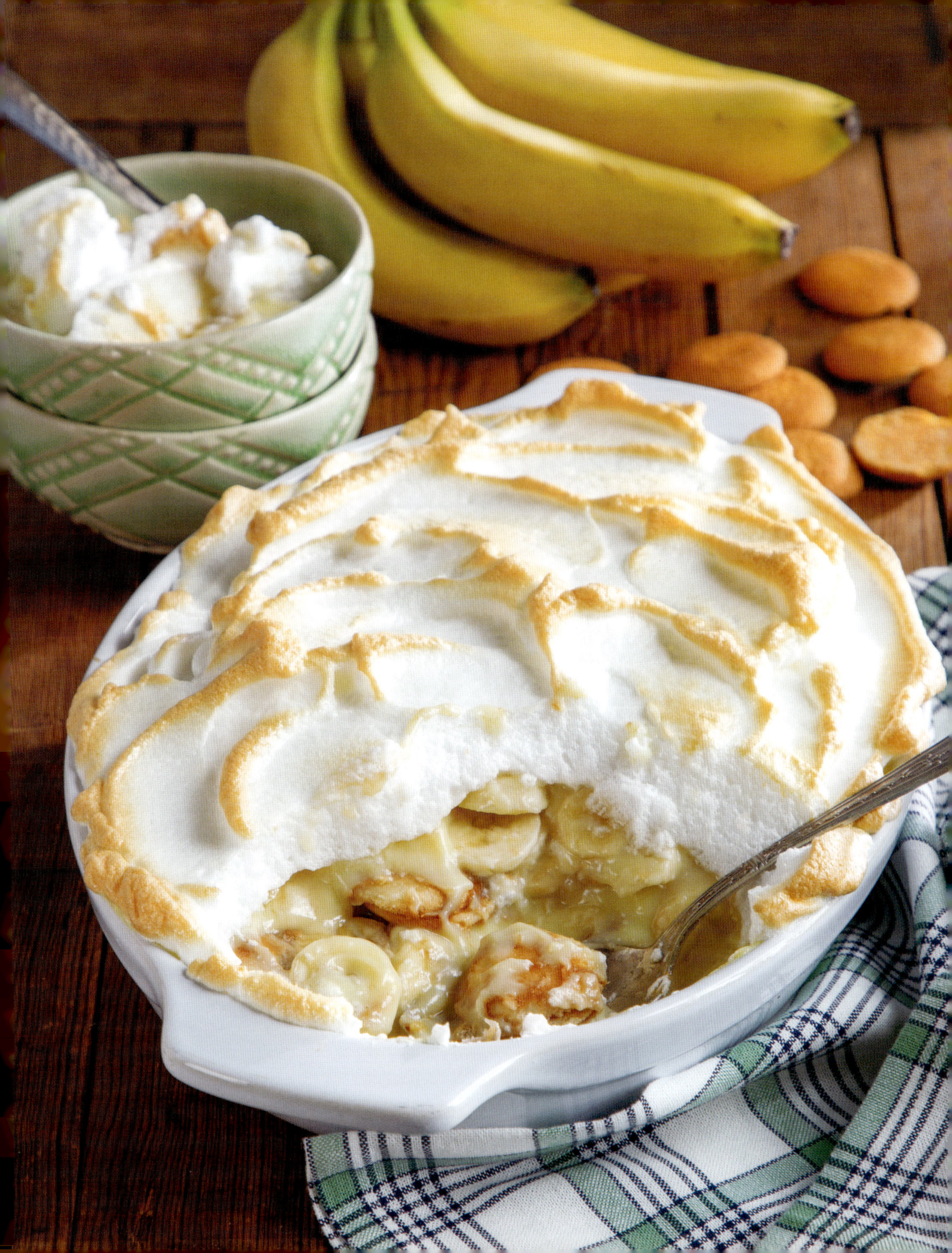

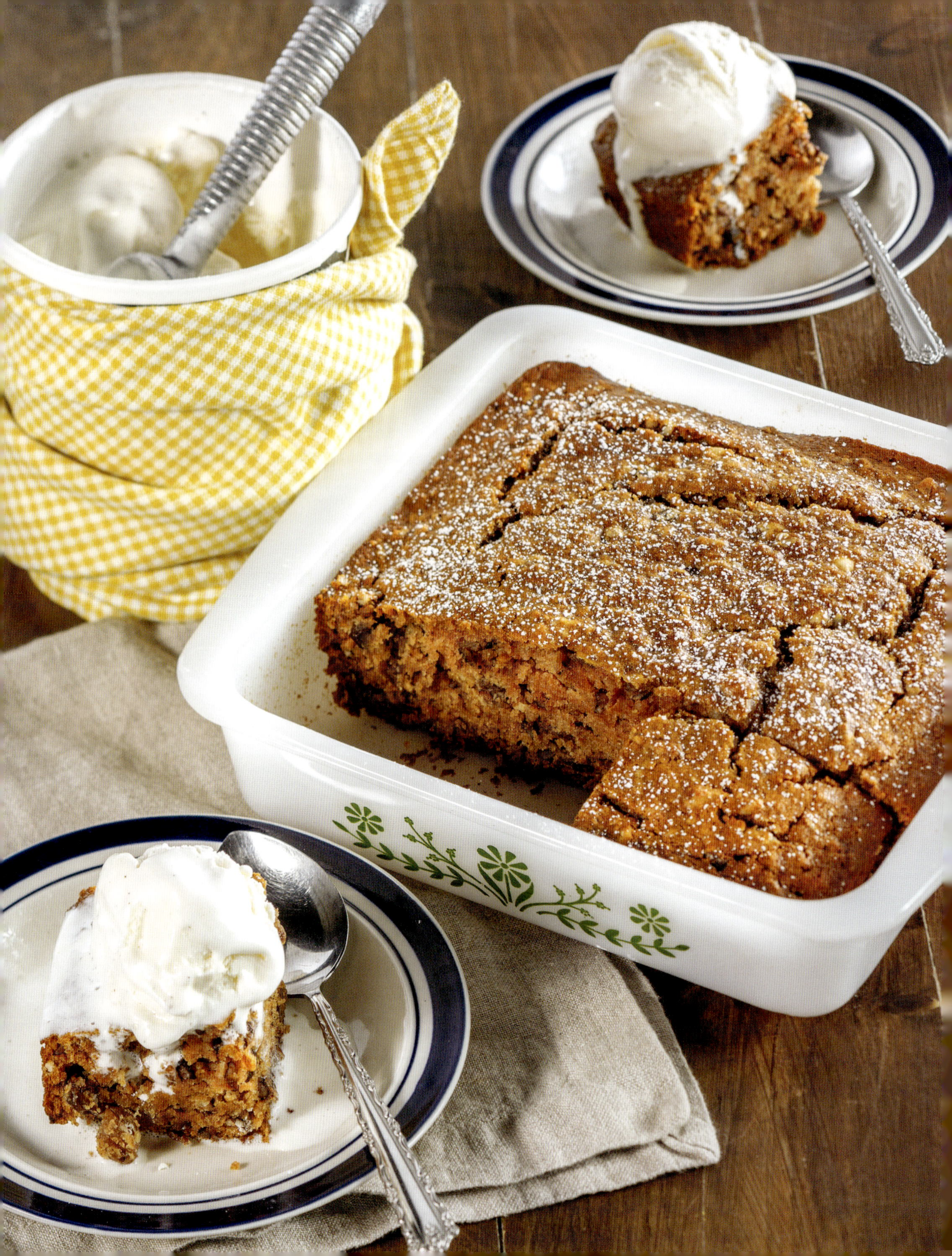

JOHNNY APPLESEED CAKE

There are many versions of this cake, just like there are many tales of Johnny Appleseed. I love this version because you can enjoy it at any time of day, especially with ice cream!

Makes 1 (8-inch) cake

- 2 cups all-purpose flour
- 1 cup sugar
- 1 teaspoon salt
- 1 teaspoon ground cinnamon
- ½ teaspoon ground nutmeg
- ¼ teaspoon ground cloves
- 1 cup raisins
- 1 cup chopped pecans
- ½ cup salted butter, melted
- 1½ cups unsweetened applesauce
- 2 teaspoons baking soda
- Ice cream, to serve

1. Preheat oven to 350°. Lightly spray an 8-inch square baking dish with cooking spray.

2. In a large bowl, sift together flour, sugar, salt, cinnamon, nutmeg, and cloves. Stir in raisins, pecans, and melted butter.

3. In a small bowl, combine applesauce and baking soda. Add applesauce mixture to flour mixture, stirring until combined. Pour batter into prepared pan.

4. Bake for 30 minutes. Cover with foil, and bake until a wooden pick inserted in center comes out clean, 10 to 15 minutes more. Serve with ice cream.

Grandmother and Granddaddy Paul in Daytona Beach in front of the motel they owned, The Casbah. This would have been in the early 1960s. I was 15 the last time I got to spend a summer there with them, and I loved it.

ELVIS PRESLEY CAKE

Anyone who knows me knows about my deep love for Elvis Presley. I've made recipes celebrating him before, and this cake is special because it is my version of his favorite pineapple cake! They say his grandmother used to make him a pineapple poke cake every time he visited her.

Makes 1 (13x9-inch) cake

- 1 (15.25-ounce) box yellow cake mix
- 1 (15.25-ounce) can crushed pineapple in juice
- 1 cup granulated sugar
- 1 (8-ounce) package cream cheese, softened
- 2¼ cups confectioners' sugar, sifted
- Garnish: toasted sweetened flaked coconut

1. Spray a 13x9-inch baking dish with baking spray with flour.

2. Prepare cake mix according to package directions; pour into prepared dish.

3. Bake as directed. Using a wooden skewer, poke holes all over hot cake.

4. In a small saucepan, combine crushed pineapple and granulated sugar. Cook over medium heat, stirring frequently, until sugar dissolves, about 6 minutes. Pour over warm cake. Let cake cool completely on a wire rack.

5. In a medium bowl, beat cream cheese with a mixer at medium speed until smooth. Gradually beat in confectioners' sugar until smooth. Gently spread over cooled cake. Garnish with coconut.

When my first husband, Jimmy Deen, and I were married, we went to see Elvis Presley—my absolute idol!—in concert. I didn't have any money for a new outfit but was determined to look my best. I bought some fabric and made a blouse and a pair of what we called hot pants—short shorts—and paired the outfit with my knee-high white leather boots! The show was in Atlanta at the Omni, and we had the very last seats in the house. I just knew I could impress Elvis with my new outfit and he'd dump Priscilla for me! Obviously, that didn't happen, but it was worth a shot!

Bubba acting like Elvis.

CHAPTER TWO

PASSED DOWN

After my grandparents sold River Bend, my family and I moved into town. Life became so different! We were no longer living in a business but in an actual neighborhood where I had plenty of other kids to play with. As I grew into a teenager, I didn't give two flips about school in the academic sense, but I was very social and had a lot of friends. My daddy always told me he better never hear about me being mean or rude to anyone and that I was no better than the next fella. He expected me to show kindness to everybody.

My only plans for after high school were to either become a model or just go ahead and get married and have children. When I was 18, I was madly in love with the man who would become my first husband—Jimmy Deen. The first time I saw him, I was walking down the halls of school. I remember he had his arm around another girl, and I thought, "That might be the best-looking boy I ever laid my eyes on." I didn't think anything of it after that because I was already going steady with a guy named Ronnie.

One day, Ronnie and I had to go to a service station because he was having problems with his Volkswagen Beetle. Guess who was there to work on his car! That pretty boy I'd seen in the hallway! Turns out he worked there after school and on weekends, and I thought, "Oh, my gosh, he is so good-looking."

One night after Ronnie and I had been broken up, I had a date with a guy named Johnny, and my friend Marilyn had a date with Jimmy. We made it a double date, and Johnny and I sat in the backseat while Jimmy and Marilyn sat up front. Jimmy was driving, but he spent nearly the whole drive turned around to the backseat talking to me. He'd practically asked me out before we got out of the car.

My mother later told me that when Jimmy came to the front door to pick me up for a date and meet her, she went to her bedroom and cried after we left. She took one look at him and knew that it was all over for me—she knew I was head over heels in love.

For graduation, Momma and Daddy gifted me a two-week trip to New York City to visit my Uncle Bob. Honey, I'd never been anywhere, and I was so excited! Uncle Bob was Daddy's baby brother, and he was a model. I used to see him on TV doing commercials sometimes—oh, he was so handsome. Uncle Bob really wanted me to continue to stay with him so he could help me break into modeling, and sometimes, I wish I'd done that instead of running back to be with Jimmy. Truth be told, though, I didn't have what it took. I wasn't tall enough or probably thin enough, but back then, curves were in fashion.

My daddy had a different dream for me. He told me, "Blue, I want you to go to school at Florida State. They've got a great dental hygienist program, and that's a wonderful profession for a woman." I said, "Daddy! I am not smelling people's bad breath for the rest of my life." So, I got married instead.

Opposite page, left to right: Bubba and me heading to school. Me, Paula Ann. Me striking a pose for the camera. **This page, top to bottom:** Me in my graduation gown. My escort and me when I was crowned the March of Dimes Queen.

"Blue"

Daddy called me "Blue" because my hair was so black that it had a blue shine. I've noticed that when I talk about my family and childhood, I mainly talk about my father. He and I were so much alike. I always knew Bubba was my momma's favorite, but I also knew I was my daddy's favorite.

BAYOU CASSEROLE

This is a favorite from Aunt Trina. It is hearty and so flavorful! It would be perfect to serve on a late Sunday morning.

Makes 8 to 10 servings

- ½ large loaf day-old French bread, torn into small pieces
- 6 tablespoons salted butter, melted
- ½ pound Genoa salami, julienned
- 2 cups shredded Monterey Jack cheese
- 10 large eggs
- 1½ cups whole milk
- ⅓ cup dry white wine
- 3 green onions, minced
- 2 teaspoons Dijon mustard
- ¼ teaspoon ground black pepper
- ¼ teaspoon crushed red pepper
- 1 cup sour cream
- Freshly grated Parmesan cheese

1. In a 3-quart baking dish, place bread pieces. Drizzle melted butter over bread; scatter salami and Monterey Jack on top.

2. In a large bowl, whisk together eggs, milk, wine, green onion, mustard, and peppers until frothy. Pour over bread mixture. Cover and refrigerate overnight.

3. Let casserole stand at room temperature for 30 minutes.

4. Preheat oven to 325°.

5. Bake, covered, for 1 hour until set. Spread sour cream on top of casserole, and sprinkle with Parmesan; bake uncovered until lightly browned, about 10 minutes more.

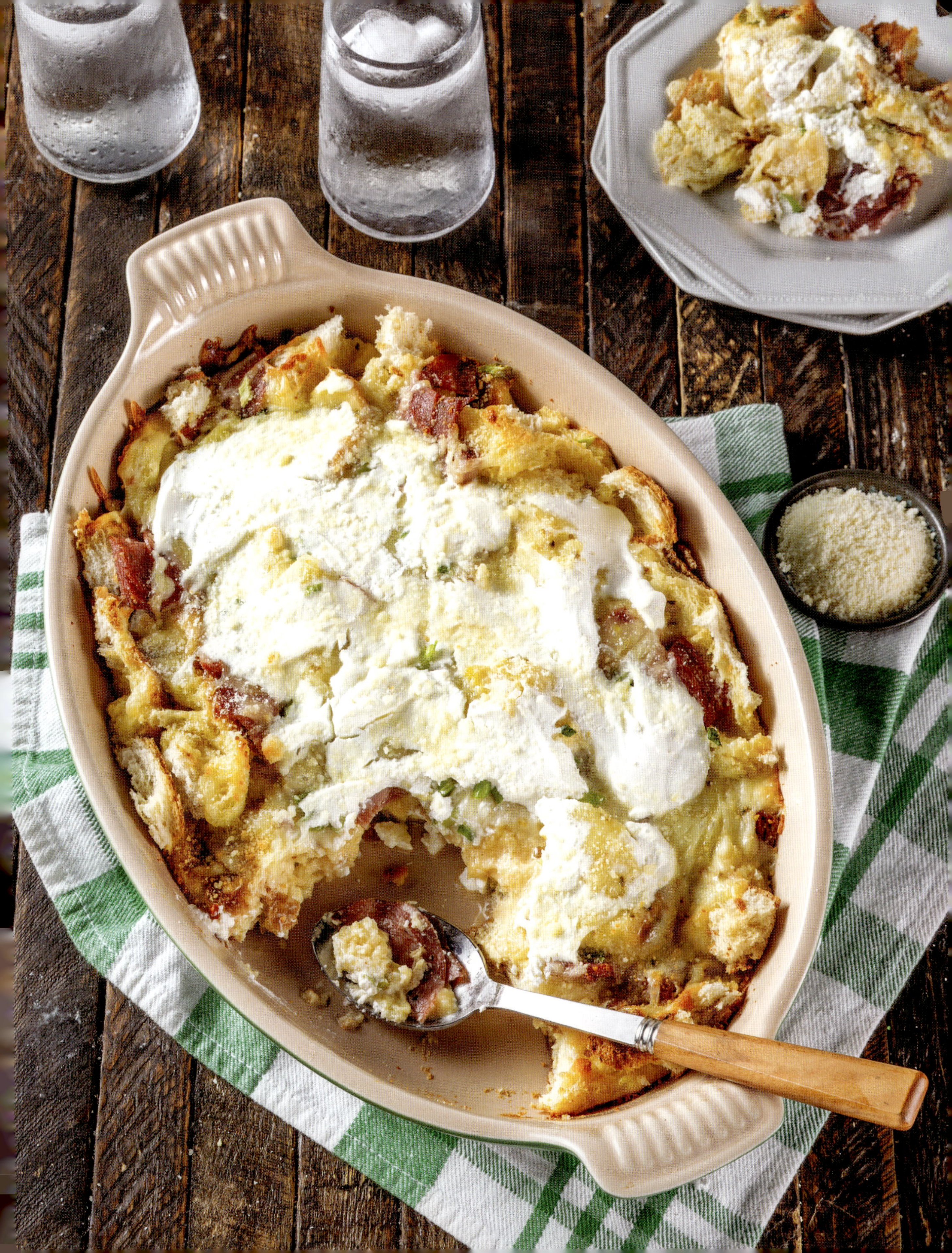

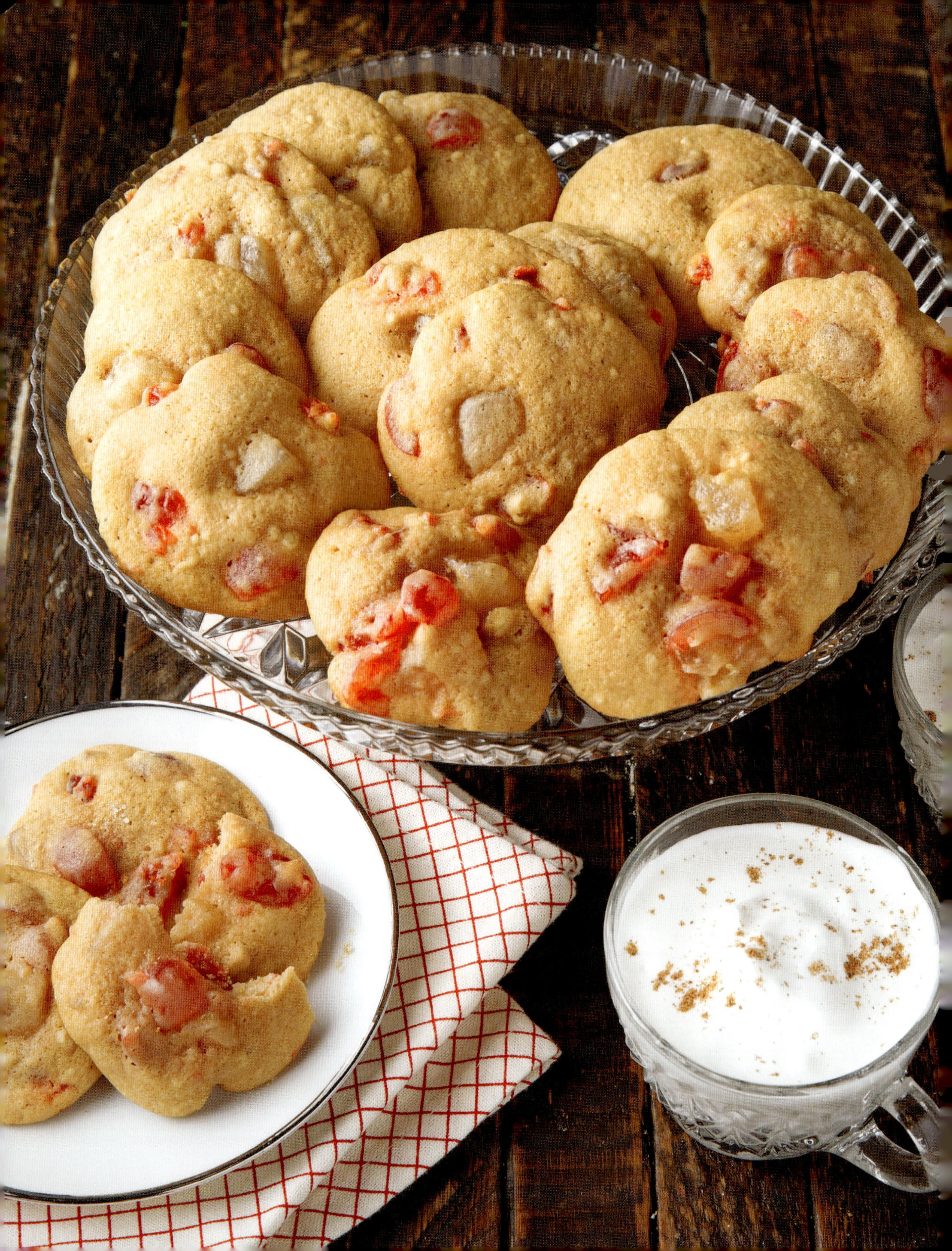

AUNT TRINA'S FRUITCAKE COOKIES

My Aunt Trina was only three and a half years older than me, so we were more like sisters than aunt and niece. When her momma first told her she was going to be an aunt, she thought she meant "ant" and got under the table to start crawling around like a bug and crying.

Makes 50

- 1 cup salted butter, softened
- 1 cup firmly packed dark brown sugar
- 3 large eggs
- 1 teaspoon vanilla extract
- 3 cups self-rising flour, sifted
- 1 teaspoon baking soda
- 1 teaspoon ground cinnamon
- ½ cup whole milk
- 2 cups candied cherries, chopped
- 6 slices candied pineapple, chopped into small pieces

1. Preheat oven to 350°. Line 4 baking sheets with parchment paper.

2. In the bowl of a stand mixer fitted with the paddle attachment, beat butter and brown sugar at medium speed until creamy, 2 to 3 minutes, stopping to scrape sides of bowl. Add eggs, one at a time, beating well after each addition. Beat in vanilla.

3. In a medium bowl, whisk together flour, baking soda, and cinnamon. With mixer on low speed, add flour mixture to butter mixture in two additions alternately with milk, beginning and ending with flour mixture, beating just until combined after each addition. Fold in fruit. Using a 1½-tablespoon spring-loaded scoop, scoop dough onto prepared pans.

4. Bake until light golden brown and set around edges, 10 to 12 minutes. Let cool on pans for 3 minutes. Remove from pans, and let cool completely on wire racks.

CORRIE'S EGGNOG

My momma, Corrie, used to make this wonderful eggnog every holiday season. She made Bubba and me our own nonalcoholic version as kids, but once I was a teenager, she'd let me sample a little bit with the bourbon. It's a very special memory.

Makes about 12 servings

- 6 large pasteurized eggs, separated
- ¾ cup sugar, divided
- 2 cups cold heavy whipping cream
- 2 cups cold whole milk
- 1 cup bourbon
- 2 teaspoons vanilla extract

Garnish: ground nutmeg, cinnamon sticks

1. In large bowl, beat egg yolks and ½ cup sugar with a mixer at medium speed until thickened.

2. In another large bowl, using clean beaters, beat egg whites with a mixer at high speed just until soft peaks form; gradually add remaining ¼ cup sugar, beating just until stiff peaks form.

3. In another large bowl, beat cold cream with a mixer at high speed until thickened; fold into egg yolk mixture. Fold in egg white mixture. Stir in cold milk, bourbon, and vanilla. Freeze until chilled. Garnish with nutmeg and cinnamon sticks, if desired.

My sweet momma. She was such a softspoken and ladylike woman. I always thought she was so strong, and never understood how she managed raising Bubba and me on US 19 while also running a business. I wouldn't have been able to stand the worry. I was 23 when she passed away and my brother was only 16. I cherish my memories of her more than I can express.

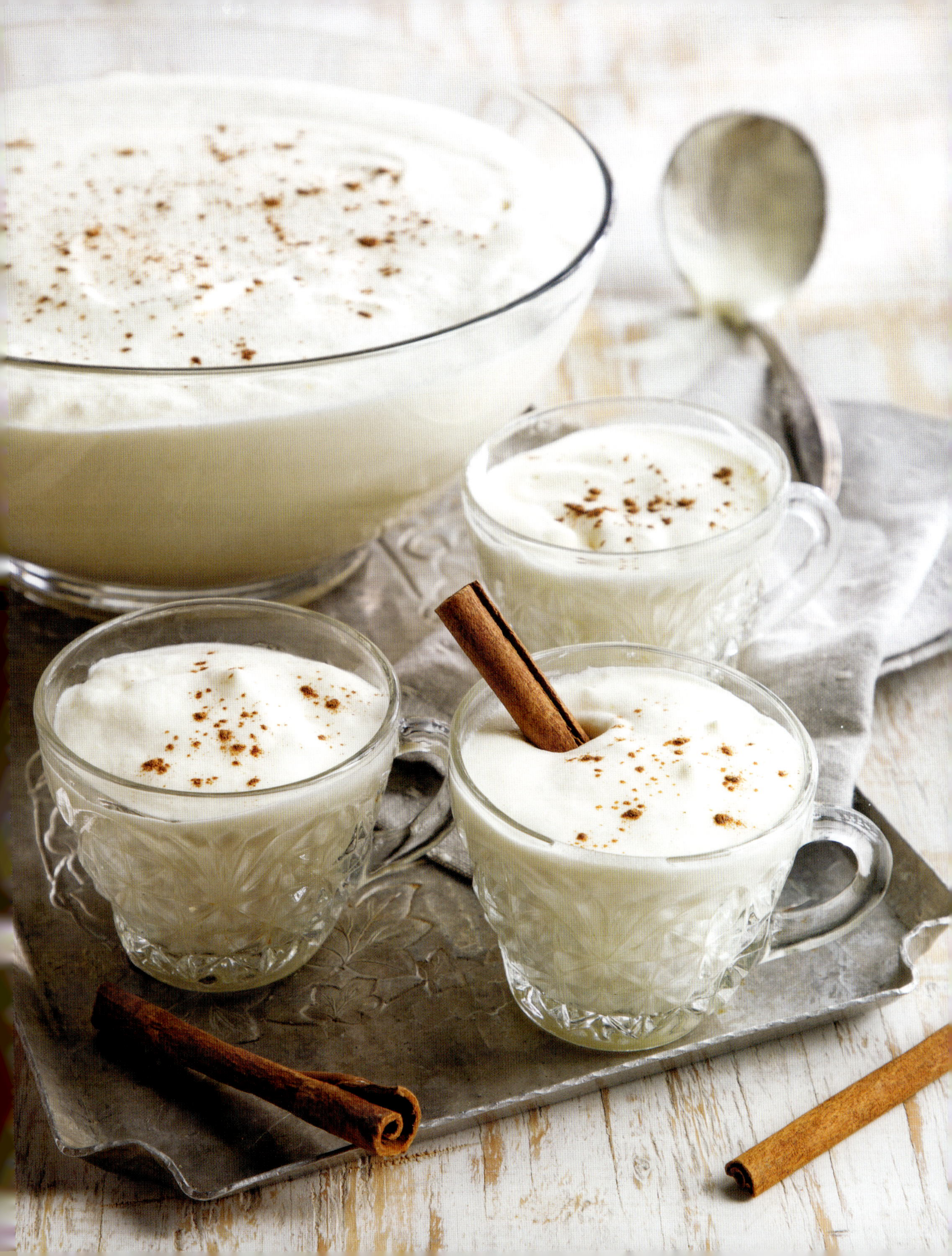

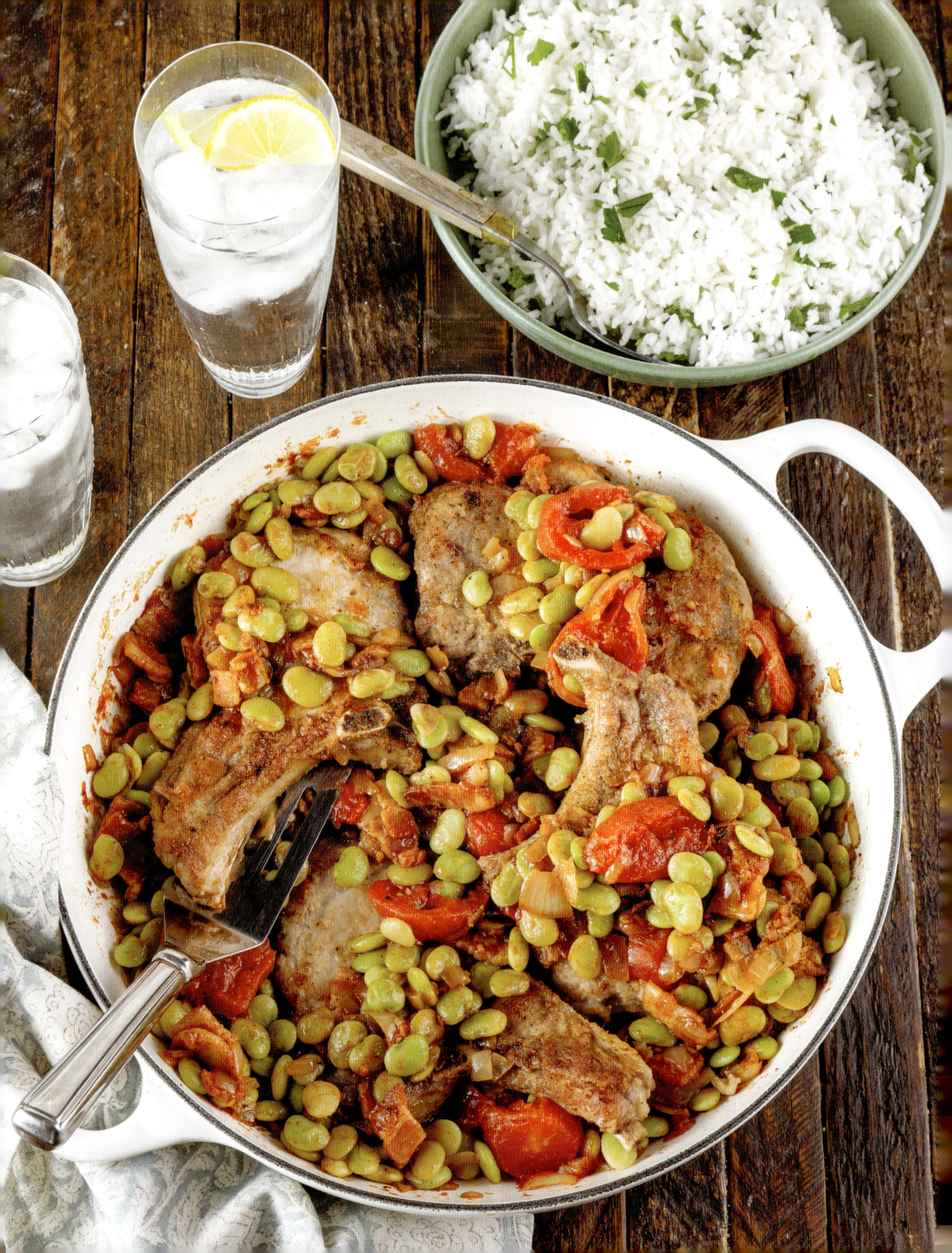

PORK CHOPS

Aunt Trina's pork chops are a family favorite! The bone-in chops have so much flavor, and you get your serving of veggies in with this recipe, too.

Makes 4 to 6 servings

- 1 teaspoon salt
- ½ teaspoon paprika
- ¼ teaspoon ground black pepper
- 4 to 6 bone-in pork chops
- 2 tablespoons oil
- 4 slices bacon, chopped
- 1 large onion, thinly sliced
- 1 (16-ounce) can stewed tomatoes
- 1 (16-ounce) package frozen lima beans
- Hot cooked rice, to serve

1. Sprinkle salt, paprika, and pepper all over pork.

2. In a large skillet, heat oil over medium-high heat. Add pork chops and cook for 2 to 3 minutes per side. Remove pork chops from skillet, and keep warm.

3. In same skillet, cook bacon and onion over medium-high heat, stirring frequently. Add pork chops and tomatoes. Cover and cook over medium-low heat, stirring occasionally, for 30 minutes.

4. Add lima beans to pork mixture. Reduce heat to low; cover and cook for 30 minutes. Serve over rice.

My Aunt Trina was such a great cook. When she was in her 40s, she moved to Louisiana and became so good at Creole and Cajun cooking. She passed a lot of those recipes on to me. Cajun food is probably my second favorite type of food to eat! I was so glad Aunt Trina moved there so she could pass on those great tips to me.

SHRIMP PUFFS

Oh my, these are so good! This recipe was always a crowd-pleaser when Aunt Trina would whip them up. They are crispy, and the Creole seasoning gives them a kick.

Makes 40

- 1 tablespoon vegetable oil
- 1 cup all-purpose flour
- 2 teaspoons Creole seasoning
- 1½ teaspoons baking powder
- ½ teaspoon garlic powder
- ¾ cup whole milk
- 2 large eggs, separated
- 2 cups chopped, peeled, and deveined fresh shrimp
- 2 cups cooked rice
- 1 medium onion, chopped
- ⅓ cup chopped green onion

1. In a Dutch oven, pour oil to a depth of 1½ inches. Heat over medium-high heat until a deep-fry thermometer registers 350°.

2. In a large bowl, whisk together flour, Creole seasoning, baking powder, and garlic powder. Whisk in milk, egg yolks, and oil. Stir in shrimp, rice, and onion.

3. In a medium bowl, beat egg whites with a mixer at medium-high speed until glossy stiff peaks form. Fold egg whites into shrimp batter.

4. Drop batter by tablespoonfuls into hot oil, and fry until golden brown, 3 to 4 minutes, turning halfway through frying. Remove from oil, and let drain on paper towels. Sprinkle with Creole seasoning.

I was very social in school and loved being friends with everybody! I was a cheerleader, and PE was probably the only subject I didn't fail. I was just not interested in academics—school was my social gathering place!

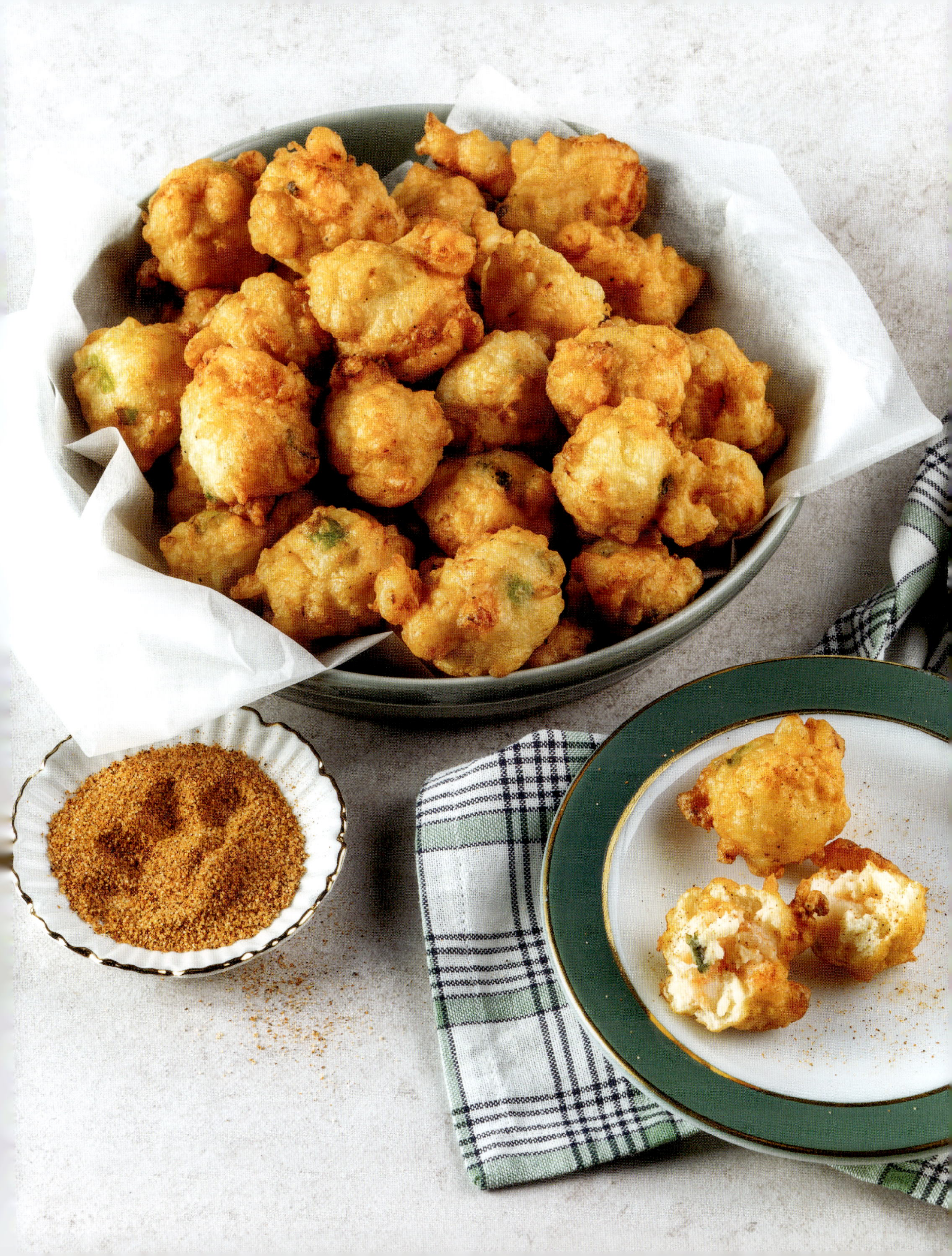

Me, Aunt Jessie, Grandmother Paul, and Grandmother Hiers,

CHOCOLATE POUND CAKE

I have so many wonderful memories of my precious Aunt Jessie who gave me this recipe. The texture of the cake combined with the flavor makes it a go-to.

Makes 1 (10-inch) cake

- 1 cup salted butter, softened
- ½ cup all-vegetable shortening
- 3 cups sugar
- 5 large eggs
- 1 tablespoon vanilla extract
- 3 cups all-purpose flour
- ¼ cup unsweetened cocoa powder
- ½ teaspoon baking powder
- ½ teaspoon salt
- 1 cup whole milk

CHOCOLATE FROSTING

- ½ cup evaporated milk
- 2 (1-ounce) squares unsweetened chocolate, chopped
- ¼ cup salted butter, diced
- 1 (1-pound) box confectioners' sugar, sifted
- 1 teaspoon vanilla extract

Garnish: chopped toasted pecans

1. Preheat oven to 350°. Spray a 10-inch tube pan with baking spray with flour.

2. For cake: In a large bowl, beat butter, shortening, and sugar with a mixer at medium speed until fluffy, 3 to 4 minutes, stopping to scrape sides of bowl. Add eggs, one at a time, beating well after each addition. Beat in vanilla.

3. In a medium bowl, whisk together flour, cocoa, baking powder, and salt. Gradually add flour mixture to butter mixture alternately with milk, beginning and ending with flour mixture, beating at low speed just until combined after each addition. Spoon batter into prepared pan, smoothing top. Tap pan on a kitchen towel-lined counter 3 times.

4. Bake until a wooden pick inserted near center comes out clean, about 1 hour and 10 minutes. Let cool in pan for 10 minutes. Run a knife around edge of pan to help loosen cake. Invert cake onto wire rack and let cake cool completely.

5. For frosting: In a small Dutch oven, cook evaporated milk, chocolate, and butter over medium-low heat, whisking constantly, until chocolate and butter are melted. Gradually whisk in confectioners' sugar and vanilla until smooth. Let cool for 3 minutes.

6. Place cake on a serving plate. Drizzle with frosting. Garnish with pecans, if desired.

JAMBALAYA

My Aunt Trina's jambalaya can compete with the best of them! Nothing will make your kitchen smell better than this recipe simmering on the stove.

Makes 6 servings

- ½ pound bacon, chopped
- 2 cups diced smoked sausage
- 2 tablespoons salted butter
- 1½ cups long-grain rice
- Salt, ground black pepper, and dried parsley, to taste
- 3 cups water
- 1 cup chopped onion
- ½ cup chopped celery
- 2 beef bouillon cubes
- 3 tablespoons Worcestershire sauce
- 1 tablespoon browning and seasoning sauce
- Garnish: chopped, fresh parsley

1. In a large Dutch oven, cook bacon and sausage over medium heat until crispy. Remove meat mixture using a slotted spoon, and let drain on paper towels. Wipe Dutch oven clean.

2. In same Dutch oven, melt butter over medium heat. Add rice, and season with salt, pepper, and dried parsley. Cook, stirring constantly, for 5 minutes. Add 3 cups water, onion, celery, bouillon, Worcestershire, and browning and seasoning sauce. Increase heat to high, and bring to a boil, stirring constantly. Cover, reduce heat to low, and cook for 30 minutes.

3. Remove from heat, and let stand, covered, for 20 minutes before serving. Garnish with fresh parsley, if desired.

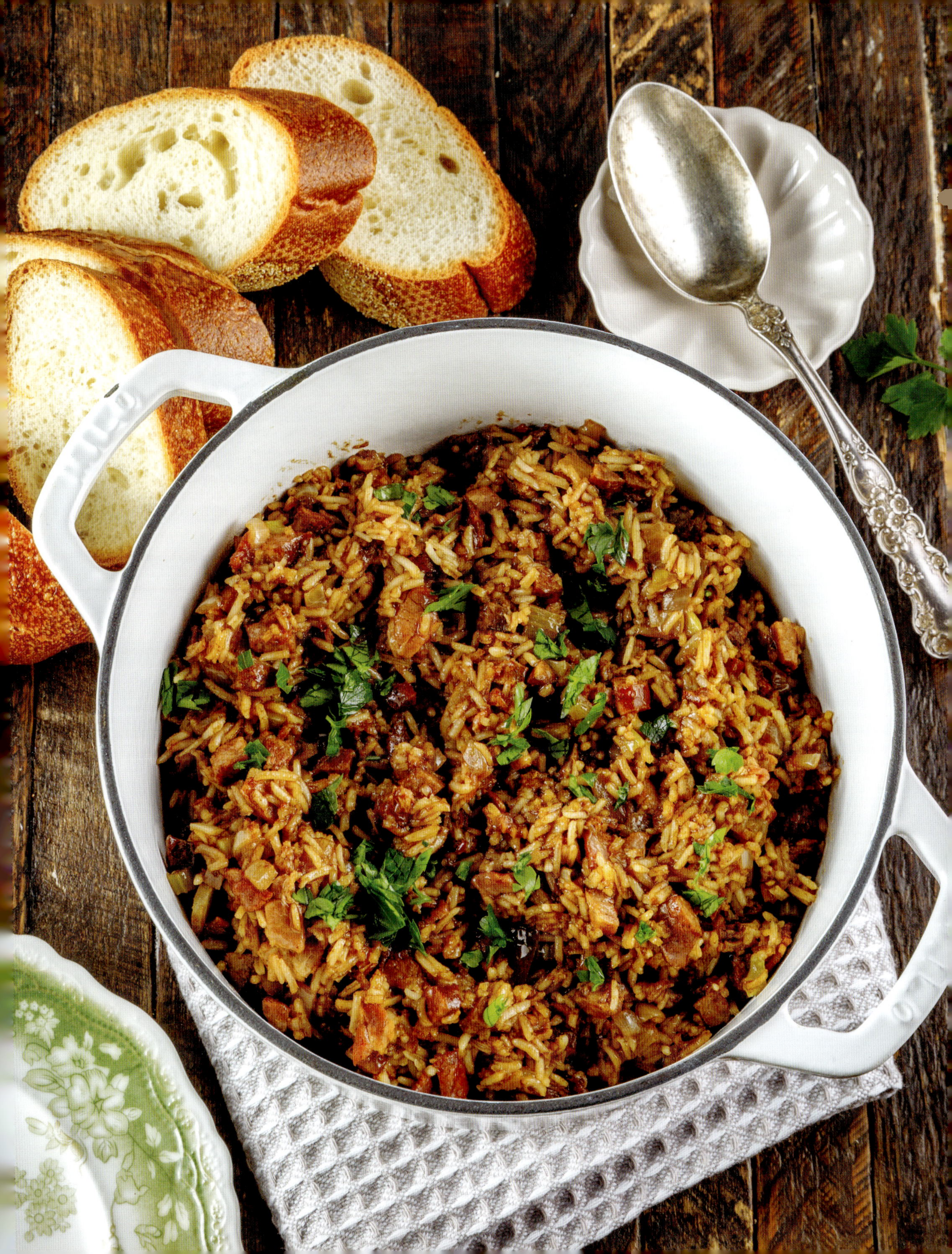

PARMESAN ASPARAGUS

My first cousin Don Hiers gave me this recipe, and I think it is so delicious with the garlic, red pepper, and Parmesan cheese!

Makes about 4 servings

- 1 pound fresh asparagus, trimmed
- 2 tablespoons olive oil
- ¼ teaspoon crushed red pepper
- 1 large clove elephant ear garlic, thinly sliced
- 2 tablespoons shaved Parmesan cheese

Salt, to taste

1. Preheat oven to 425°. Line a large rimmed baking sheet with foil.

2. On prepared pan, toss together asparagus, oil, red pepper, and garlic.

3. Bake until tender, about 15 minutes, stirring halfway through baking. Transfer to a serving plate. Top with cheese, and season to taste with salt.

CAJUN CLAM DELIGHT

This is another Aunt Trina favorite that I am excited to share. If you love seafood and a creamy, cozy meal, this one is for you!

Makes about 6 cups

- 2   (8-ounce) bottles clam juice
- 2   (6.5-ounce) cans chopped clams, drained
- 1   (10.75-ounce) can golden mushroom soup
- 1   cup diced Yukon gold potatoes
- 1   cup pan-boiled diced salt pork
- ½   teaspoon Creole seasoning
- ½   cup salted butter
- Saltines, to serve

1. In a stockpot, bring clam juice, clams, soup, potatoes, pork, and Creole seasoning to a boil over medium-high heat. Reduce heat, and simmer, stirring occasionally, for 40 minutes.

2. Add butter to clam mixture, and stir until butter is melted and combined. Serve with saltines.

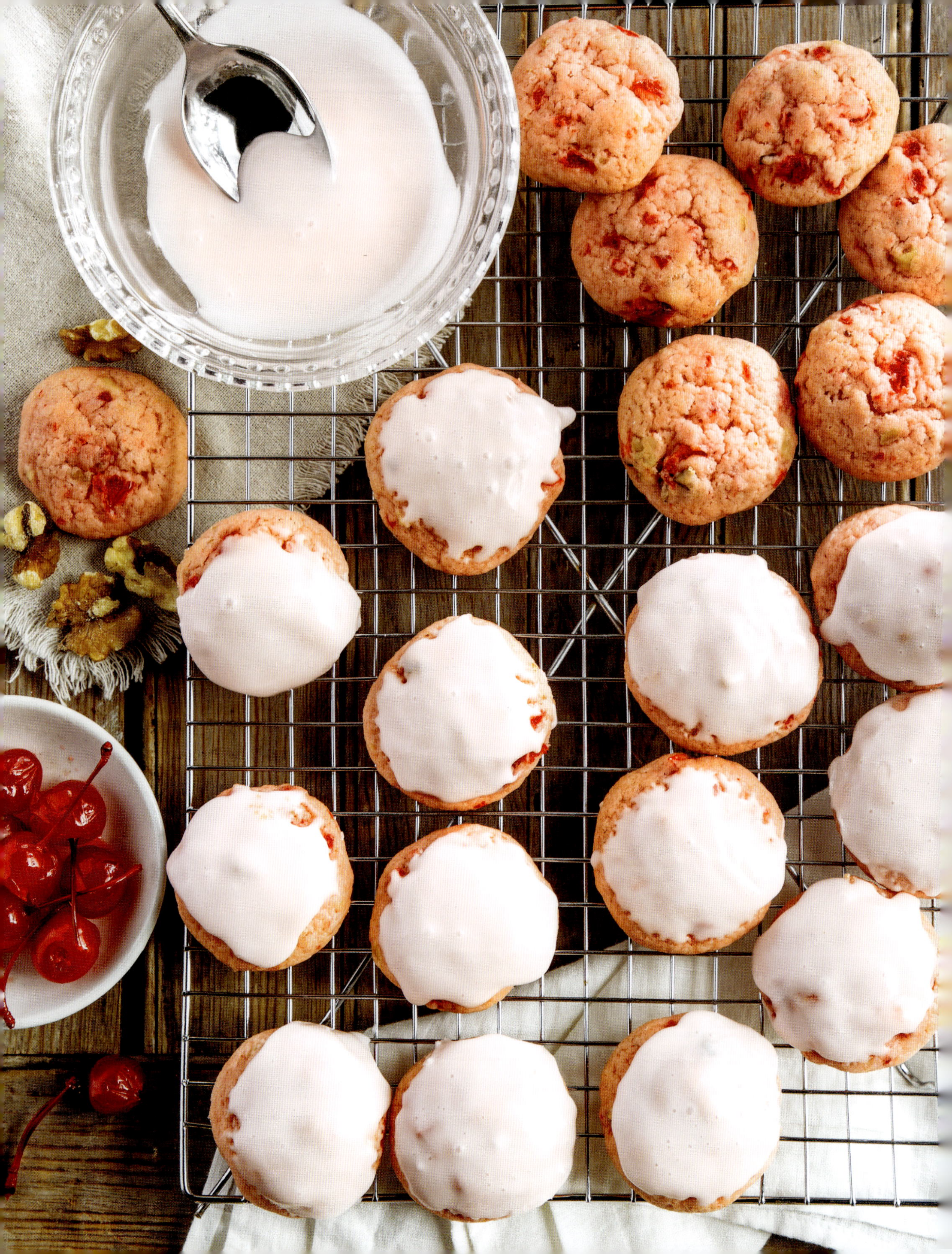

CHERRY CHRISTMAS COOKIES

This is a classic from my cousin Don. We have been close since we were children, and I always begged him to bring these wonderful cookies when he and his wife visited for Christmas.

Makes about 34

- ½ cup all-vegetable shortening
- 1 cup sugar
- ½ cup maraschino cherry juice (from cherry jar)
- 1 large egg
- ¼ teaspoon almond extract
- 3 cups all-purpose flour
- 2 teaspoons baking powder
- ½ teaspoon salt
- ½ cup chopped maraschino cherries, patted dry
- ½ cup finely chopped walnuts

GLAZE

- 1½ cups confectioners' sugar
- 2 tablespoons whole milk
- ½ tablespoon maraschino cherry juice (from cherry jar)

1. Preheat oven to 350°. Line baking sheets with parchment paper.

2. For cookies: In a large bowl, beat shortening and sugar with a mixer at medium speed until fluffy, 3 to 4 minutes, stopping to scrape sides of bowl. Add cherry juice and egg, beating until well combined. Beat in almond extract.

3. In a medium bowl, whisk together flour, baking powder, and salt. Gradually add flour mixture to shortening mixture, beating at low speed just until combined. Stir in chopped cherries and walnuts. Using a 1½-tablespoon spring-loaded scoop, scoop dough, and roll into smooth balls. Place at least 1½ inches apart on prepared pans.

4. Bake until bottoms are lightly browned, 12 to 14 minutes. Let cool on pans for 2 minutes. Remove from pans, and let cool completely on wire racks.

5. For glaze: In a small bowl, whisk together all ingredients until smooth. Dip top of cooled cookies in glaze, and return to wire racks. Let stand until glaze is set, about 2 hours.

FRESH CRANBERRY SALAD

This recipe is a Southern favorite! Everyone loves this cool treat after a hot meal.

Makes 10 servings

- 1 (12-ounce) package fresh or frozen cranberries (thawed if frozen)
- 1 cup sugar
- 1 (16-ounce) package miniature marshmallows
- 1 (20-ounce) can crushed pineapple packed in heavy syrup
- 2 cups heavy whipping cream
- 1 cup coarsely chopped pecans

1. In the work bowl of a food processor, process cranberries until chopped into small pieces. Transfer to a large bowl, and add sugar, tossing until combined. Cover and refrigerate for at least 2 hours or up to overnight.

2. Add marshmallows and pineapple to cranberry mixture. Cover and refrigerate for at least 2 hours.

3. In another large bowl, beat cream with a mixer at medium-high speed until stiff peaks form. Fold whipped cream and pecans into cranberry mixture.

Top: Grandmother and Granddaddy Hiers and their four children—my aunt Jessie, my uncle Burney, my daddy, and my uncle Bob.
Left: My mother and daddy on their wedding day. I just love this picture!

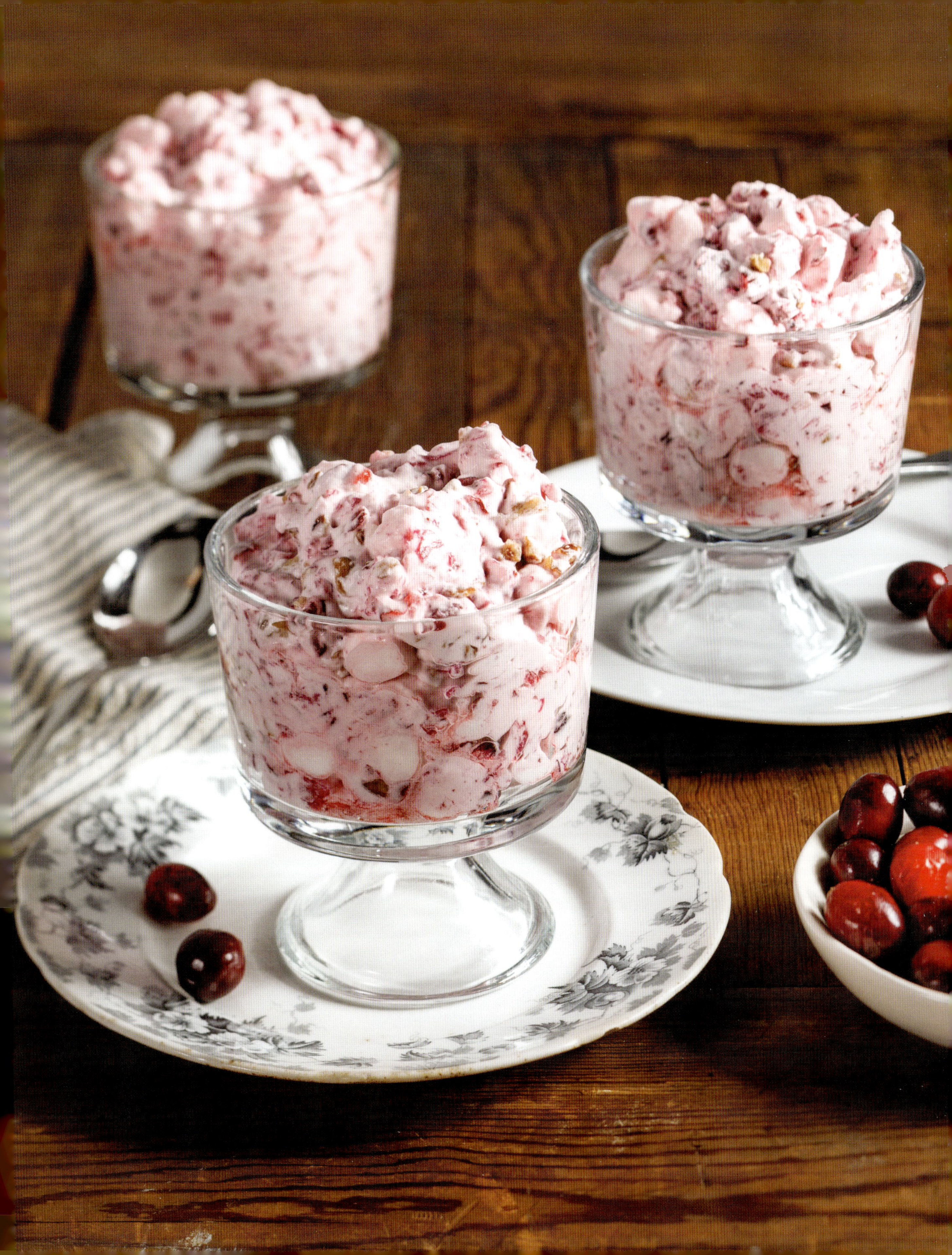

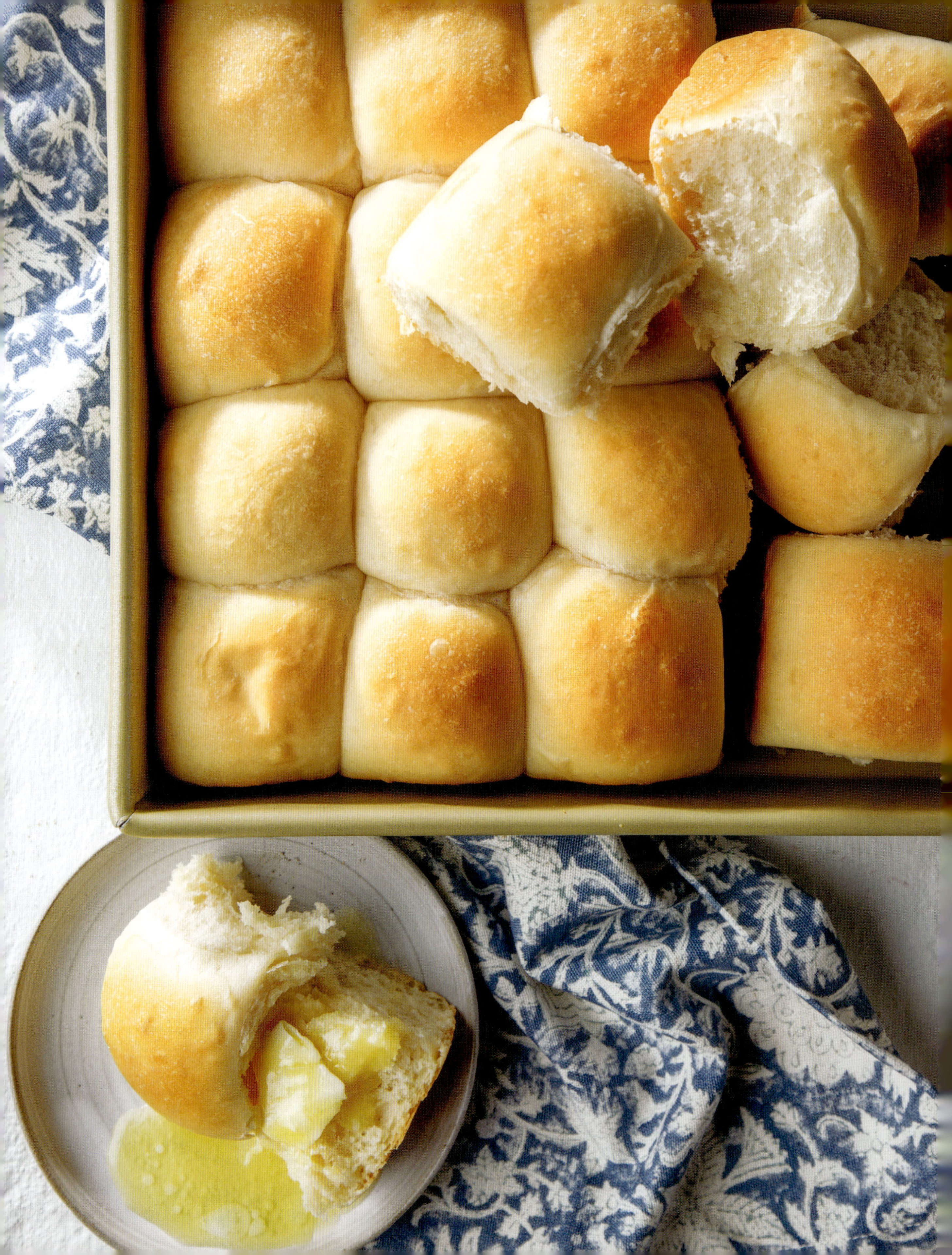

SOUTH GEORGIA ICEBOX ROLLS

Honey, these rolls will melt in your mouth! This recipe came from Aunt Trina.

Makes 24

- ½ cup all-vegetable shortening
- ⅓ cup sugar
- 2 cups whole milk
- 1 (0.25-ounce) package active dry yeast
- 4½ cups all-purpose flour, divided
- 2 teaspoons salt
- 1 teaspoon baking powder

1. In the bowl of a stand mixer fitted with the paddle attachment, beat shortening and sugar.

2. In a small saucepan, heat milk over medium-low heat just until bubbles form around sides of pan. (Do not boil.) Pour hot milk over shortening and sugar, stirring until sugar dissolves and shortening is melted. Let stand until an instant-read thermometer registers 105° to 110°. Add yeast, and stir until dissolved. Cover and let stand until foamy, 5 to 10 minutes.

3. Add 2 cups flour to shortening mixture, and beat until fully combined. Cover and let stand until bubbly, about 1 hour.

4. Switch to the dough hook attachment. Add salt, baking powder, and remaining 2½ cups flour, and beat at medium-low speed until a smooth, elastic dough forms, 5 to 6 minutes. Spray a large bowl with cooking spray. Place dough in bowl, turning to grease sides. Cover and refrigerate until ready to use.

5. Lightly spray a 13x9-inch baking pan with cooking spray.

6. Divide dough into 24 equal portions. Roll each portion into a ball, and place in prepared pan. Cover and let stand in a warm, draft-free place (75°) until puffed, 45 minutes to 1 hour.

7. Preheat oven to 350°.

8. Bake until golden brown, 20 to 25 minutes.

AUNT GLENNIS'S POUND CAKE

Aunt Glennis and Uncle Burney played a big part in my life. For about 25 years, my whole family spent Thanksgivings in Statesboro, Georgia. The times we had were wonderful. We always looked forward to being in their home. We lost Uncle Burney in 1996, and we will continue to feel this loss for a long time.

Makes 1 (10-inch) cake

- 1 cup salted butter, softened
- ½ cup all-vegetable shortening
- 2¾ cups sugar
- 6 large eggs
- 1 teaspoon vanilla extract
- 3 cups plus 2 tablespoons all-purpose flour, sifted and divided
- 1 teaspoon baking powder
- 1 cup whole milk
- 1 (12-ounce) package semisweet chocolate chips
- 1 cup chopped pecans

1. Spray a 10-inch tube pan with baking spray with flour.

2. In a large bowl, beat butter, shortening, and sugar with a mixer at medium speed until fluffy, 3 to 4 minutes, stopping to scrape sides of bowl. Add eggs, one at a time, beating until combined after each addition. Beat in vanilla.

3. In a medium bowl, sift together 3 cups flour and baking powder. Gradually add flour mixture to butter mixture alternately with milk, beginning and ending with flour mixture, beating at low speed just until combined after each addition.

4. In a medium bowl, toss together chocolate chips, pecans, and remaining 2 tablespoons flour. Stir into batter. Spoon into prepared pan.

5. Place in cold oven, and bake at 325° until a wooden pick inserted near center comes out clean, about 1½ hours, covering with foil during final 30 minutes of baking to prevent excess browning. Let cool in pan on a wire rack for 30 minutes. Remove from pan, and let cool on a wire rack. Serve warm or at room temperature.

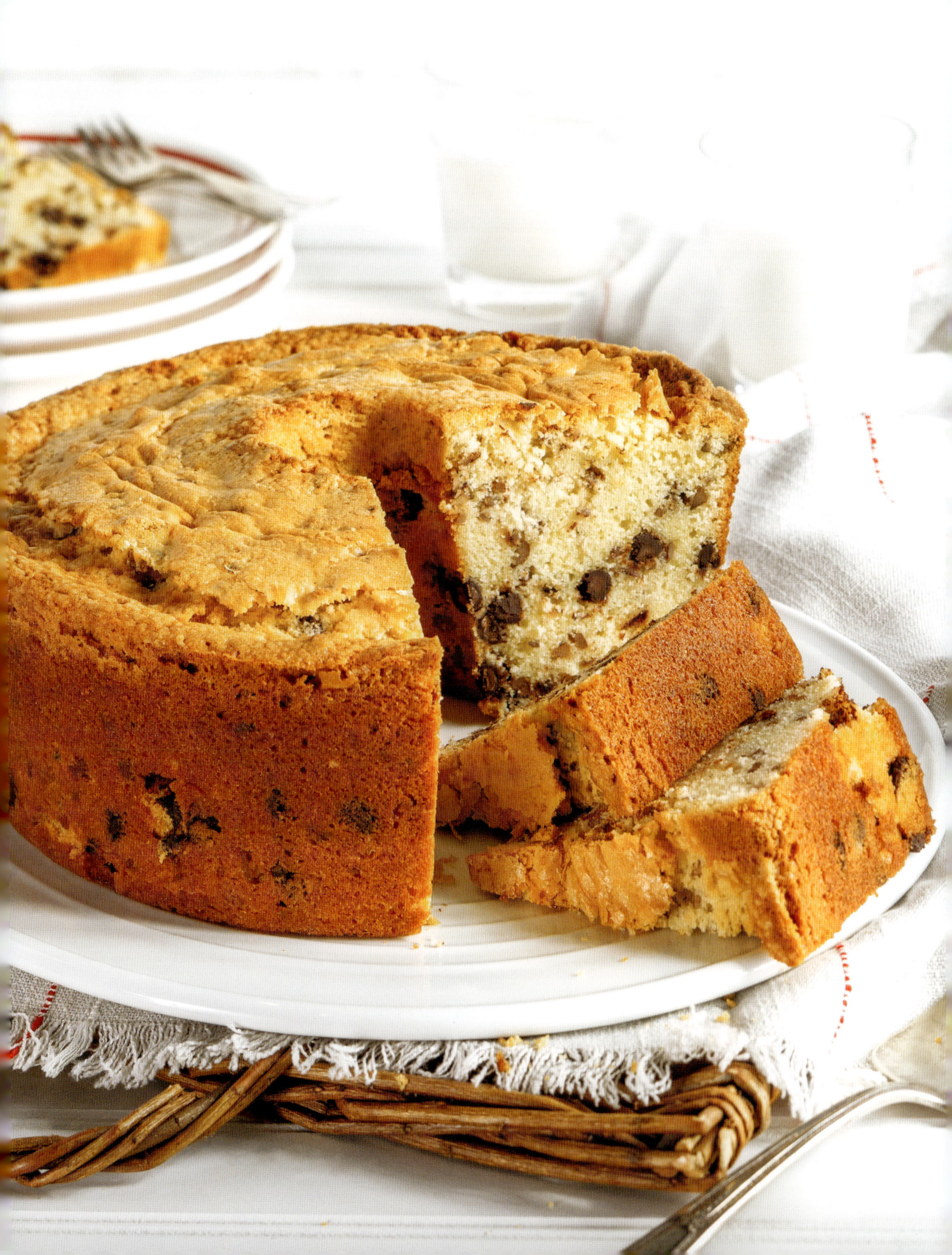

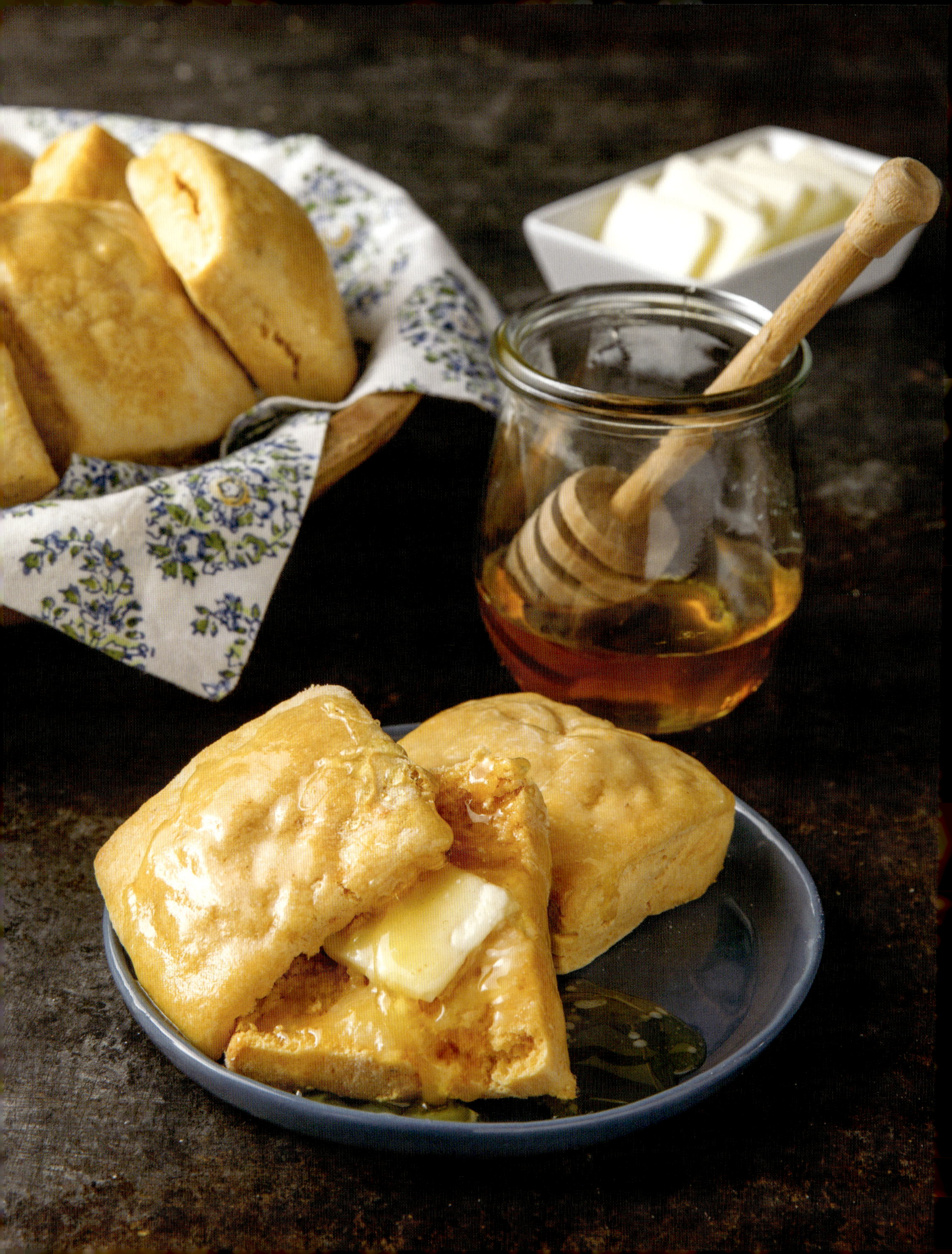

SWEET POTATO BISCUITS

*These biscuits are pure love and comfort!
Serve these up warm with plenty of honey and butter.*

Makes 12

- ¾ cup canned sweet potatoes, drained and mashed
- 4 tablespoons salted butter, softened
- ¼ cup sugar
- 2 cups all-purpose flour
- 2½ teaspoons baking powder
- 1 teaspoon salt
- ½ teaspoon baking soda
- ⅓ cup whole buttermilk
- Butter and honey, to serve

1. Preheat oven to 400°. Spray a baking sheet with cooking spray, or line a baking sheet with parchment paper.

2. In the bowl of a food processor, process sweet potatoes, butter, and sugar until combined.

3. In a large bowl, sift together flour, baking powder, salt, and baking soda. Add flour mixture to sweet potato mixture, and pulse until flour mixture is evenly distributed. Add buttermilk, and pulse until mixture forms into a ball.

4. Turn out dough ball onto a lightly floured surface, and knead until dough holds together, flouring fingers as needed. Gently roll dough out into a 10x8-inch rectangle (about ½ inch thick). Using a pizza cutter, cut dough into 12 rectangular biscuits. Transfer to prepared pan.

5. Bake until tops are golden and bottoms are beginning to turn light brown, about 10 minutes. Serve hot with honey and butter.

CHAPTER THREE

BECOMING A MOMMA

Jimmy and I had been married about seven months when Daddy died. He had rheumatic fever as a child, and it damaged his heart. He was sent to Emory Hospital in Atlanta, and they performed a valve replacement. It was such a new surgery in 1966 that Daddy was basically a guinea pig. The surgery was in February of 1966, and he died that June.

I was traumatized and heartbroken. The night after his death, I remember, I had to sleep in the bed between my momma and my new husband because I was overcome with terror. I didn't know what was happening to me at the time, but that was the beginning of my 20-year battle with agoraphobia. I went from being an outgoing, fun-loving girl to someone who was insecure and frightened of life.

I never shared my struggles with anxiety with anybody, not even my mother. Jimmy was the only one I told my fears and thoughts to, and he probably thought I was crazy. No one knew anything about mental health back then. When I became pregnant with my first son, Jamie, my fears grew even more intense. I was scared that something would happen to my baby, and it continued to get worse once my second son, Bobby, was born. I constantly thought, "Oh, my gosh, if something happens to them, I won't be able to stand it." My life turned into one of fear.

Raising children was different in those days. We didn't have the resources modern parents have now. I was so terrified of something happening to one of my boys or myself that I could barely step outside. I did my best to put them in their strollers and take them for walks, but they mostly played at home with each other.

I remember one day when Jamie was about 6 months old—the house we lived in had a stainless steel sink. I had just decided I was going to bathe him when, suddenly, it went pitch black outside and started pouring rain. I put him in his little baby seat on the table and said, "We're just gonna sit right here for now, buddy. We're not supposed to be in the tub when there's lightning outside."

It was just minutes later that as I was sitting there with Jamie at the table, lightning struck through the kitchen window and hit that metal sink. Holy moly! I was in shock. We could have both been electrocuted. I was so glad I was a scaredy cat about things like that because it saved his life, but of course, it just made my day-to-day fears even worse.

Oh, how I love my boys, though. You talk about two totally different personalities—Jamie and Bobby were and are as different as night and day. As kids, Jamie could never sit still and was always active, while Bobby was content and quiet. Even their looks are different.

Opposite page, left to right: Me, Jamie, and Bobby. Me and Jamie. Christmas Eve with Bobby and Jamie. **This page, clockwise:** Me and my boys. Jamie in a shirt I added the watermelon stitching to. Bobby with another hand-stiched shirt. Bobby blowing out his birthday candles.

Brothers

Jamie is tall and fair, with blue eyes and dimples, and Bobby is shorter, with black hair, dark eyes, and a darker skin tone. They were the best of friends growing up and I loved how close they were.

GREEN ONION MINI QUICHES

These bite-size quiches are an easy and delicious addition to any breakfast or brunch spread.

Makes 24

- ¾ cup crushed saltine crackers
- 4 tablespoons salted butter, melted
- 2 tablespoons salted butter, cubed
- 1 cup chopped green onion
- 2 large eggs
- 1 cup shredded Swiss cheese
- 1 cup whole milk
- ½ teaspoon salt
- ¼ teaspoon ground black pepper
- Garnish: paprika

1. Preheat oven to 300°. Spray a 24-cup mini muffin pan with cooking spray.

2. In a small bowl, stir together crushed crackers and melted butter. Divide crumbs among prepared muffin cups.

3. In a small saucepan or small skillet, melt cubed butter over medium heat. Add green onion, and cook until tender, about 4 minutes. Remove from heat, and let cool. Divide green onion among muffin cups.

4. In a medium bowl, whisk eggs; whisk in cheese, milk, salt, and pepper. Spoon on top of green onion in muffin cups. (Do not fill to top, as they will run over.)

5. Bake until set, 15 to 20 minutes. (Do not overbake.) Let cool in pan on a wire rack for 5 minutes. Run a knife around edges of quiches. Gently remove from pans. Serve warm. Refrigerate or freeze in an airtight container, and reheat in oven before serving. Garnish with paprika, if desired.

My boys and me! My sons are so precious to me, and we have overcome and achieved so much together.

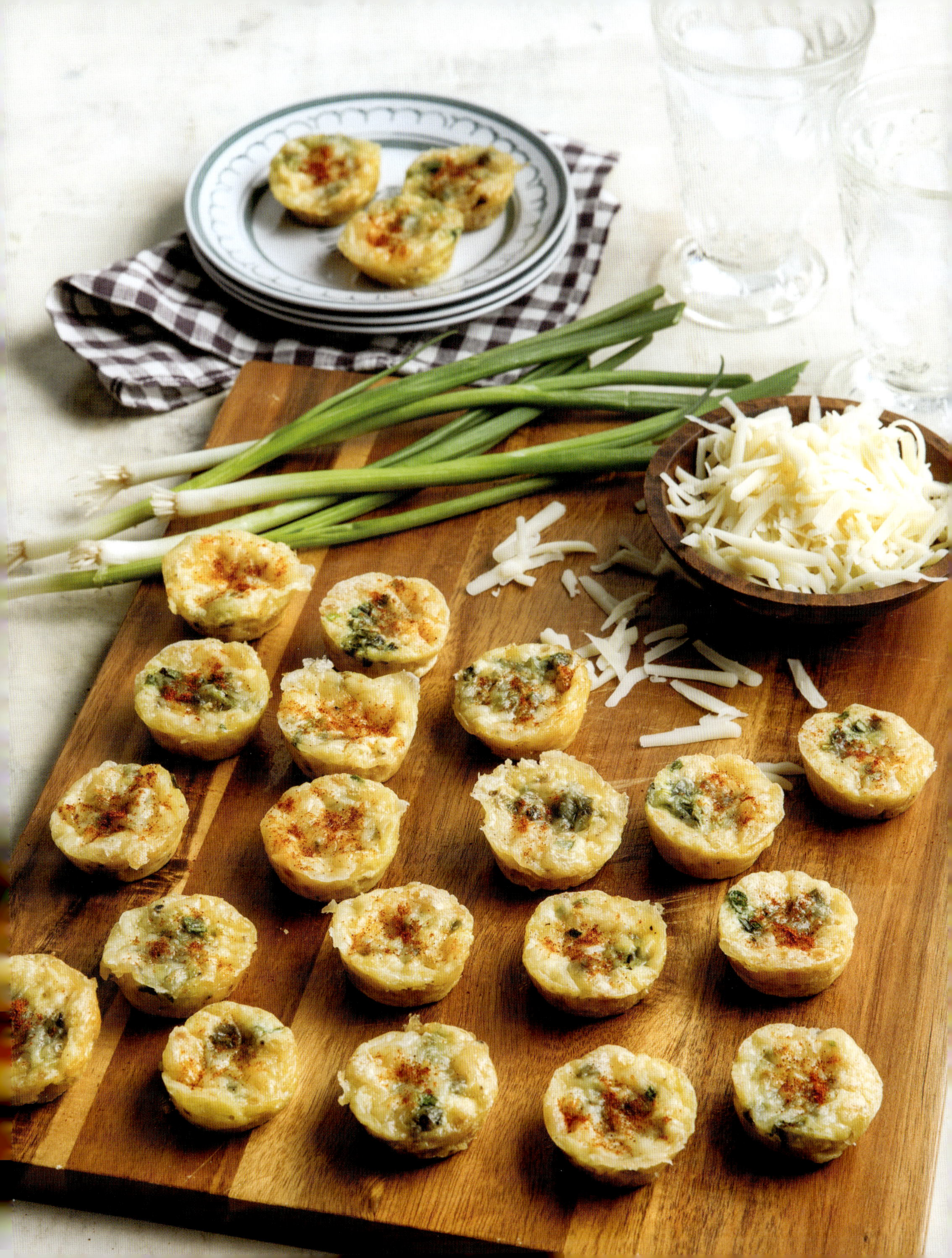

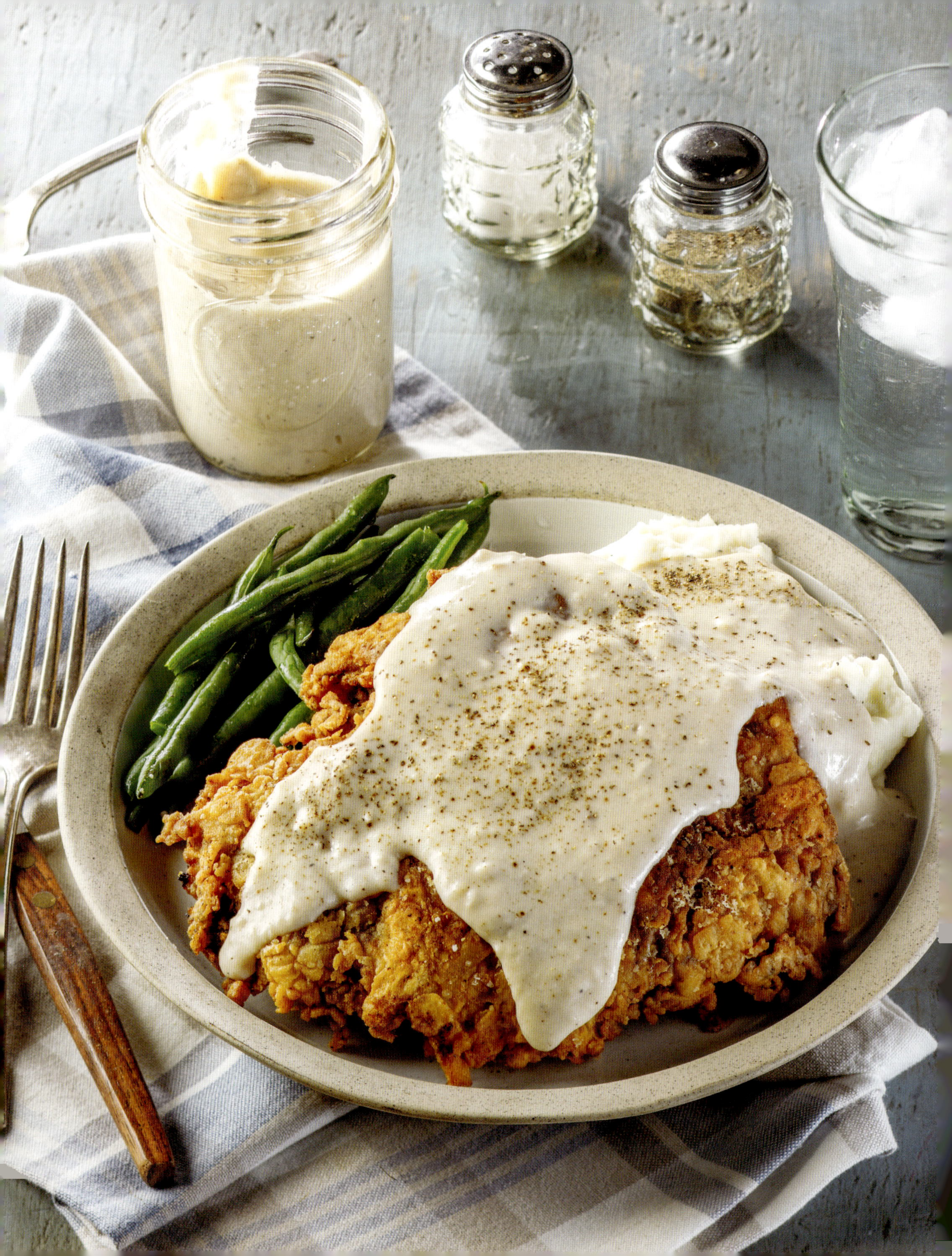

CHICKEN-FRIED STEAK WITH MILK GRAVY

Hearty, comforting, and Southern! Who doesn't crave this classic topped with creamy gravy? Serve it with green beans or your favorite vegetable.

Makes 6 servings

- 1¼ cups all-purpose flour, divided
- 4 teaspoons salt, divided
- 3½ teaspoons ground black pepper, divided
- ½ teaspoon paprika
- 1 cup whole buttermilk
- 1 large egg, lightly beaten
- Vegetable oil, for frying
- 6 cube steaks (about 1½ pounds)
- 2 cups whole milk

1. Preheat oven to 200°. In a shallow dish, whisk together 1 cup flour, 3 teaspoons salt, 3 teaspoons pepper, and paprika. In a separate shallow dish, whisk together buttermilk and egg.

2. In a large heavy-bottomed skillet, pour oil to a depth of 2 inches, and heat over medium heat until a deep-fry thermometer registers 350°.

3. Working in batches, dredge cube steaks in flour mixture, gently shaking off excess. Dip in buttermilk mixture, letting excess drip off. Dredge steaks in flour mixture again to coat.

4. Fry steaks, in batches, until an instant-read thermometer inserted in center registers 165°, 3 to 5 minutes per side, adjusting heat as needed to maintain a temperature of 350°. Let drain on paper towels. Place in single layer on a baking sheet, and keep warm in oven.

5. Drain oil into a heatproof container, reserving ¼ cup oil in skillet. Heat reserved oil over medium heat. Whisk in remaining ¼ cup flour. Cook, whisking constantly, until thickened, 1 to 2 minutes. Gradually whisk in milk until smooth. Stir in remaining 1 teaspoon salt and remaining ½ teaspoon pepper. Cook, whisking constantly, until thickened, 4 to 5 minutes. Serve immediately over steaks.

CORN CASSEROLE

This is a great dish to bring to a gathering or serve with your favorite main.

Makes about 4 servings

- 1 (15-ounce) can whole kernel corn
- 1 large egg
- 1 (14.75-ounce) can cream-style corn
- ⅓ cup half-and-half
- 3 tablespoons salted butter, melted
- 2 tablespoons diced pimiento, drained
- ¼ teaspoon salt
- ¼ teaspoon ground black pepper
- 30 saltine crackers, crushed

1. Preheat oven to 350°. Spray a 1-quart baking dish with cooking spray.

2. Drain whole kernel corn, reserving 3 tablespoons liquid.

3. In a medium bowl, whisk egg until foamy. Stir in whole kernel corn, reserved 3 tablespoons liquid, cream-style corn, half-and-half, melted butter, pimiento, salt, and black pepper. Reserve ¼ cup crushed crackers; stir remaining crushed crackers into corn mixture. Pour into prepared dish. Sprinkle with reserved ¼ cup crushed crackers.

4. Bake until set in the center, about 35 minutes.

My Grandmother Paul with Bobby and Jamie. She always said she wanted to be where the children were at Christmas. I was so lucky she always wanted to spend Christmas with us! I made those stockings in 1971, and I still have them now.

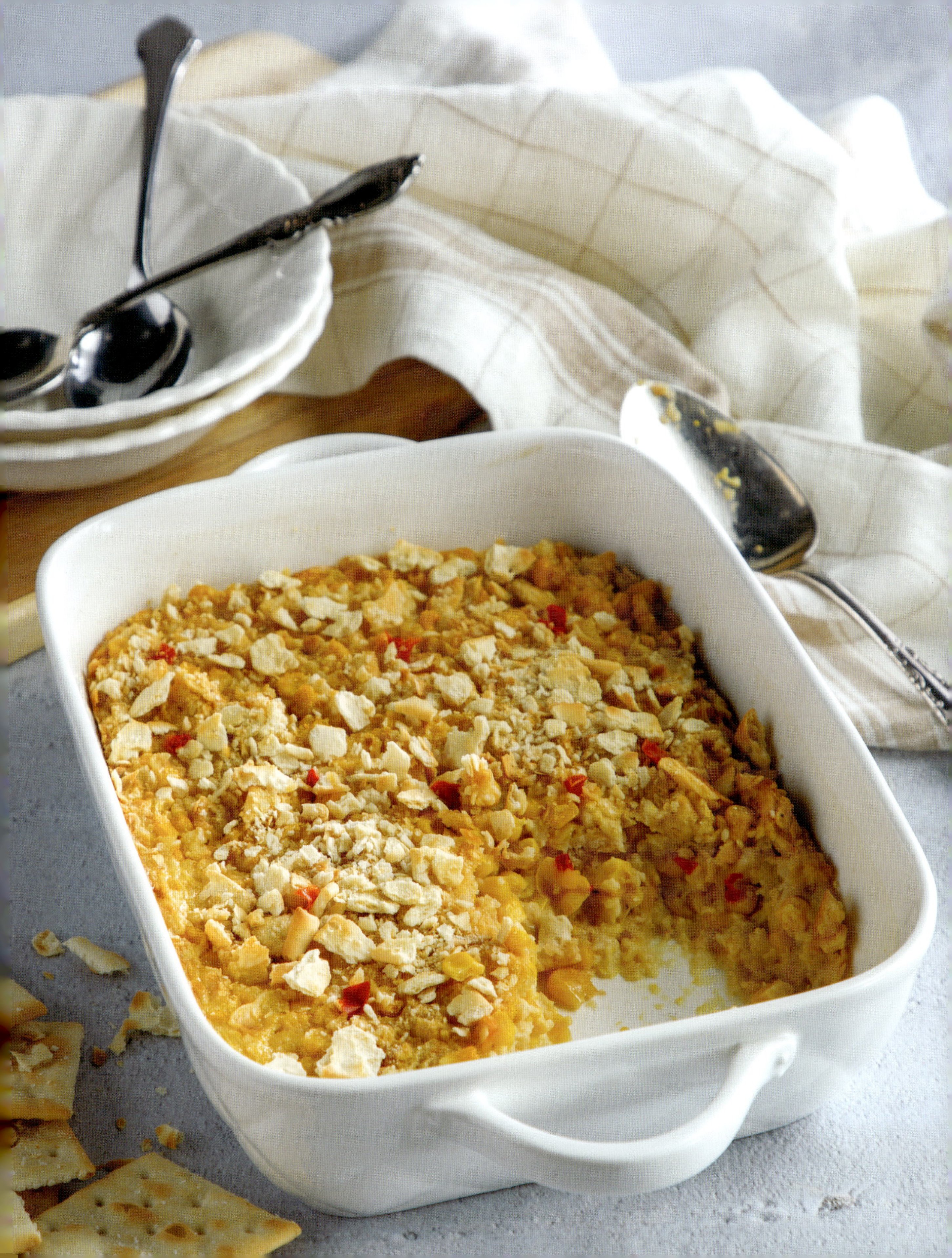

Recipe Tip

If you prefer a three-layer cake, simply do not cut the cake layers in half.

COCONUT CREAM CAKE

This cake chills for three days before you frost it, but it is worth the wait!

Makes 1 (9-inch) cake

- 1 cup salted butter, softened
- 2 cups sugar
- 5 large eggs
- 2 teaspoons vanilla extract
- 3½ cups all-purpose flour
- 1 tablespoon baking powder
- 1 cup whole milk

FILLING

- ¾ cup sugar
- 1 cup sour cream
- 4 tablespoons milk
- ½ cup sweetened flaked coconut

7-MINUTE FROSTING

- 1½ cups sugar
- ⅓ cup water
- 2 egg whites
- ¼ teaspoon cream of tartar or 1 tablespoon white corn syrup
- ⅛ teaspoon salt
- 1½ teaspoons vanilla extract
- Sweetened flaked coconut

1. Preheat oven to 350°. Spray 3 (9-inch) round cake pans with baking spray with flour.

2. For cake: In a large bowl, beat butter and sugar at medium speed until light and fluffy, 3 to 4 minutes, stopping to scrape sides of bowl. Add eggs, one at a time, beating well after each addition. Beat in vanilla.

3. In a medium bowl, whisk together flour and baking powder. Gradually add flour mixture to butter mixture alternately with milk, beginning and ending with flour mixture, beating at low speed until combined after each addition. Divide batter among prepared pans.

4. Bake until firm to the touch, 25 to 30 minutes. Let cool in pans for 10 minutes. Remove from pans, and let cool completely on wire racks. Cut cooled layers in half.

5. For filling: Stir together sugar, sour cream, milk, and coconut. Using the wrong end of a wooden spoon, poke holes in each layer about 1 inch apart. Spread filling onto cut side of each cake layer; stack layers. Cover and refrigerate for 3 days.

6. For frosting: In a large heatproof bowl, beat sugar, ⅓ cup water, egg whites, cream of tartar or corn syrup, and salt with a mixer at medium speed for 1 minute. Place bowl over a saucepan of rapidly boiling water, and beat at high speed for 7 minutes. Remove bowl from heat, and gently stir in vanilla with a spatula.

7. Spread frosting on top and sides of cake. Refrigerate in an airtight container for up to 3 days. When ready to serve, coat with coconut.

BROCCOLI SOUFFLÉ

Forget what you know about broccoli casserole! This soufflé will become your new favorite.

Makes 10 servings

- 3 (10-ounce) packages fresh broccoli florets, chopped
- ¾ cup chicken broth
- ¾ cup heavy whipping cream
- ½ cup salted butter, melted
- ½ cup all-purpose flour
- 4 large eggs, separated
- 3 tablespoons minced onion
- 2 teaspoons chopped fresh parsley
- Salt and ground black pepper, to taste
- ½ cup grated Parmesan cheese

1. Preheat oven to 425°. Butter a 3-quart baking dish.

2. In a large Dutch oven, bring broccoli and water to cover to a boil over medium-high heat; cook until broccoli is tender, 2 to 3 minutes. Drain well, and set aside.

3. In a small saucepan, combine broth and cream. Heat over medium heat, stirring occasionally, just until bubbles form around sides of pan. (Do not boil.) Remove from heat.

4. In a small bowl, place melted butter; whisk in flour. Gradually whisk into broth mixture; cook over medium heat, stirring constantly, until thick. Remove from heat, and whisk in egg yolks, onion, parsley, salt, and pepper. Stir in broccoli and cheese.

5. In a medium bowl, beat egg whites with a mixer at high speed until stiff peaks form. Gently fold into broccoli mixture. Transfer to prepared pan.

6. Bake until golden brown and center is set, 30 to 45 minutes. Serve immediately.

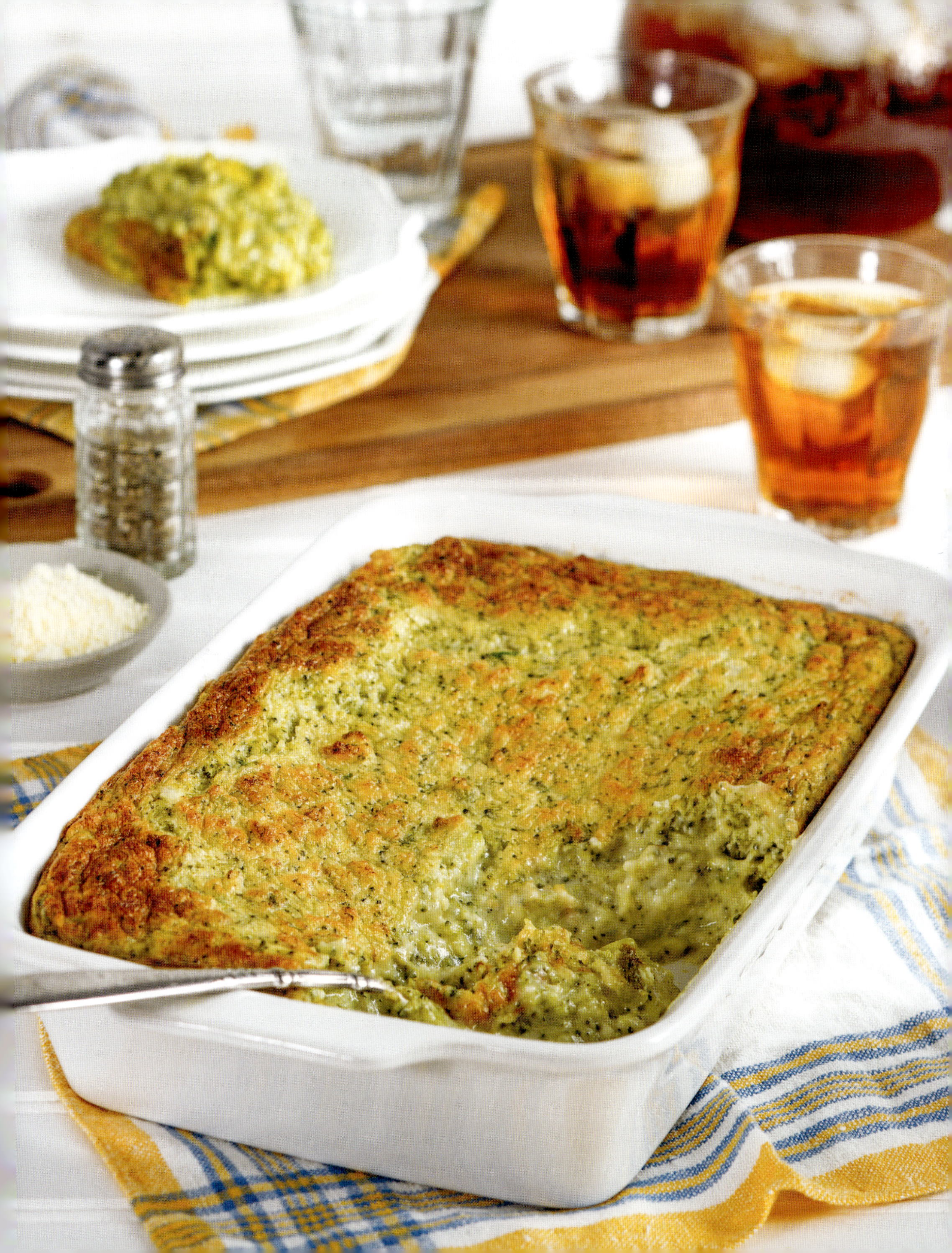

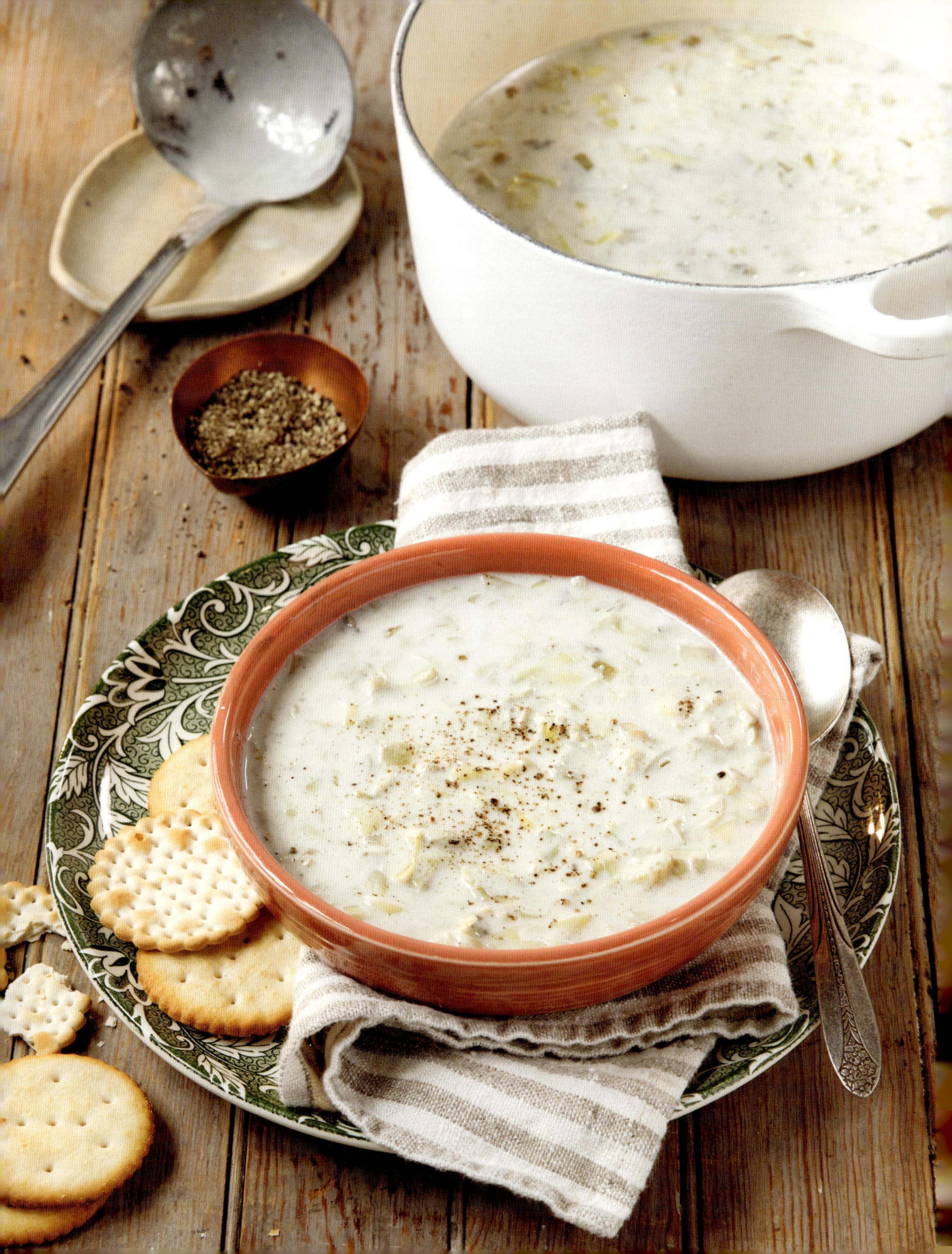

CREAM OF ARTICHOKE SOUP

This creamy soup is full of flavor and comfort, perfect for a cozy day at home or making a big batch for your loved ones.

Makes about 5½ cups

- 4 tablespoons salted butter
- 1 cup chopped yellow onion
- 2 (13.75-ounce) cans artichoke hearts, drained and chopped
- 1½ cups chicken stock
- 1 (10.5-ounce) can cream of mushroom soup
- ½ cup heavy whipping cream
- ¼ teaspoon salt
- ¼ teaspoon ground black pepper

1. In a medium saucepan, melt butter over medium heat. Add onion, and cook, stirring occasionally, until tender, 6 to 8 minutes. Add artichoke and stock; increase heat, and bring to a boil. Reduce heat to medium, and stir in soup; stir in cream, salt, and pepper. Serve immediately.

Bobby feeding a goat.

BLUEBERRY CREAM PIE

*This pretty pie tastes even better than it looks!
The chopped pecans give it the perfect amount of crunch.*

Makes 1 (9-inch) deep-dish pie

- ½ (14.1-ounce) package refrigerated piecrusts
- ¾ cup finely chopped pecans or walnuts
- 2 (3-ounce) packages cream cheese, room temperature
- 1 cup confectioners' sugar
- 1 cup heavy whipping cream
- ¼ cup sugar
- 1 (21-ounce) can blueberry pie filling

1. Preheat oven to 425°.

2. On a lightly floured surface, unroll piecrust. Roll into a 12-inch circle. Transfer to a 9-inch pie plate, pressing into bottom and up sides. Fold edges under, and crimp as desired. Lightly press nuts into bottom of prepared crust. Refrigerate for 10 minutes.

3. Bake until golden brown, 8 to 9 minutes. Let cool completely.

4. In a large bowl, beat cream cheese and confectioners' sugar with a mixer at medium speed until smooth and creamy.

5. In a medium bowl, beat cream and sugar with a mixer at medium-high speed until soft peaks form. Fold whipped cream mixture into cream cheese mixture. Spoon into cooled crust, and refrigerate for at least 1 hour.

6. Top pie with blueberry pie filling. Refrigerate until well chilled before serving.

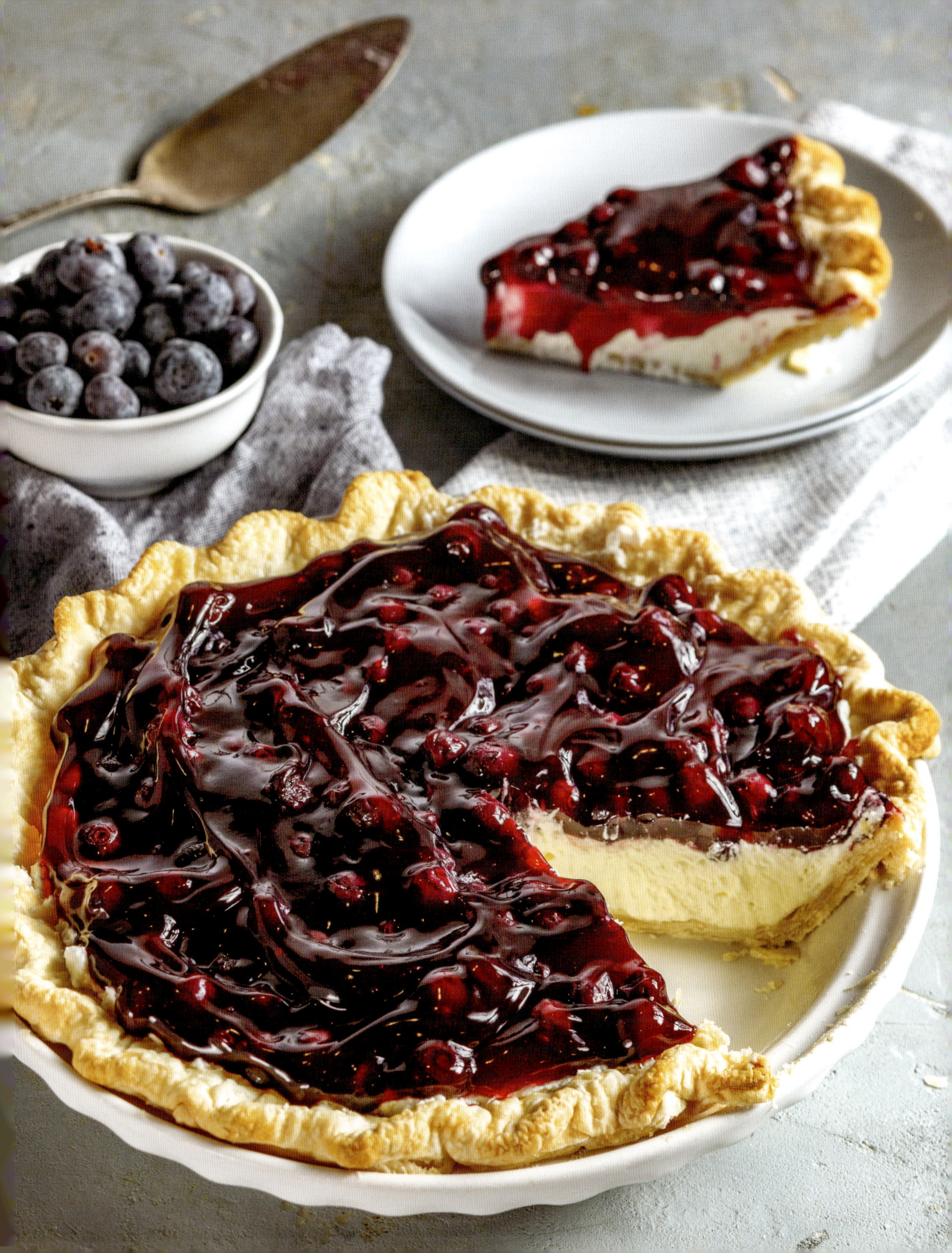

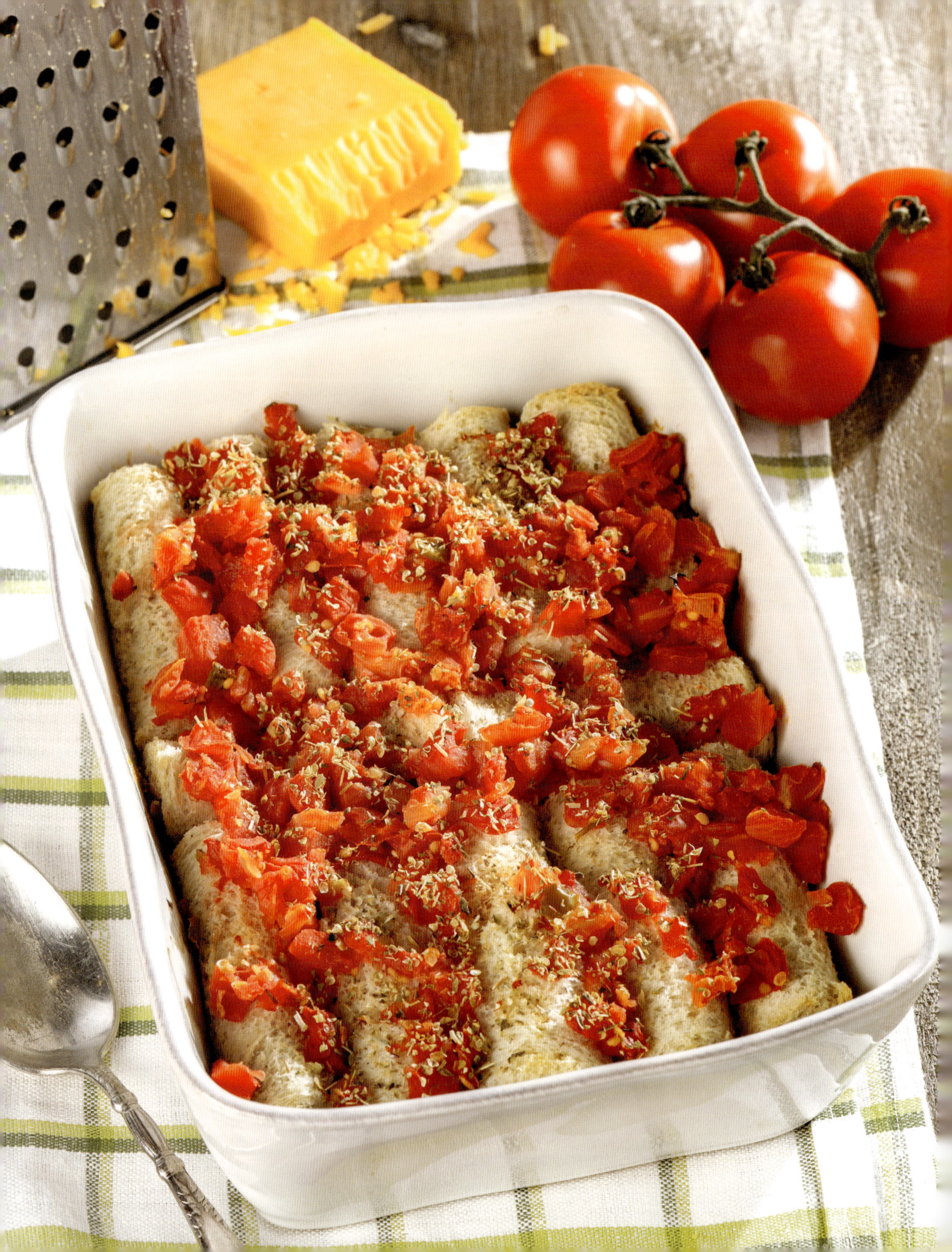

PIMIENTO CHEESE TOMATO BAKE

Oh, I love this recipe! You can't have just one serving. The sharp Cheddar cheese mixed with the fresh tomatoes is pure heaven.

Makes 8 to 10 servings

- 1 cup grated Monterey Jack cheese
- 1 cup grated sharp Cheddar cheese
- ½ cup mayonnaise
- 1 (3-ounce) package cream cheese, room temperature
- 3 tablespoons mashed pimientos
- 1 teaspoon grated onion
- ½ teaspoon House Seasoning (recipe on page 119), plus more to taste
- Cracked black pepper, to taste
- 12 slices white bread, crusts trimmed
- 2 to 3 ripe tomatoes, sliced
- 1 (10-ounce) can diced tomatoes with green chiles
- 2 teaspoons chopped fresh oregano or 1 teaspoon dried oregano

1. Preheat oven to 350°.

2. In a medium bowl, beat Monterey Jack, Cheddar, mayonnaise, cream cheese, pimientos, onion, House Seasoning, and cracked pepper at medium speed until creamy. Spread mixture on one side of each slice of bread. Roll up each slice up, jelly roll style.

3. In an 11x8-inch baking dish, place sliced tomatoes. Place roll-ups on top of sliced tomatoes. Sprinkle rolls with diced tomatoes and oregano.

4. Bake until golden brown, about 30 minutes. Serve warm.

My brother, Bubba, with his nephews, Jamie and Bobby. Bubba was at the perfect age to love playing with my boys and teasing them the way uncles do!

SATURDAY NIGHT VIDALIA ONIONS

You don't have to limit yourself to enjoying these delicious onions to just Saturday night, but they make a meal so extra special. I love mine with steak and salad!

Makes 1 onion

- 1 large Vidalia onion, or a comparable sweet onion, per person (about ¾ pound each)
- 1 beef bouillon cube per onion
- 1 tablespoon salted butter per onion, cut into slivers
- Ground black pepper, to taste

1. Prepare a fire in a charcoal grill.

2. Trim a slice from top of onion; peel onion without cutting off root end. Using a potato peeler, cut a small cone-shaped section from center of onion. Cut onion into quarters from top down, stopping within ½ inch of root end. Place bouillon cube in center, and place slivers of butter in between sections. Season with pepper. Wrap onion in a double layer of heavy-duty foil.

3. Place directly onto hot coals, and cook for 45 minutes, turning occasionally. (Alternatively, place on a rimmed baking sheet and bake at 350° until tender and bouillon cube dissolves, 45 minutes to 1 hour.) Serve in individual bowls.

When I was first married, back in the late 1960s and early '70s, going out to eat was reserved for very special occasions. Because of our tight budgets and young children, our social lives consisted of cooking out with our friends on Saturday nights. When the steaks and Vidalia onions were piled on our plates and we took our first bites, I think for a short while we all forgot that we were as poor as church mice. We were eating like kings! What fond memories these Vidalia onions bring back.

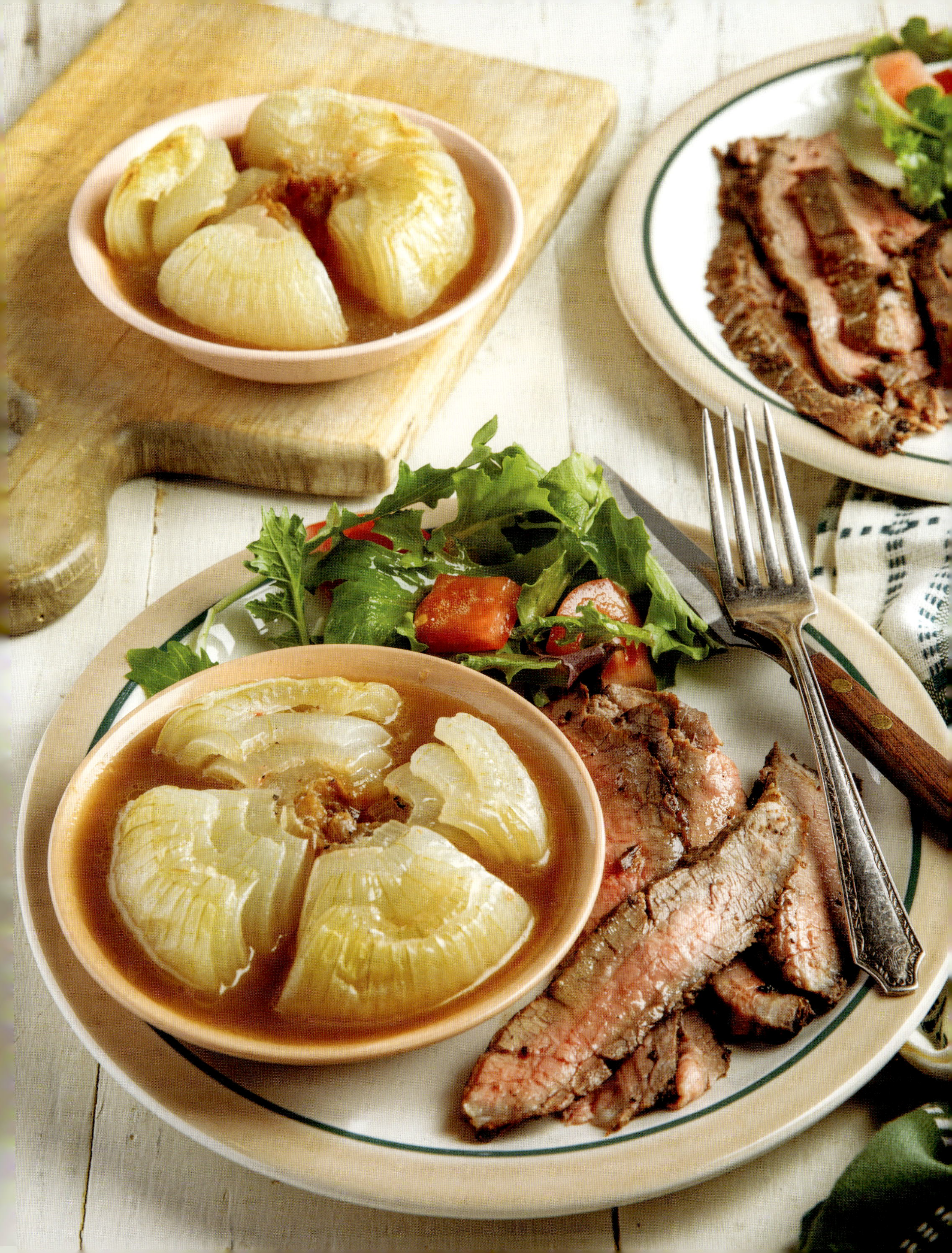

CHAPTER FOUR

SETTLING INTO SAVANNAH

I was 40 years old when we moved to Savannah. I counted once, and throughout our marriage, Jimmy and I ended up moving 23 times. The day he came home and told me we were moving to Savannah—four hours away from Albany—I was devastated. My agoraphobia had become so bad that I didn't know how I'd ever get myself back home.

Not only did I have my boys to worry about, but I was also very close to Bubba's daughter, Corrie, whom he'd named after our mother. I adored her and was heartbroken to leave.

The first two months we lived in Savannah, all I could do was lie in my bed and cry. I couldn't do anything. I was absolutely terrified to leave the house and couldn't accept that I was so far from home. I was also scared for my boys. I was married to someone who couldn't be depended on to keep a job for very long, and alcohol was always a problem, which later led to our divorce.

One morning during those months of crying in bed, I woke up and something was different. I knew I had to get better. I can tell you exactly where I was standing in my bedroom when suddenly the Serenity Prayer went through my head:

God, grant me the serenity to accept the things I cannot change, the courage to change the things I can, and the wisdom to know the difference.

Obviously, I'd heard that prayer so many times, but I was floored. It was like hearing it for the very first time and God was speaking it directly to me. I finally realized what He was trying to tell me and what I should be asking Him for. I needed to accept the things I could not change. I had to accept that my parents were both gone. I had to accept that I was far away from everything I knew. I asked Him to help me take control of my life. After that, things started to get better.

I got out that day and decided to just ride around Savannah. I had barely set foot outside the house, and I told myself to just get acquainted with the city. Oh, honey, I just fell in love with her! It is such a magical place with something for everyone. She has the old, beautiful architecture, the beaches, the squares, and so much history.

After that day, I decided to take responsibility for myself. I was worried about my marriage, and I was determined to find a way to take care of my boys and myself. Since I made that decision, God hasn't missed a day of blessing me.

I began lying awake at night dreaming up what I wanted to do to make money. I told myself, "OK, Paula. It's time to put your big girl panties on. You don't have your parents and you can't rely on your husband. What are your talents?" The only thing I could think of was cooking.

After we got our tax return that year, Jimmy gave me $200 to start my business. I decided to call it The Bag Lady, and I wanted to carry lunches to local businesses to sell. I took that $200 and bought a cooler, a business license, and $50 worth of groceries.

Jamie and I ran the first route together, and after that, he ran our five routes and I made the food. I think I made about 50 tuna fish sandwiches wrapped in plastic wrap that first day. I had no idea what I was doing, but I started by selling to the nearby hospital that I had worked for as a temp.

For the next year and a half, Jamie and I ran The Bag Lady. Bobby also quit his other job to come help us full-time. It was hard work, but I was able to grow slowly, and my little business took off. I think it was a good thing I had no money in those days. No money meant I couldn't afford to make any mistakes. I couldn't and wouldn't quit.

Opposite page, left to right: Me standing in front of where The Bag Lady was born—my house. Me while visiting Wisconsin. Me with baby Corrie in my arms. **This page, right:** Me next to our new building we'd leased downtown.

JAMIE'S CHICKEN SALAD

My son Jamie has perfected this recipe and enjoys altering it to accommodate different occasions. He does a wonderful job in the kitchen as well as looking after the business management of the restaurant.

Makes 6 servings

- 1 (3½- to 4-pound) whole chicken, giblets removed
- 1 onion, quartered
- 2 stalks celery
- Salt and ground black pepper to taste
- 4 large hard-cooked eggs, peeled and chopped
- 1 cup chopped celery
- ½ cup mayonnaise
- 2 teaspoons House Seasoning (recipe on page 119)
- Dash lemon pepper seasoning
- Small amount of chicken stock

1. In a large stockpot, combine chicken, onion, celery stalks, salt, and black pepper. Bring to a boil over medium-high heat; cook until an instant-read thermometer inserted in thickest portion of chicken registers 165°, about 45 minutes. Reserve stock for another use, if desired. Remove chicken from pot; let cool enough to handle. Discard chicken skin and bones. Chop cooked chicken.

2. In a large bowl, combine diced chicken, eggs, chopped celery, mayonnaise, House Seasoning, lemon pepper seasoning, and stock, and stir until combined. Refrigerate for at least 1 hour before serving.

Variation: Try adding walnuts and canned mandarin oranges or grapes for a Hawaiian taste.

Recipe Tip

If your chicken salad is a little dry after it's been in the refrigerator, add more mayo to suit your taste.

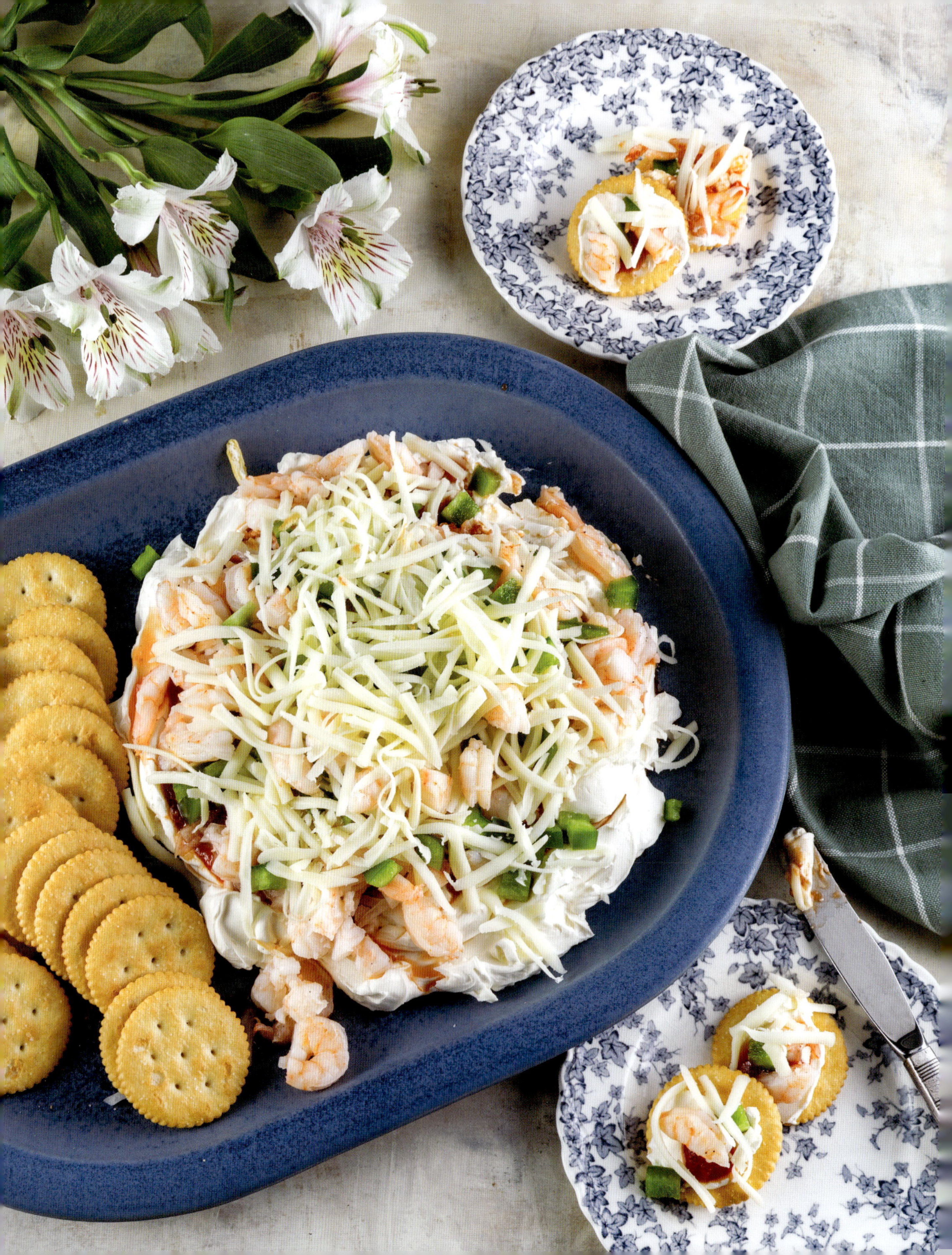

LAYERED SHRIMP DIP

My dear friend Bubbles gave me this delicious recipe! It's a refreshing, flavorful snack everyone can enjoy.

Makes 8 to 10 servings

- 1 (8-ounce) package cream cheese, room temperature
- 2 tablespoons sour cream
- 2 teaspoons Worcestershire sauce
- 1 teaspoon fresh lemon juice
- ½ teaspoon ground red pepper
- 1 clove garlic, minced
- 1 (12-ounce) bottle chili sauce
- ½ cup chopped onion
- 1½ pounds medium fresh shrimp, peeled, deveined, cooked, and chopped
- 1 small green bell pepper, finely chopped
- 2 cups shredded mozzarella cheese

Buttery round crackers, to serve

1. In a medium bowl, stir together cream cheese and sour cream. Stir in Worcestershire, lemon juice, red pepper, and garlic. Spread mixture in bottom of 12-inch platter. Layer chili sauce, onion, shrimp, bell pepper, and cheese on top. Refrigerate until ready to serve. Serve with crackers.

Jamie and Bobby with baby Corrie.

SAVANNAH BREAKFAST CASSEROLE

This filling casserole is perfect for making ahead and baking for your overnight guests.

Makes 6 to 8 servings

- 1 small onion, chopped
- 1 green bell pepper, chopped
- ½ cup fresh mushrooms
- 1 pound ground sausage
- 8 slices bacon, chopped
- 9 large eggs, lightly beaten
- 4 cups whole milk
- 8 slices white bread, cubed
- 1½ cups sharp Cheddar cheese, grated
- ½ cup Parmesan cheese, grated
- 1½ teaspoons dry mustard
- ½ teaspoon salt
- Ground black pepper and ground red pepper, to taste

1. Spray a 13x9-inch baking dish with cooking spray.

2. In a large skillet, cook onion, bell pepper, and mushrooms over medium-high heat for 1 to 2 minutes; let cool.

3. Scramble sausage and bacon until half-cooked; drain and set aside.

4. In a large bowl, stir together eggs, milk, bread, cheeses, dry mustard, salt, black pepper, and red pepper; add cooled onion mixture and half of sausage mixture. Pour into prepared pan. Place remaining sausage mixture on top. Cover and refrigerate overnight.

5. Let casserole stand at room temperature for 30 minutes.

6. Preheat oven to 350°.

7. Bake, covered, for 45 minutes to 1 hour. Uncover and bake until bubbly and set in center, about 15 minutes.

Me and Jamie working in the kitchen.
Our air conditioner had broken on this day, and it was so hot that we had to put cold, wet rags on our heads to keep from fainting!

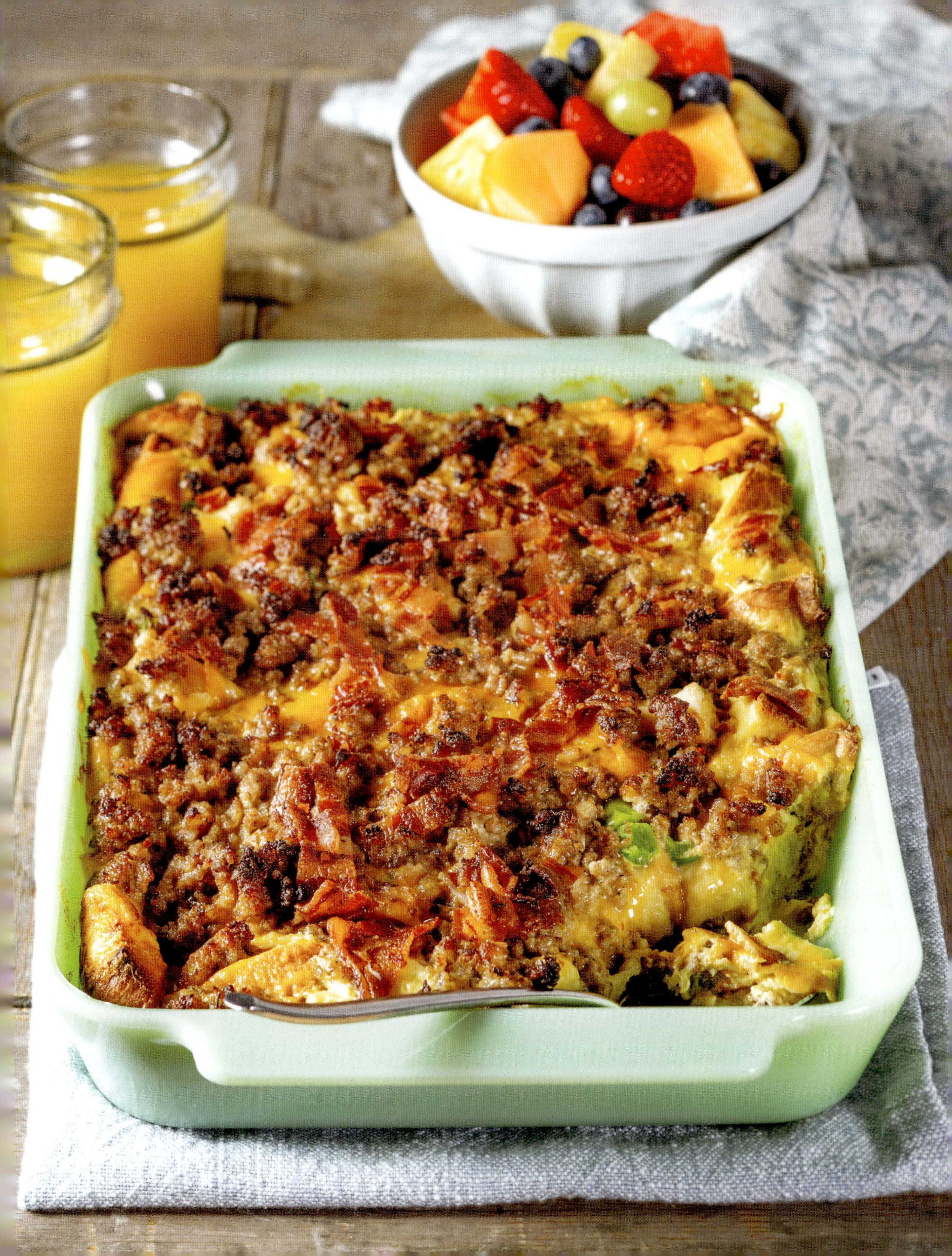

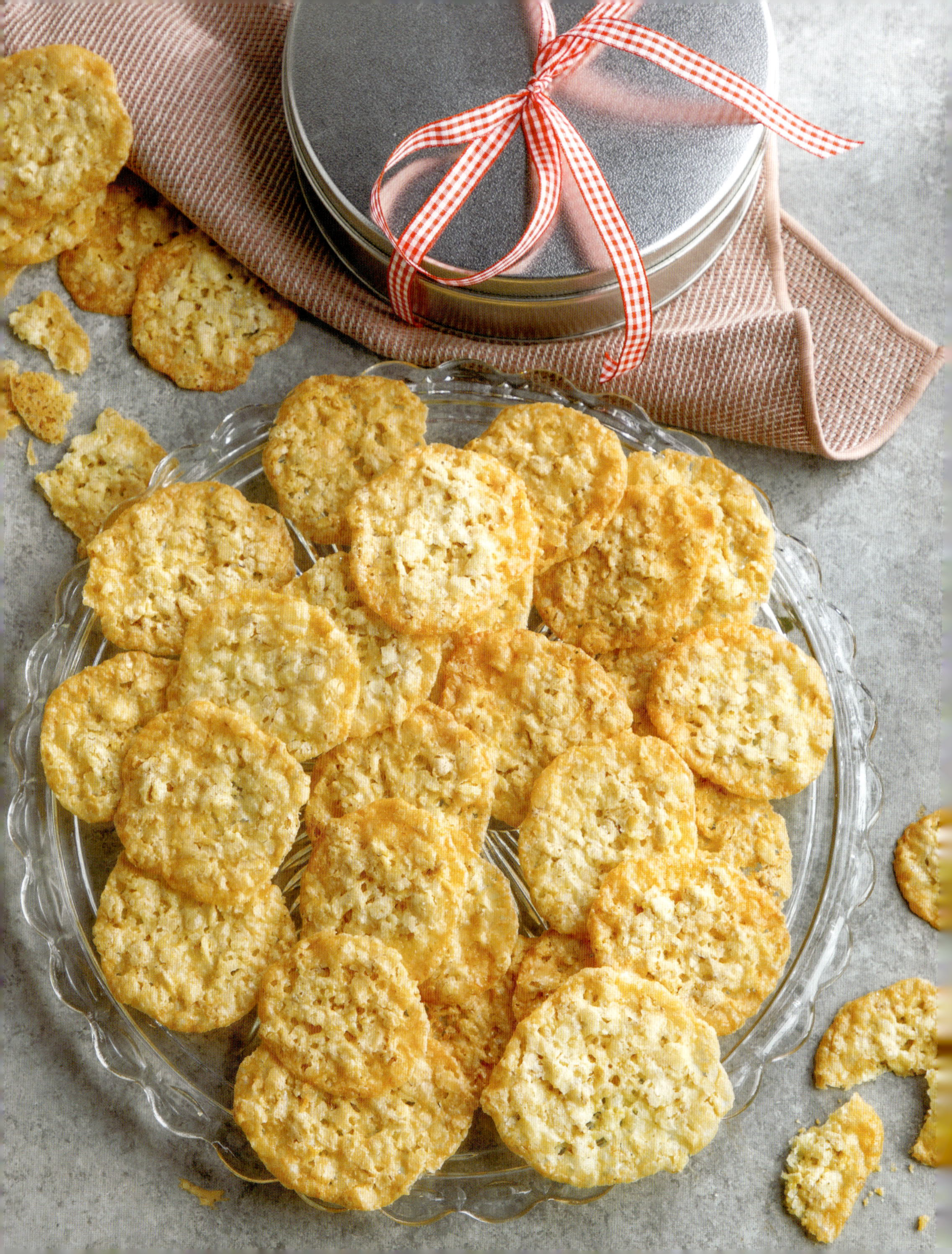

LACE COOKIES

Bubbles is famous for these delicate and perfectly crisp cookies! There is truly nothing better than sharing great food with great friends.

Makes about 75

- 1 cup sugar
- 1 cup old-fashioned oats
- 1½ teaspoons all-purpose flour
- ¼ teaspoon salt
- ½ cup salted butter, melted and very hot
- 1 large egg, beaten
- ½ teaspoon vanilla extract

1. Preheat oven to 350°. Line baking sheets with parchment.

2. In a large bowl, stir together sugar, oats, flour, and salt. Pour melted butter over mixture, and stir until sugar is melted. Add egg and vanilla. Stir well. Scoop mixture by ½ teaspoonfuls, and drop 2 inches apart onto prepared pans.

3. Bake until lightly browned, 10 to 12 minutes. Let cool on pans until cookies can be easily removed with a spatula. Gently remove from pan.

My amazing friend Susan, a.k.a. Bubbles. She has been with me through thick and thin, and I love her so very much.

PIMIENTO CHEESE

This is my son Bobby's recipe for pimiento cheese. Whenever we have pimiento cheese sandwiches at our home, everyone wants Bobby to make them because this recipe is a definite favorite.

Makes 2 cups

- 1 (8-ounce) package cream cheese, room temperature
- 1 cup shredded sharp Cheddar cheese
- 1 cup shredded Monterey Jack cheese
- ½ cup mayonnaise
- 2 to 3 tablespoons mashed pimientos
- 1 teaspoon grated onion (optional)
- ½ teaspoon House Seasoning (recipe on page 119)
- Cracked black pepper, to taste
- Buttery round crackers and vegetables, to serve

1. In a medium bowl, beat cream cheese with a mixer at medium speed until fluffy; add Cheddar, Monterey Jack, mayonnaise, pimientos, grated onion (if using), House Seasoning, and black pepper, and beat until well blended. Cover and refrigerate for at least 1 hour. Serve with crackers and vegetables or use to make a sandwich.

Me with my son Bobby. Bobby was known for his delicious desserts at the restaurant along with this Pimiento Cheese. I taught Jamie how to make chicken salad and Bobby how to make pimiento cheese—they both ended up creating recipes better than mine!

Bobby also ran the front of house and was good at talking to every single customer and making all feel welcome and special.

Recipe Tip

If your pimiento cheese is a little dry after it's been in the refrigerator, add more mayo to suit your taste.

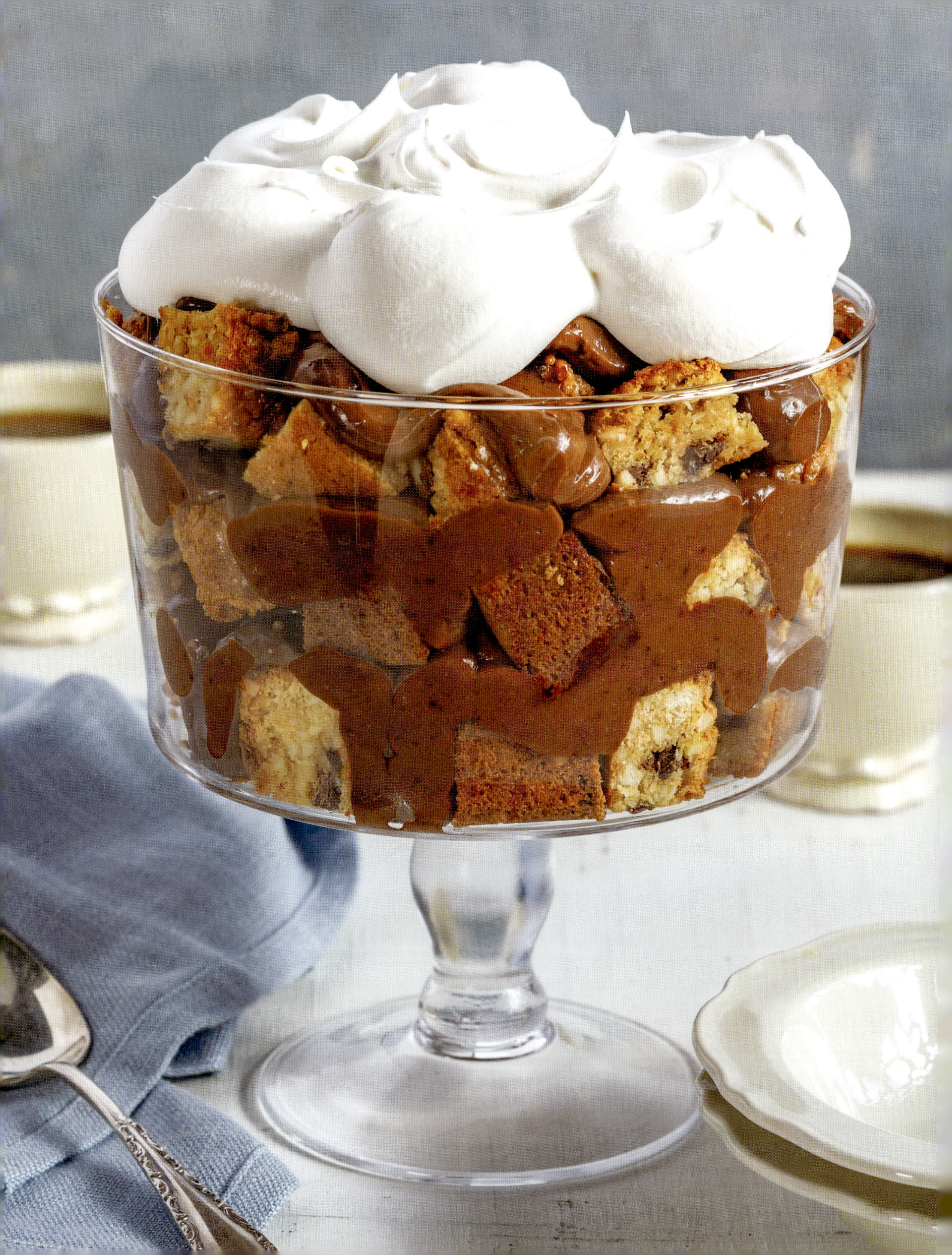

CHOCOLATE TRIFLE

This dessert comes together quickly and tastes just as good as it looks!

Makes 20 to 25 servings

- 3 large eggs
- ½ cup salted butter
- 1 (16-ounce) package light brown sugar
- 1 tablespoon vanilla extract
- 2 cups self-rising flour
- 2 cups chopped almonds
- 6 ounces chocolate chips
- 1 cup flaked sweetened coconut (optional)
- 2 (3.4-ounce) packages chocolate cook-and-serve pudding mix
- ¼ cup sherry
- 2 cups heavy whipping cream
- ½ cup granulated sugar

1. Preheat oven to 375°. Spray a 13x9-inch glass baking dish with baking spray with flour.

2. In a large bowl, beat eggs and butter with a mixer at medium speed until combined. Beat in brown sugar and vanilla; gradually add flour, beating until combined. Fold in almonds, chocolate chips, and coconut (if using). Spread batter into prepared pan.

3. Bake until wooden pick inserted in the center comes out clean, 25 to 30 minutes. Let cool completely. Cut into 1-inch squares.

4. Prepare pudding mixes according to package directions. Let cool slightly.

5. Place a layer of blondies in a 4-quart dish, and sprinkle with sherry. Spoon pudding on top. Repeat layers.

6. In another large bowl, beat cream and granulated sugar at medium-high speed until stiff peaks form. Spoon whipped cream mixture onto trifle. Refrigerate until ready to serve.

In the restaurant kitchen on a particularly harried day, the baker had put a pan of blondies in the oven and in the rush, had left them in too long—the blondies were burned. But we had to have that dessert. "Don't worry," I told her, "I'll think of something." I cut the blondies into pieces and carefully trimmed off the burned edges. I crumbled up the good part, sprinkled it with sherry, covered it with chocolate pudding, and topped it with fresh whipped cream—and our Chocolate Trifle was born. Today, it is one of our most requested desserts. Oh, by the way, you don't have to go to the trouble of burning the blondies!

FRENCH CREAM

This recipe is simple and adds so much flavor and fun to your favorite fresh fruit and fruit salads.

Makes about 9 servings

- 1 (8-ounce) package cream cheese, softened
- 1 cup confectioners' sugar
- 1 teaspoon lemon zest
- 2 tablespoons fresh lemon juice
- 1 tablespoon pineapple juice
- 1 teaspoon orange zest
- 1 cup cold heavy whipping cream
- ¼ cup granulated sugar

Fresh fruit or fruit salad, to serve

Garnish: orange zest

1. In a large bowl, beat cream cheese and confectioners' sugar with a mixer at medium speed until smooth. Beat in lemon zest and juice, pineapple juice, and orange zest until blended.

2. In a medium bowl, beat cold cream and granulated sugar with a mixer at high speed just until stiff peaks form. Fold whipped cream into cream cheese mixture. Serve immediately, or cover and refrigerate up to 4 hours. Serve over fruit. Garnish with orange zest, if desired.

Jamie, Bobby, and me. This was right before we moved to Savannah. I was terrified of the change, but it turned out to be the most wonderful move I could have made.

Recipe Tip

If your French Cream is a little too thick for your liking, you can always thin it out with some orange juice.

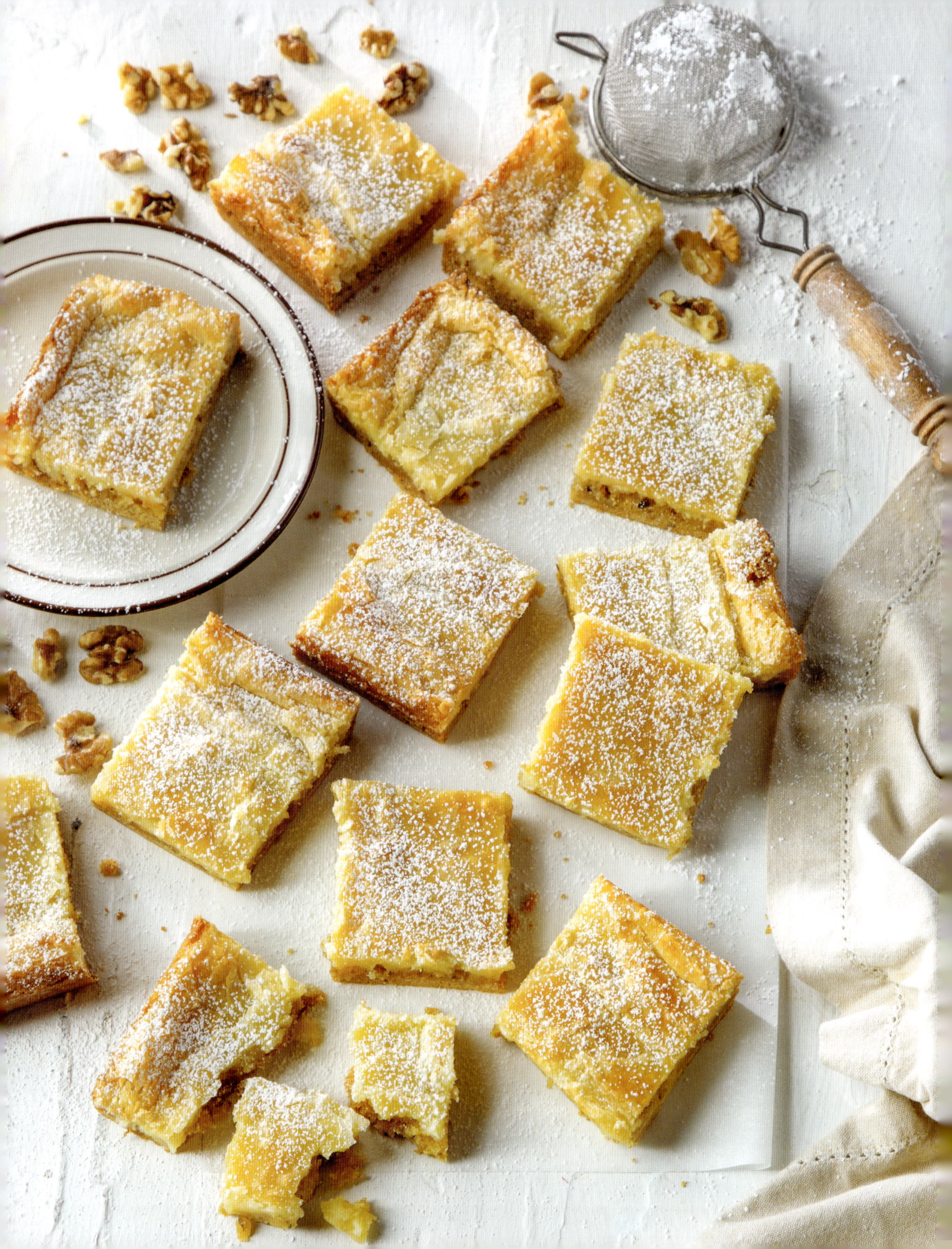

GOOEY BUTTER CAKE BARS

Y'all know I love gooey butter cake! These have been my go-to for decades, and it's one of the recipes that really put our business on the map.

Makes about 24

- 1 (15.25-ounce) box yellow cake mix
- 3 large eggs, divided
- 1 cup salted butter, melted and divided
- ½ cup finely chopped walnuts
- 1 (8-ounce) package cream cheese, softened
- 1 teaspoon vanilla extract
- 1 (16-ounce) package confectioners' sugar

Garnish: confectioners' sugar

1. Preheat oven to 350°. Spray a 13x9-inch baking pan with baking spray with flour.

2. In a large bowl, beat cake mix, 1 egg, ½ cup melted butter, and walnuts with a mixer at medium speed just until combined. Press mixture into prepared pan.

3. In another large bowl, beat cream cheese with a mixer at medium speed until smooth. Beat in vanilla and remaining 2 eggs until combined. With mixer on low speed, add confectioners' sugar, beating until well combined. Slowly add remaining ½ cup melted butter, beating until well combined. Pour filling onto prepared crust.

4. Bake until center is just set but still has some movement, 40 to 45 minutes. (Do not overcook.) Let cool completely on a wire rack. Cut into bars, and garnish with confectioners' sugar, if desired.

We started The Bag Lady on June 19, 1989. I made gooey butter cakes every single day. I swear, I don't know how I did it. I made so many! By the time October came around, I was so sick of cooking gooey butter cakes that I wanted to make a pumpkin version to change things up. They were a hit and are still so popular in the fall.

CHEESE APPETIZERS

Another favorite from Bubbles! These are so easy and tasty as a presupper snack.

Makes about 72

2   cups shredded Cheddar cheese
½   cup chopped green onion
½   cup mayonnaise
1   (2.25-ounce) can black olives, chopped
½   teaspoon curry powder
Square whole wheat wafers
Garnish: chopped green onion

1. Position oven rack to lowest level. Preheat oven to broil.

2. In a medium bowl, stir together cheese, green onion, mayonnaise, olives, and curry powder. Spread on wafers, and place on a rimmed baking sheet.

3. Broil until cheese is melted, about 2 minutes. Garnish with green onion, if desired.

SWEET POTATO CHIPS

A wonderful friend of my Aunt Peggy's gave me this recipe. They are the perfect combination of salty and sweet!

Makes 4 to 6 servings

- ½ cup salted butter, melted
- 2 large sweet potatoes, sliced crosswise ¼ inch thick
- 1 cup honey-roasted peanuts, finely chopped
- Salt (optional)

1. Preheat oven to 450°. Line 2 large baking sheets with foil. Lightly spray foil with cooking spray.

2. In a small bowl, place melted butter. Dip potatoes in melted butter, and place in a single layer on prepared pans. (Do not overlap.) Sprinkle with peanuts.

3. Bake until tender and edges are lightly browned, 15 to 20 minutes. Sprinkle with salt (if using).

SETTLING INTO SAVANNAH | LOVE AND BEST DISHES

BENNE WAFERS

If you've never tried baking with benne or sesame seeds, you are in for a treat with these wafers!

Makes 40

- 1 cup benne or sesame seeds
- ¼ cup salted butter, softened
- 1 cup firmly packed light brown sugar
- 1 large egg
- 1 tablespoon lemon zest
- ½ teaspoon vanilla extract
- ½ cup all-purpose flour
- ⅛ teaspoon salt
- ⅛ teaspoon baking powder

1. Preheat oven to 325°. Line a rimmed baking sheet with parchment paper.

2. On prepared pan, spread benne seeds in a single layer.

3. Bake until lightly browned, 5 to 7 minutes. Let cool. Leave oven on.

4. Line 4 rimmed baking sheets with parchment paper.

5. In a large bowl, beat butter and brown sugar with a mixer at medium speed until fluffy, 3 to 4 minutes, stopping to scrape sides of bowl. Add egg, beating well. Beat in lemon zest and vanilla.

6. In a small bowl, whisk together flour, salt, and baking powder. Gradually add flour mixture to butter mixture, beating at low speed until combined. Beat in toasted seeds. Using a 2-teaspoon spring-loaded scoop, drop batter 3 inches apart onto prepared pans. (Wafers will spread.)

7. Bake until deep golden brown, about 15 minutes. Let cool on pans for 5 minutes. Remove from pans, and let cool completely on wire racks. Store in an airtight container with layers separated by wax paper.

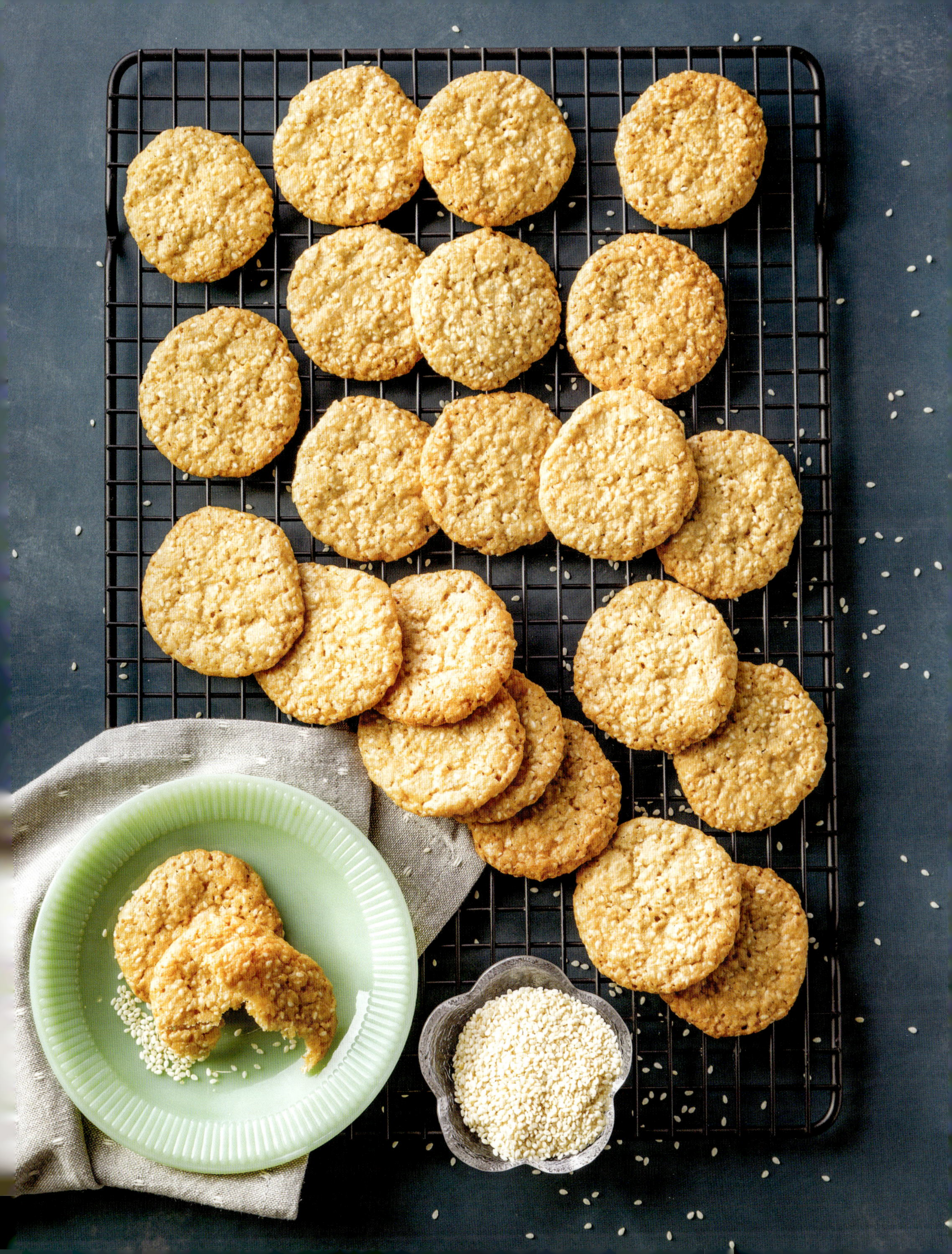

CHAPTER FIVE

THE LADY & SONS

After a year and a half of running The Bag Lady, I knew it was time to make a big leap. I still wanted to run my catering business, but I also heard that the nearby Best Western had a vacancy in their restaurant space.

It was perfect for me! It was already fully furnished—all I had to do was bring in my groceries. When I interviewed with the owner of the motel, he said he was going to take a chance on me because he could see the determination in my eyes.

We were there for five long, hard years. Seven days a week, three meals a day. The kitchen was small and hot—the ventilation was so bad—but business was good, and catering was a great supplement. It was the hardest work of my life, though. Some nights, I'd work so late in the kitchen and have a catering job early the next morning, so I'd just curl up in one of the booths and sleep there. I never took a day off.

I knew I couldn't stay at the Best Western forever. Business was good, but it was only locals who spent time in that part of town. I had my sights set on downtown—I wanted to be able to serve both the locals and the tourists. I saved up $20,000 to make our next move, and I got in touch with a man who owned an available building downtown. I walked in and thought, "Oh, my gosh. This is it!"

All improvements to the building would be up to the tenant to finance—the landlord would do none of it. I had an estimated cost of $150,000—which I did not have—but I signed the lease right then and there. I had to make it work.

I went to the bank for a loan with my $20,000 to offer as collateral. Every bank I talked to said that would not be enough—I needed at least $40,000.

I tried everything but could not figure out a way to get that money. I was ready to lay my head down on my desk and cry when the phone rang. It was my Uncle George. He said, "Paula, your Aunt Peggy and I want to help you. We believe you can do it." So, my dear Aunt Peggy loaned me her $25,000 CD to use as collateral. I was over the moon with joy and so grateful to her.

Naming the restaurant was a no-brainer for me. I was running the place with my two sons, so naturally, The Lady & Sons was born. Later, I realized that other women really loved the name and what it stood for. People loved our story. I was a single lady who built up a phenomenal business with my two boys—I truly could not have done it without them.

By the time the restaurant opened, I had racked up about $1,000 in parking tickets. We had no money for anything, let alone parking meters! Within less than a year, though, The Lady & Sons had become so successful, the bank released that money back to my Aunt Peggy.

So many wonderful things started happening once we were up and running. I remember the Friday morning Jamie called me at 6 a.m. all excited. He said, "Momma. Momma, Momma! Every December, the *USA Today* reporters name the best meal they'd eaten as they traveled the world for work. We were the number one most delicious meal they had this year!" We couldn't believe our humble little buffet had taken the top honors. That was when I realized we were going to be just fine.

Opposite page, from left: Me with my boys. Me going through the dumpster at Barnett's Novelty Company—we had just started renovating this building for the restaurant. **This page, top:** My sweet Aunt Peggy. She would drive up to help me for a couple of weeks at a time when I was so tired I couldn't go on. Her support kept me going for all those years! **Above:** Jamie, Bobby, and me.

Name Game

It's common to see businesses that fathers and sons run together but not so much mothers and sons. The Lady & Sons was a unique name and people loved our story.

CRAB FRIED RICE

A long-time employee and dear friend of mine, Nita, who goes by "Jellyroll," taught me how to make this fried rice. She says she's retired from the restaurant now, but I know she still goes in every day! Our guests just adore her, and so do I.

Makes 4 to 6 servings

- 1½ cups basmati rice
- 1¼ teaspoons salt, divided
- ⅓ cup salted butter
- 1 cup chopped onion
- ¾ cup chopped red bell pepper
- ⅔ cup chopped celery
- 2 cloves garlic, minced
- ½ teaspoon Creole seasoning
- ½ pound lump crabmeat, picked free of shell
- 2 tablespoons chopped fresh parsley

1. Cook rice according to package directions, adding ½ teaspoon salt. Spread cooked rice onto a baking sheet; let cool.

2. In a 12-inch skillet, melt butter over medium-high heat. Add onion, bell pepper, and celery; cook, stirring frequently, until softened, about 5 minutes. Add garlic; cook for 1 minute. Add rice, Creole seasoning, and remaining ¾ teaspoon salt. Reduce heat to medium; cook, stirring frequently, until rice is heated through, about 5 minutes. Gently stir in crab; cook until heated through, about 2 minutes. Sprinkle with parsley. Serve immediately.

Jellyroll ringing the bell for lunchtime.

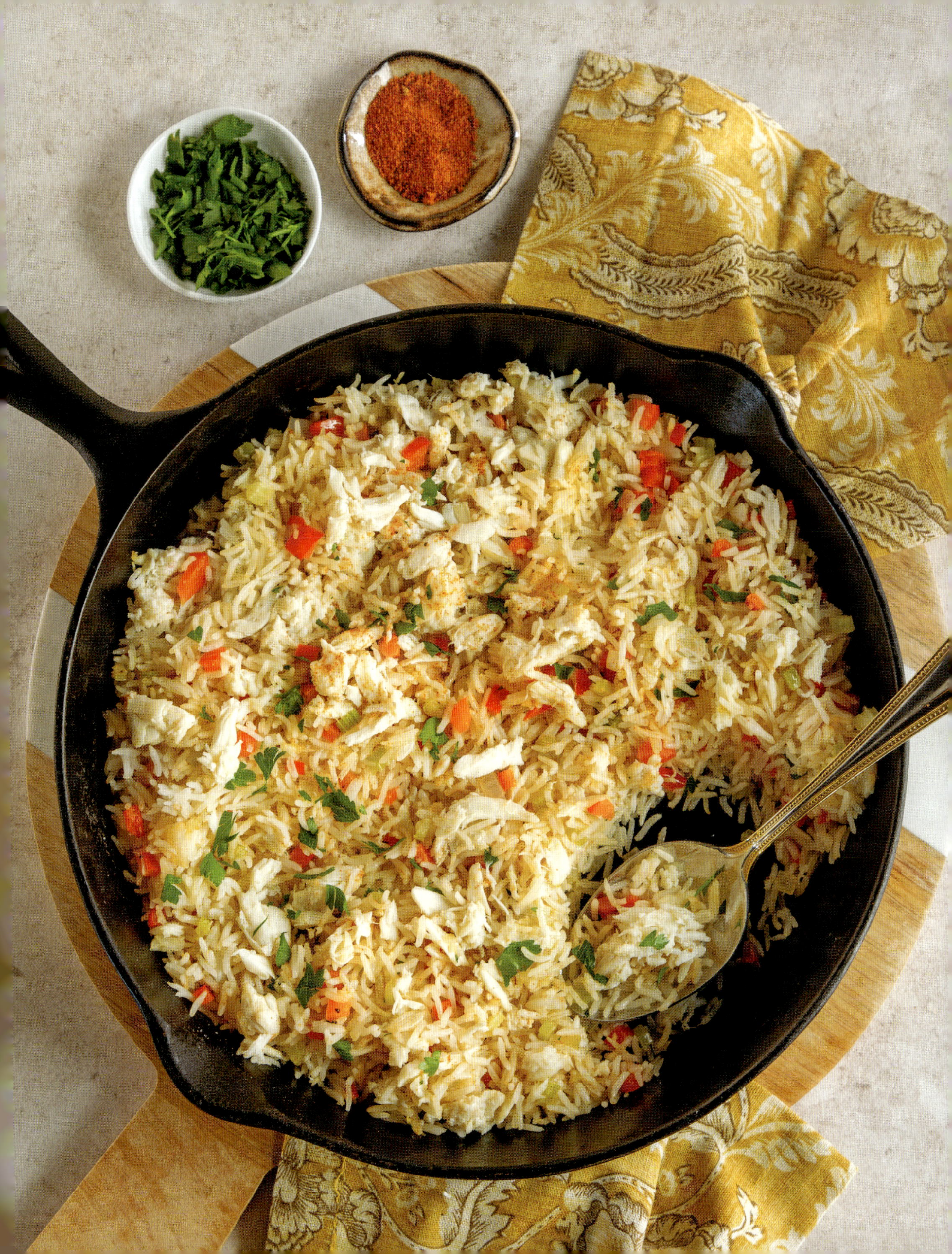

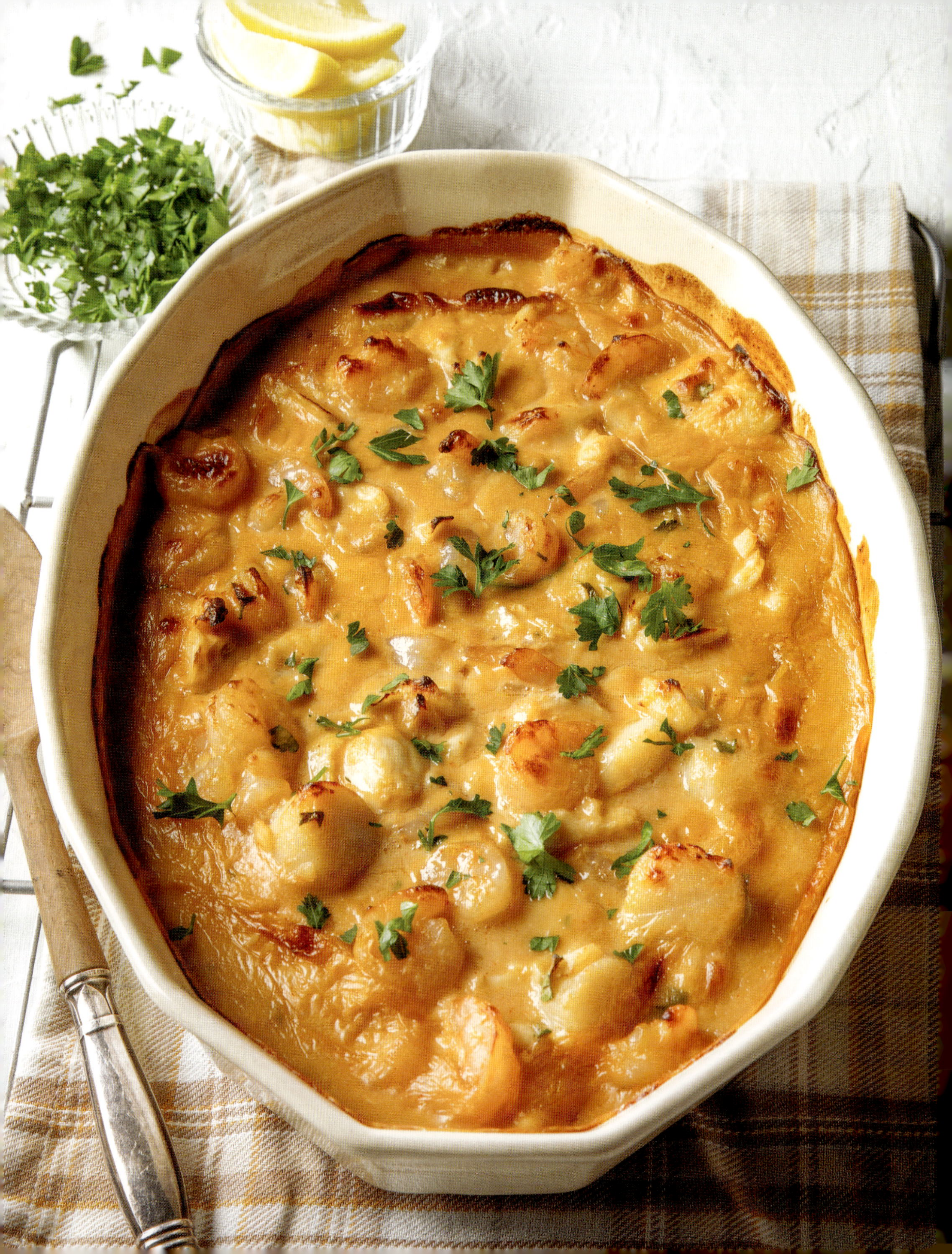

DEVILED SEAFOOD CASSEROLE

Fresh shrimp and scallops combine in this dish, and oh, my gosh, honey, you will not be disappointed in the flavor! This casserole reminds me so much of the rich food and culture we have here in Savannah.

Makes 8 servings

- ¾ cup salted butter, divided
- 1½ pounds fresh shrimp, peeled and deveined
- 1 pound fresh sea scallops
- 1 (1-pound) haddock fillet
- ½ cup plus 1 tablespoon all-purpose flour
- 1 cup evaporated milk
- 1 cup consommé or beef broth
- ⅓ cup whole milk
- 2 tablespoons cornstarch
- 2 tablespoons chopped fresh parsley
- 4 teaspoons ketchup
- 1 tablespoon prepared horseradish
- 1 tablespoon fresh lemon juice
- 1 tablespoon Worcestershire sauce
- 1 teaspoon garlic powder
- 1 teaspoon dry mustard
- 1 teaspoon soy sauce
- ½ teaspoon salt
- ¼ teaspoon ground red pepper
- ½ cup dry sherry

Garnish: chopped fresh parsley

1. Preheat oven to 400°. Spray a 3-quart baking dish with cooking spray.

2. In a 12-inch skillet, melt ¼ cup butter over medium-high heat. Add shrimp and scallops, and cook, stirring frequently, until scallops are no longer translucent and shrimp begin to curl, 3 to 5 minutes. Remove from skillet.

3. In a large saucepan, pour water to a depth of 2 inches, and heat over medium heat until bubbles form around sides of pan. Add fish, and cook until fish flakes easily with a fork, 6 to 8 minutes. Remove from pan, and let cool slightly. Cut into bite-size pieces.

4. In same skillet, melt remaining ½ cup butter over medium heat. Stir in flour and evaporated milk; add consommé or broth. Cook over medium heat, whisking constantly, until thick.

5. In a medium bowl, whisk together whole milk and cornstarch. Add parsley, ketchup, horseradish, lemon juice, Worcestershire, garlic powder, dry mustard, soy sauce, salt, and red pepper. Add to sauce in skillet, and stir well. Add seafood, and stir in sherry. Pour into prepared pan.

6. Bake until bubbly, about 30 minutes. Garnish with parsley, if desired.

GREEN PEA SALAD

My wonderful friends Donna and Curtis Foltz gave me this recipe. Simple and tasty, this is a perfect side dish!

Makes about 6 servings

- 1 (32-ounce) bag frozen peas, steamed
- ½ cup bacon bits
- Creole Mustard Dressing (recipe on page 135)
- Salt and ground black pepper, to taste

1. In a large bowl, toss together peas, bacon bits, and Creole Mustard Dressing; season to taste with salt and pepper. Serve immediately, or refrigerate until ready to serve.

HOUSE SEASONING

My House Seasoning can be used in so many ways. You'll find plenty of recipes throughout this book that it can be used in, too!

Makes about 1½ cups

- 1 cup salt
- ¼ cup garlic powder
- ¼ cup ground black pepper
- ¼ cup onion powder

1. In a jar with a tight-fitting lid, combine all ingredients. Store for up to 6 months.

CHEESEBURGER MEAT LOAF WITH CHEESE SAUCE

We all love meat loaf, and this version will have you coming back for a second helping.

Makes 6 to 8 servings

White bread slices
2 pounds ground beef
1 medium onion, chopped
1 medium green bell pepper, chopped
1 cup sour cream
1 cup crushed buttery round crackers
¼ cup Worcestershire sauce
2 teaspoons House Seasoning (recipe on page 119)
1 teaspoon seasoned salt

CHEESE SAUCE
1 (10.5-ounce) can cream of mushroom soup
1 cup whole milk
1½ cups shredded Cheddar cheese

1. Preheat oven to 325°.

2. For meat loaf: Line a rimmed baking sheet with bread to absorb liquid and grease.

3. In a large bowl, combine beef, onion, bell pepper, sour cream, crackers, Worcestershire, House Seasoning, and seasoned salt. Shape into a 10-inch loaf. Place on prepared pan on top of bread.

4. Bake until an instant-read thermometer inserted in center registers 160°, 45 minutes to 1 hour. Let cool for 10 minutes.

5. Meanwhile, for sauce: In a medium saucepan, bring soup and milk to a low boil over medium heat, stirring frequently; remove from heat, and stir in cheese until melted.

6. Discard bread. Serve meat loaf with cheese sauce.

Aunt Peggy and Uncle George on their wedding day.

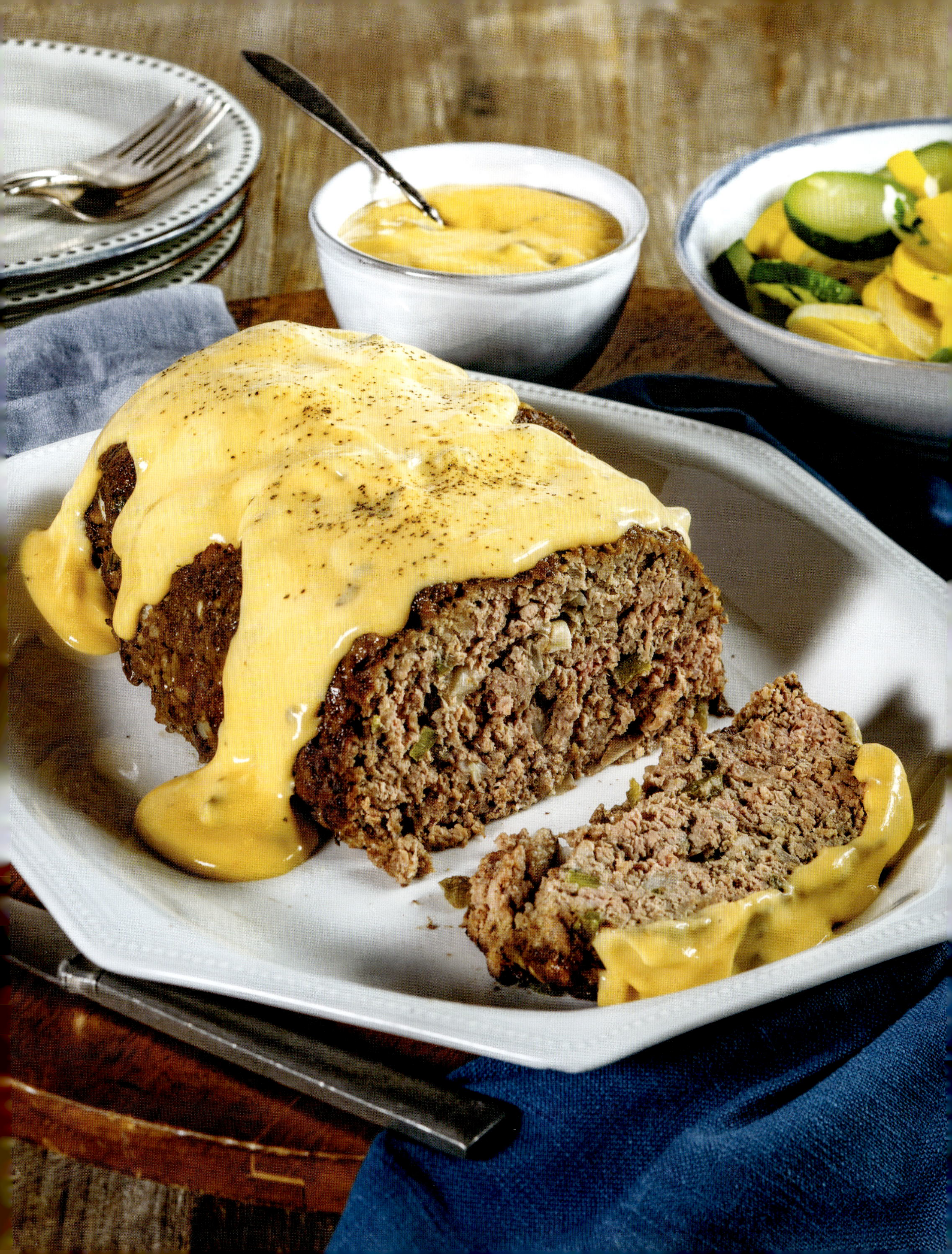

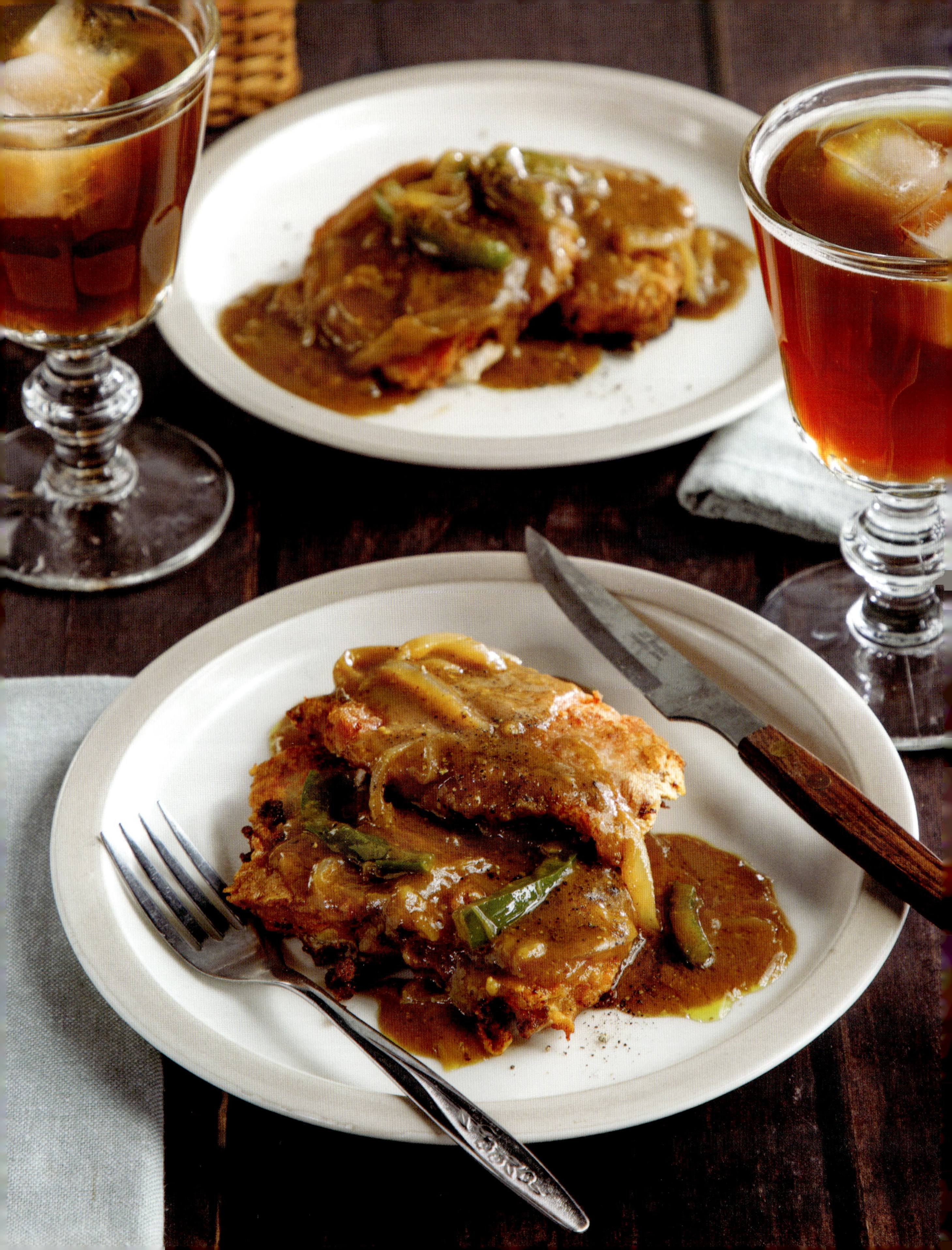

CHICKEN-FRIED PORK CHOPS WITH GRAVY

The pork chops are fried to perfection, and the gravy is pure heaven.

Makes 5 to 8 servings

9¾ cups water, divided

½ cup plus 2 teaspoons House Seasoning (recipe on page 119), divided or to taste

10 (4-ounce) pork loin cuts

1¼ cups vegetable or soybean oil, divided

1½ cups all-purpose flour, divided

2 teaspoons seasoned salt

1 medium yellow onion, julienned

1 medium to large green bell pepper, julienned

3½ tablespoons chicken base

1 teaspoon browning and seasoning sauce

1. In a large container for brining, combine 8 cups water and ½ cup House Seasoning, stirring to dissolve. Add pork; cover and refrigerate overnight.

2. Preheat oven to 200°. In a 12-inch cast iron skillet over medium heat, pour 1 cup oil and heat to 350° using a deep fry thermometer. Remove cutlets from container, discarding brine.

3. In a large shallow bowl, stir together 1¼ cups flour, seasoned salt, and remaining 2 teaspoons House Seasoning. Dredge pork in flour mixture, shaking off excess. Working in batches, add pork to skillet, and cook until golden brown and an instant-read thermometer inserted in center registers 155° to 160°, 3 to 4 minutes per side. (Reduce heat as necessary to prevent excess browning.) Transfer to a rimmed baking sheet, and keep warm in oven until ready to serve.

5. Carefully pour off all but ¼ cup oil in skillet. (If more oil is needed, then add remaining ¼ cup oil.) Heat same skillet over medium heat. Stir in remaining ¼ cup flour. Cook, stirring constantly, until roux is the color of peanut butter, 10 to 12 minutes.

6. Add onion, bell pepper, and chicken base to roux, and cook, stirring occasionally, until vegetables are softened, 8 to 10 minutes. Add browning and seasoning sauce and remaining 1¾ cups water, or to your desired thickness, and simmer, stirring occasionally, for 10 minutes. Serve on top of pork.

GARLIC POTATO SALAD

We all have our favorites when it comes to potato salad, but you need to give this garlicky version from my friends Donna and Curtis Foltz a try. It is the perfect side to bring to a party or serve with your favorite main dish.

Makes 8 to 10 servings

- 5 medium baking potatoes, cubed
- 2 cups chopped celery
- 1 cup sliced green onion
- 5 hard-cooked eggs, peeled and halved
- ⅓ cup plus 1 tablespoon yellow mustard
- ⅓ cup olive oil
- ⅓ cup mayonnaise
- 2 tablespoons tarragon vinegar
- 1 teaspoon Worcestershire sauce
- 1 large clove garlic, mashed
- Salt and ground black pepper, to taste
- Garnish: chopped fresh parsley

1. In a large saucepan, bring potatoes and water to cover to a boil over high heat; reduce heat, and simmer until tender, about 8 minutes. Drain, and let cool.

2. In a large bowl, combine potatoes, celery, and green onion.

3. Separate egg yolks from egg whites. Chop egg whites, and add to potato mixture.

4. In a medium bowl, mash egg yolks; add mustard, oil, mayonnaise, vinegar, Worcestershire, and garlic. Mix and toss with potato mixture. Season to taste with salt and pepper. Refrigerate for 1 hour before serving. Garnish with parsley, if desired.

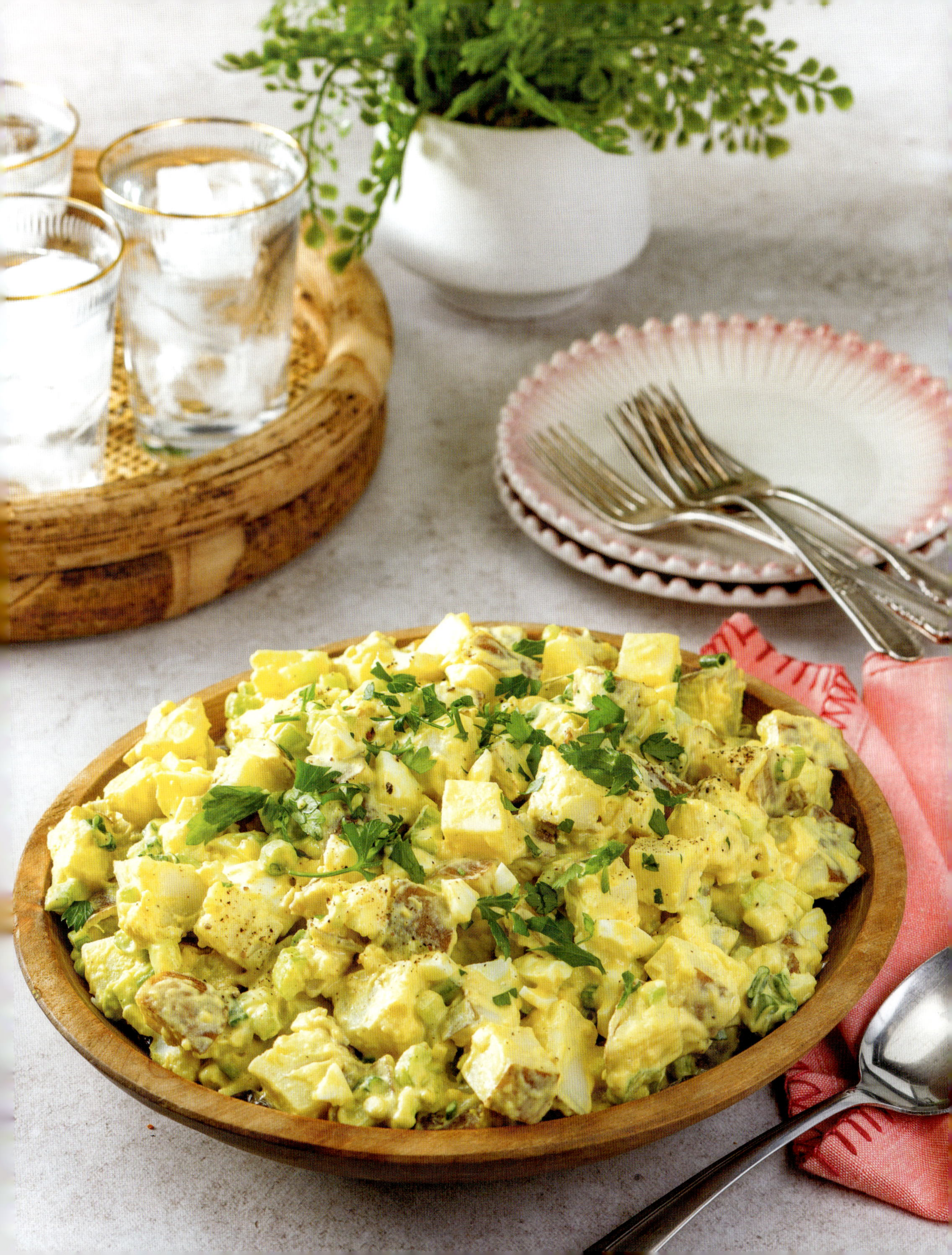

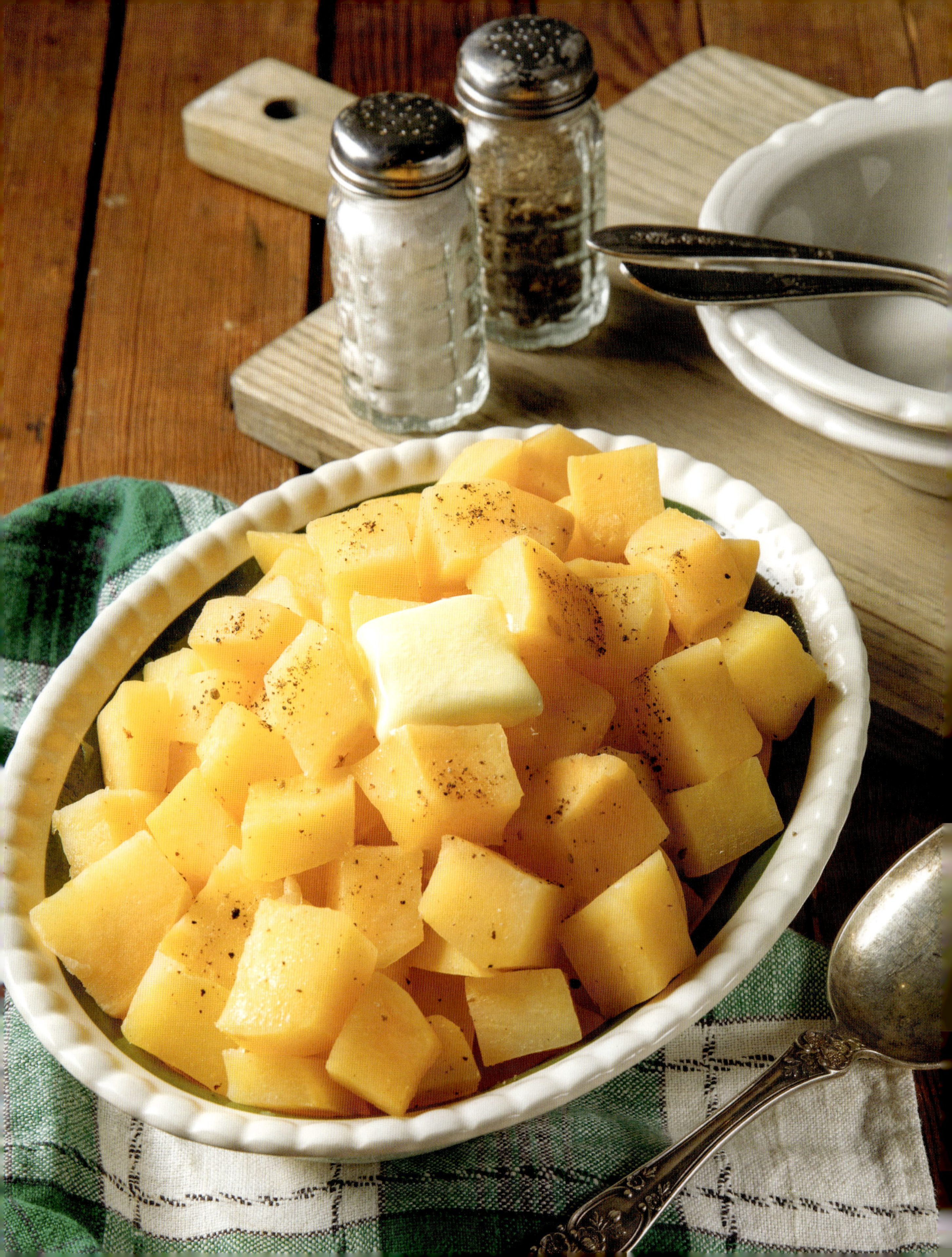

BUTTERED RUTABAGAS

Rutabagas are a winter vegetable, so make sure you enjoy them while you can! This recipe is a Southern must-try.

Makes 4 to 6 servings

- 1 large ham hock (can also use smoked turkey wings, or even chopped bacon)
- ½ teaspoon salt
- ½ teaspoon ground black pepper
- Pinch sugar
- 1 rutabaga (about 2 pounds)
- 2 tablespoons salted butter, plus more to serve

1. In a medium Dutch oven, place ham hock and enough water to cover. Add salt, pepper, and sugar. Bring to a boil; reduce heat, and simmer for 45 minutes to 1 hour.

2. Meanwhile, peel rutabaga, and cut into cubes (as you would cut up potatoes for potato salad—about the same size). Add rutabaga to meat; add more water if needed to cover rutabaga. Cover and cook until rutabaga is tender, 30 to 45 minutes. Remove rutabaga from pot, and add butter, stirring until melted. Serve with butter.

Clint Eastwood was in for dinner one night while he was here in Savannah filming *Midnight in the Garden of Good and Evil*. That particular night, we had rutabagas on the buffet. He made a point to tell me that he was a 10-year-old boy the last time he had tasted this wonderful vegetable. He said that he really enjoyed them again after all those years.

TURNIP GREENS WITH CORNMEAL DUMPLINGS

The first time I cooked a meal for my new family with Michael, I made this recipe. While it was sitting on the stove, I left the kitchen for a minute and when I came back, our daughter Michelle had eaten all but two of the dumplings! She had never had them before and fell in love with them. I still love to make them for her today!

Makes 4 to 6 servings

- 1 bunch fresh turnip greens (about 2 pounds)
- 1 pound turnip roots (about 5 medium)
- 12 cups water
- 1 ham hock, for seasoning
- 1 tablespoon bacon drippings
- 1 teaspoon House Seasoning (recipe on page 119)
- 1 teaspoon sugar

CORNMEAL DUMPLINGS DOUGH

- 1 cup fine yellow cornmeal
- ¼ cup finely chopped yellow onion
- 1 large egg
- ½ teaspoon salt
- ¼ to ⅔ cup pot likker from cooked turnips

1. For greens: Wash greens thoroughly in cold water until water runs clear. (You will need to change the water two or three times.) Strip each leaf from the stem, discarding stems. Tear leaves a few times.

2. Peel and slice turnip roots; set aside.

3. In a large stockpot, place 12 cups water and ham hock. Bring to a boil over medium-high heat. Reduce heat to low, and cook for 1½ hours.

4. Add greens, bacon drippings, House Seasoning, and sugar to pot with ham hock. Cook, stirring occasionally, for 30 minutes.

5. Add turnip roots to greens mixture; bring to a boil. Reduce heat, and simmer until roots are almost tender, about 15 minutes.

6. Meanwhile, for dumplings: In a small bowl, stir together cornmeal, onion, egg, and salt. Add pot likker, 1 tablespoon at a time, stirring just until a soft dough forms. Roll mixture into 1-inch balls.

7. Return mixture to a boil; add dumplings. Cook until dumplings are cooked through center, about 8 minutes. Adjust seasonings to taste.

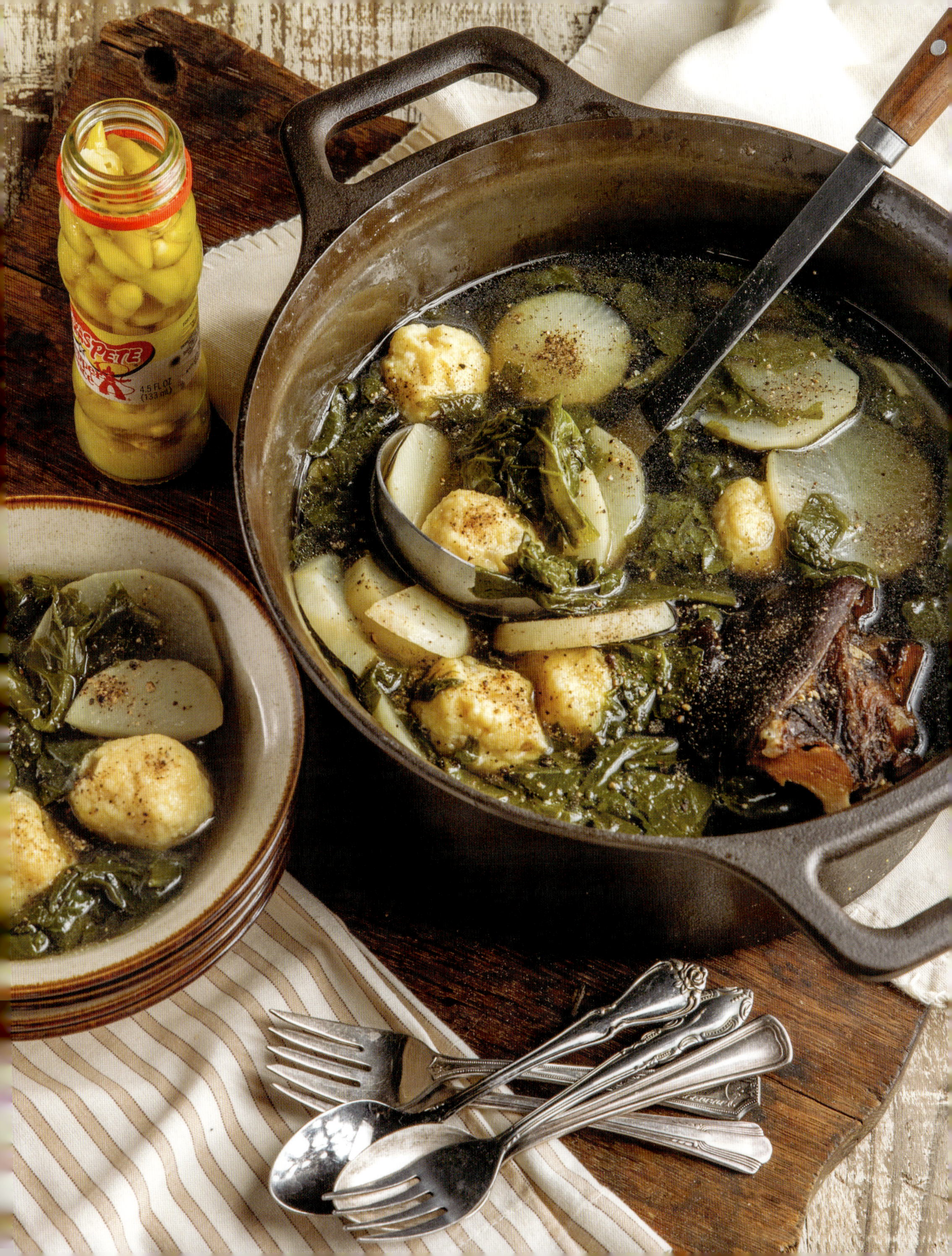
4.5 FL OZ
(133 ml)

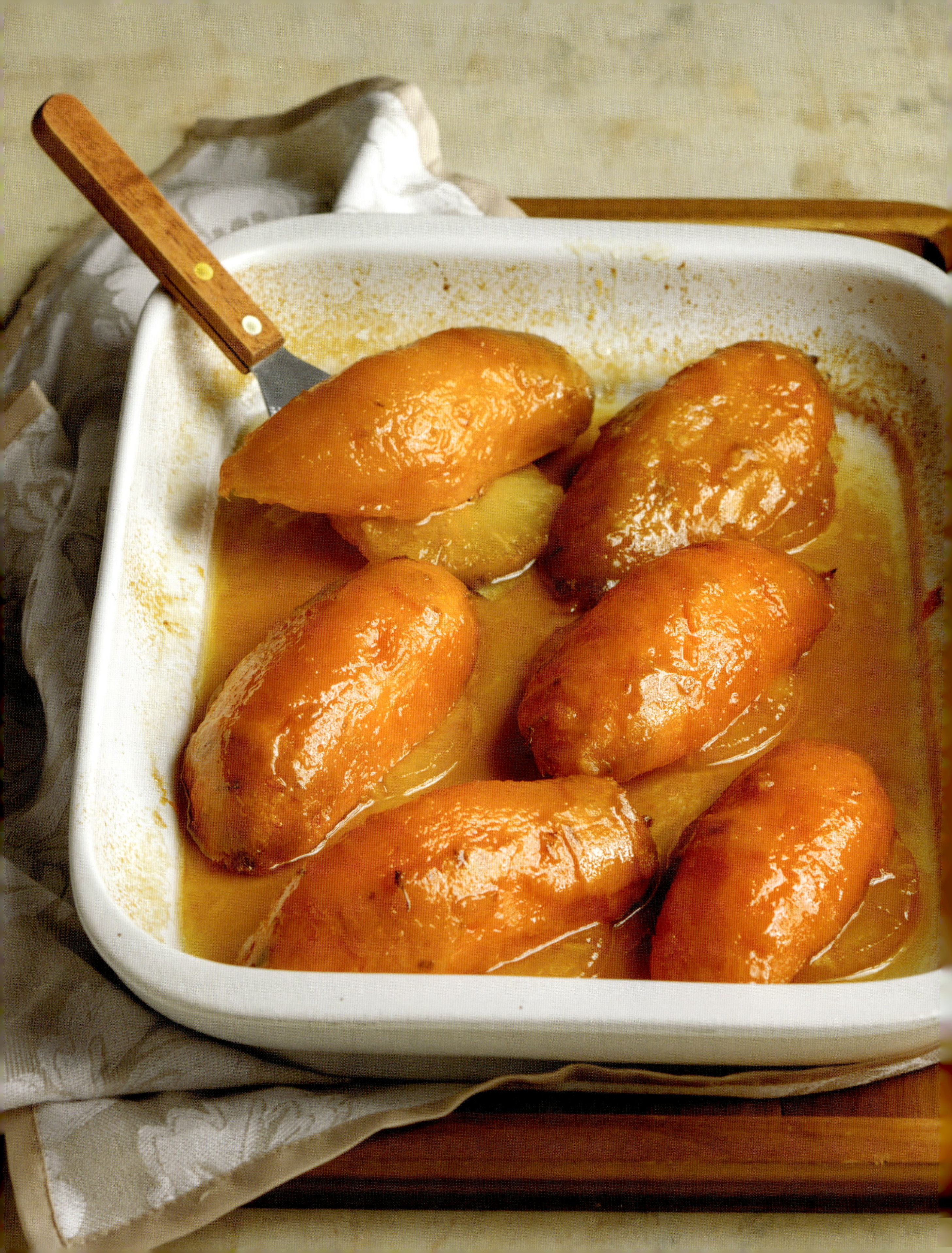

SHERRY-GLAZED SWEET POTATOES

These glazed sweet potatoes will absolutely melt in your mouth! The pineapple and brown sugar make them irresistible.

Makes 6 servings

- 3 large medium sweet potatoes (about 8 ounces each)
- 6 slices canned pineapple
- ½ cup firmly packed light brown sugar
- ½ cup dry sherry
- 4 tablespoons salted butter, softened

1. In a large stockpot, bring potatoes and water to cover to a boil over medium-high heat; cook until tender, 20 to 30 minutes.

2. Preheat oven to 375°.

3. Drain potatoes, and let cool enough to handle. Peel potatoes, and cut in half lengthwise.

4. In a 13x9-inch shallow baking dish, arrange pineapple in a single layer; place a potato half, cut side down, on top of each pineapple slice.

5. In a small saucepan, stir together brown sugar, sherry, and butter. Cook over medium heat, stirring frequently, until sugar dissolves, about 6 minutes; pour over potatoes and pineapples.

6. Bake until heated through, about 30 minutes, basting frequently with syrup.

My Granddaddy and Grandmother Hiers.

SAVANNAH TIRAMISÙ

My version of this classic dessert is fluffy and rich and looks gorgeous set on a table.

Makes 12 to 16 servings

- 24 soft macaroons, crumbled
- ½ cup bourbon or rum
- 1 cup salted butter
- 1 cup plus 3 tablespoons sugar, divided
- 6 large eggs, separated
- ½ cup chopped pecans
- 2 ounces unsweetened chocolate, melted
- ½ teaspoon vanilla extract
- 24 double soft ladyfingers
- ¾ cup heavy whipping cream

Garnish: chopped toasted pecans

1. In a medium bowl, place crumbled macaroons; add bourbon or rum, and let stand for 30 minutes.

2. In a large bowl, beat butter and 1 cup sugar with a mixer at medium speed until creamy, 3 to 4 minutes, stopping to scrape sides of bowl.

3. In a small bowl, lightly whisk egg yolks; add to butter mixture, and beat at medium speed until combined. Fold in macaroon mixture, pecans, melted chocolate, and vanilla.

4. In another medium bowl, using clean beaters, beat egg whites at high speed until stiff peaks form; fold into macaroon mixture.

5. Spray a 9-inch springform pan with cooking spray; line with separated ladyfingers, rounded side of ladyfingers out. Line bottom of pan with ladyfingers. Alternate layers of macaroon mixture and remaining ladyfingers. Cover and refrigerate overnight.

6. In another medium bowl, beat cream and remaining 3 tablespoons sugar with a mixer at high speed until stiff peaks form.

7. Remove tiramisù from pan, and top with whipped cream. Garnish with pecans, if desired.

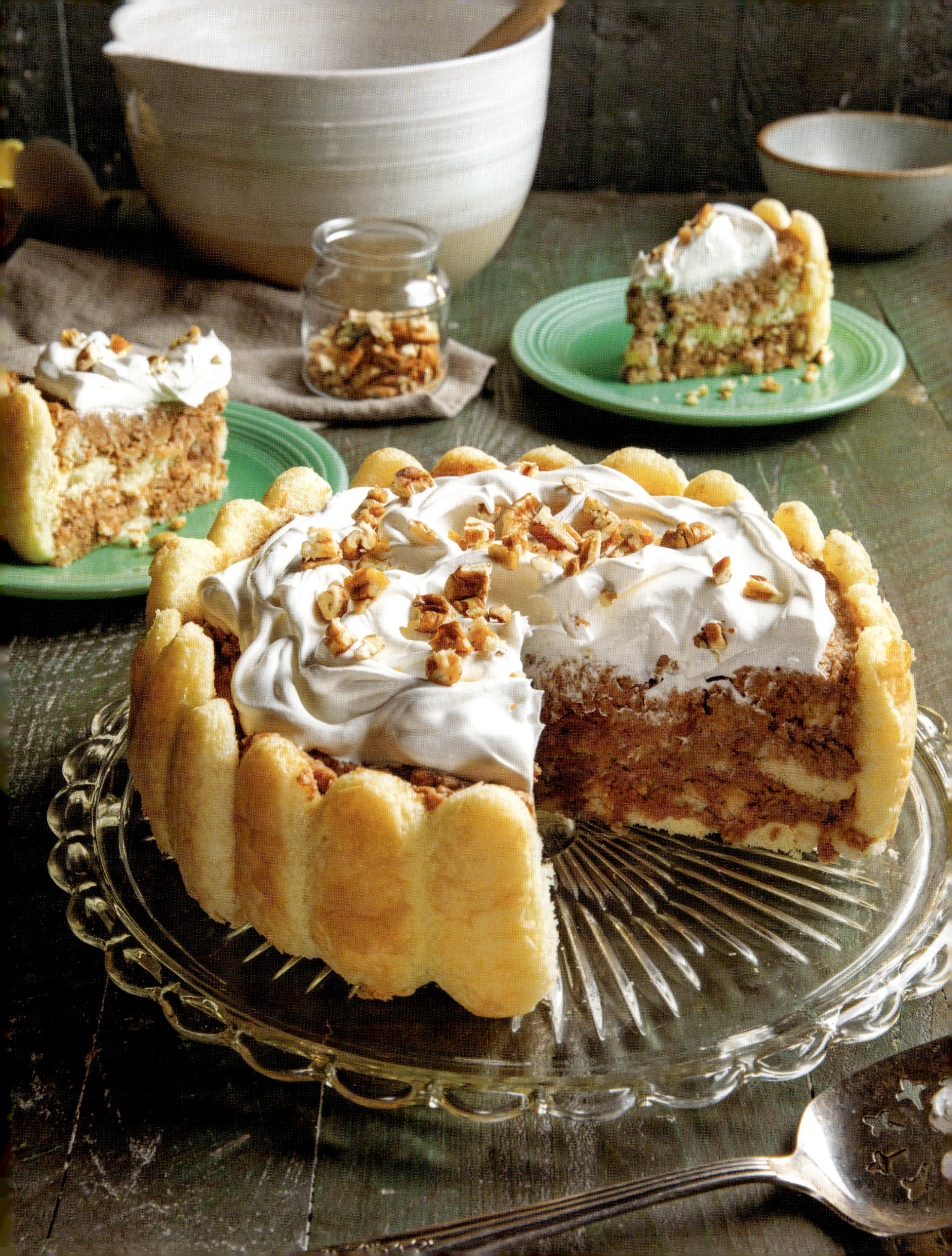

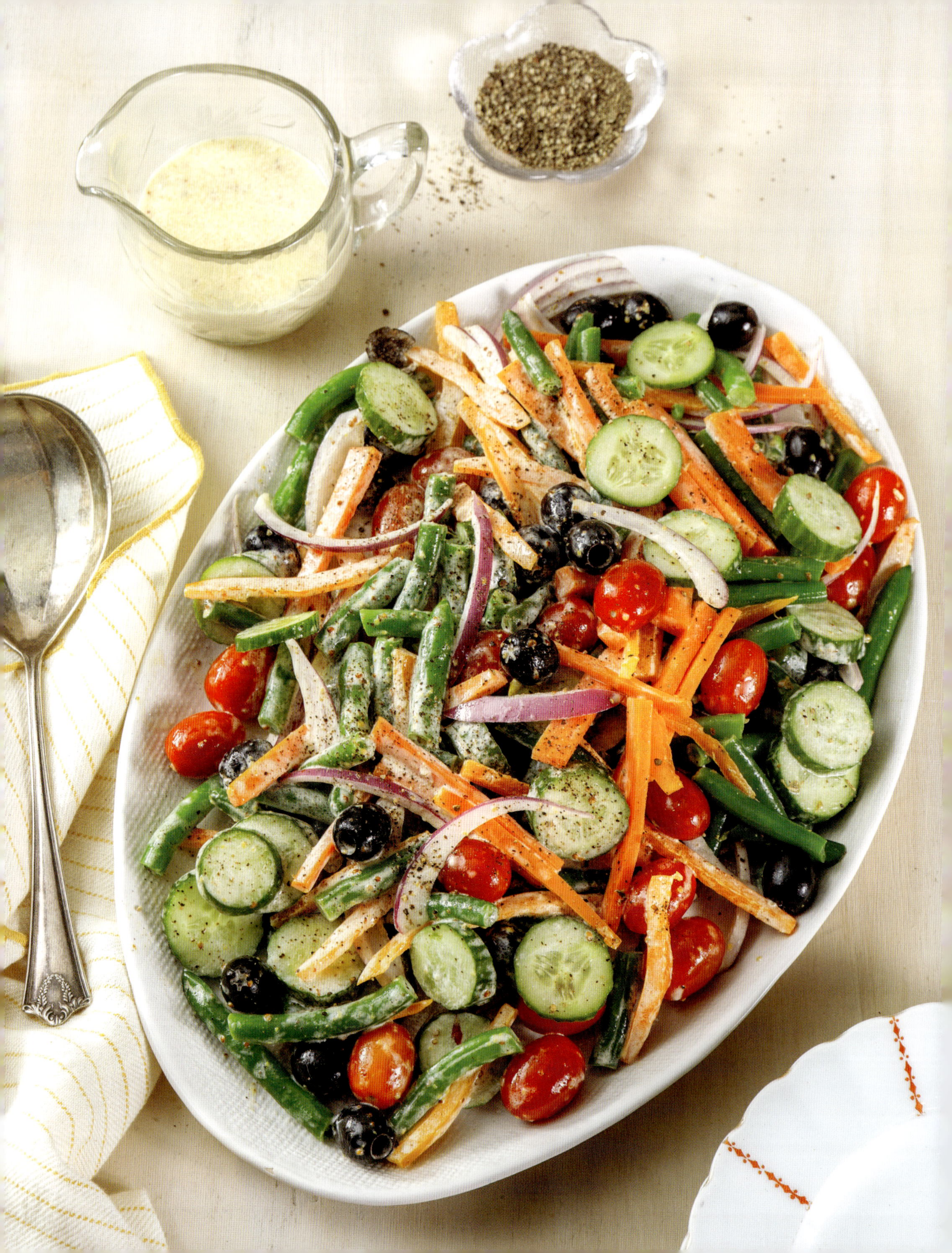

VEGGIE SALAD

This chopped salad can be whipped up in no time, and the Creole mustard dressing makes it a perfect, flavorful side dish.

Makes 8 to 10 servings

- 6 cups water
- 3 medium carrots, peeled and cut into 3x¼-inch sticks (about 1 cup)
- ¾ pound fresh green beans, cut into 2-inch pieces
- 1 medium orange bell pepper, cut into 3x¼-inch sticks (about 1 cup)
- 2 cups sliced mini cucumbers
- 1½ cups grape tomatoes
- 1 cup pitted black olives
- ⅔ cup thinly sliced red onion
- 1½ teaspoons salt
- ¼ tablespoon ground black pepper

CREOLE MUSTARD DRESSING

- ⅓ cup mayonnaise
- ¼ cup plus 1 tablespoon olive oil
- 4 teaspoons Creole mustard
- 1 teaspoon tarragon vinegar
- 1 teaspoon Worcestershire sauce
- 2 garlic cloves, mashed
- ¼ teaspoon dried oregano

1. For salad: In a large saucepan, bring 6 cups water to a boil. Add carrot and green beans; cook for 2 minutes. Drain, and rinse under cold water to stop the cooking process. Pat dry with paper towels.

2. In a large bowl, toss together carrot mixture, bell pepper, cucumbers, tomatoes, olives, onion, salt, and black pepper.

3. For dressing: In a medium bowl, whisk together mayonnaise, oil, mustard, vinegar, Worcestershire, garlic, and oregano. Pour over salad, tossing to coat. Serve immediately, or refrigerate until ready to serve.

My dear friends Donna Foltz and her husband, Curtis, shared this Veggie Salad recipe with me.

THE LADY & SONS | LOVE AND BEST DISHES

THE LADY'S CHEESY MAC

This is a classic from The Lady & Sons restaurant. I hope you'll enjoy making your own version of this perfect mac and cheese!

Makes about 8 servings

4½ cups shredded Cheddar cheese, divided
4 cups cooked elbow macaroni (about 2 cups uncooked)
1 cup whole milk
½ cup sour cream
4 tablespoons salted butter, softened
3 large eggs, beaten
½ teaspoon salt

1. Preheat oven to 350°. Spray a 13x9-inch baking dish with cooking spray.

2. In a large bowl, stir together 4 cups cheese and pasta.

3. In a medium bowl, stir together milk, sour cream, butter, eggs, and salt. Stir into cheese mixture. Pour into prepared pan.

4. Bake until set, 30 to 45 minutes. Top with remaining ½ cup cheese, and bake until melted, about 3 minutes more. Serve immediately.

Jamie, Bobby, and I are passionate about our mac and cheese! To make sure yours doesn't dry out, you want to make sure you cook your pasta very well done. This way, the noodles won't be as "thirsty" and you won't lose the liquid you need to make the mac and cheese creamy.

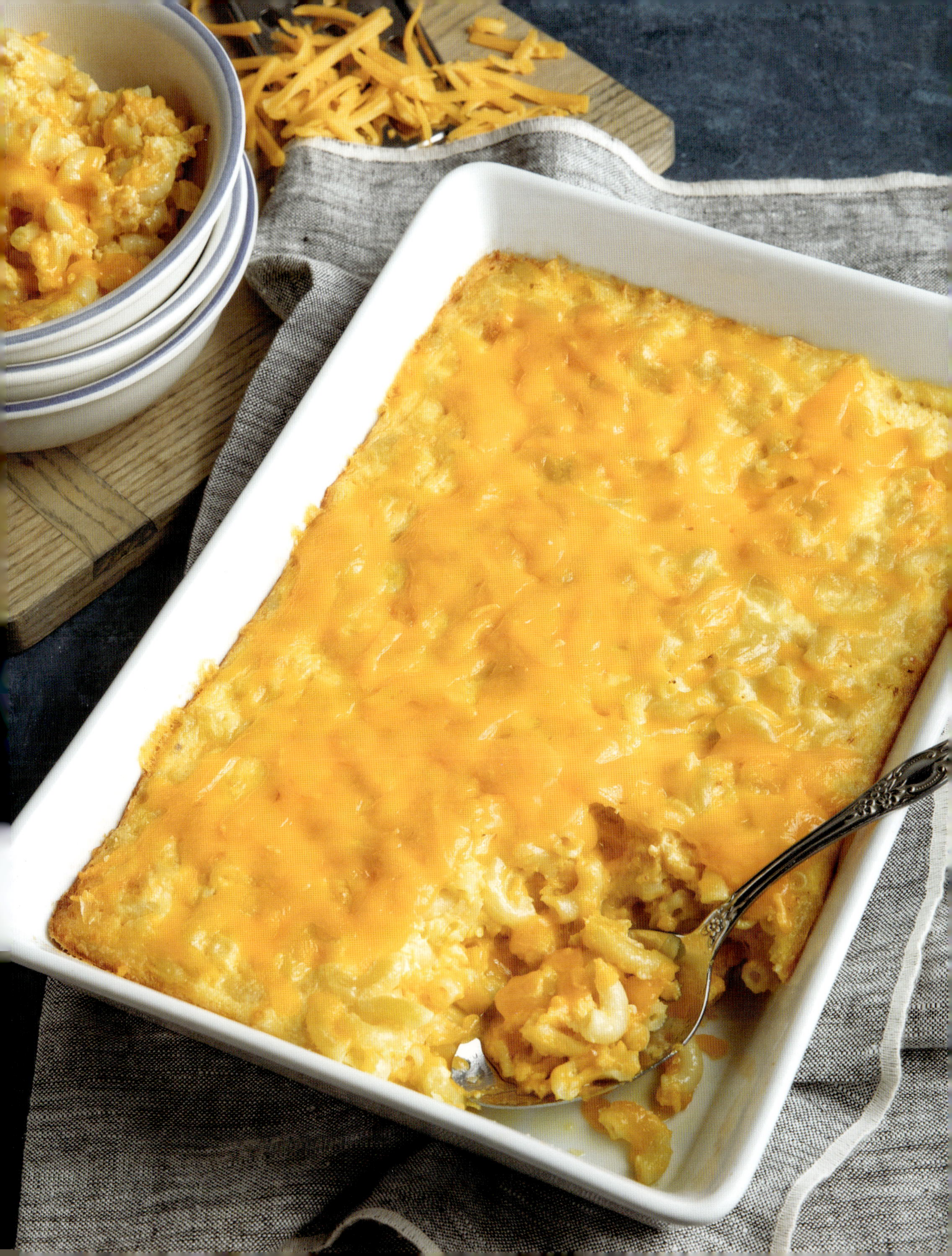

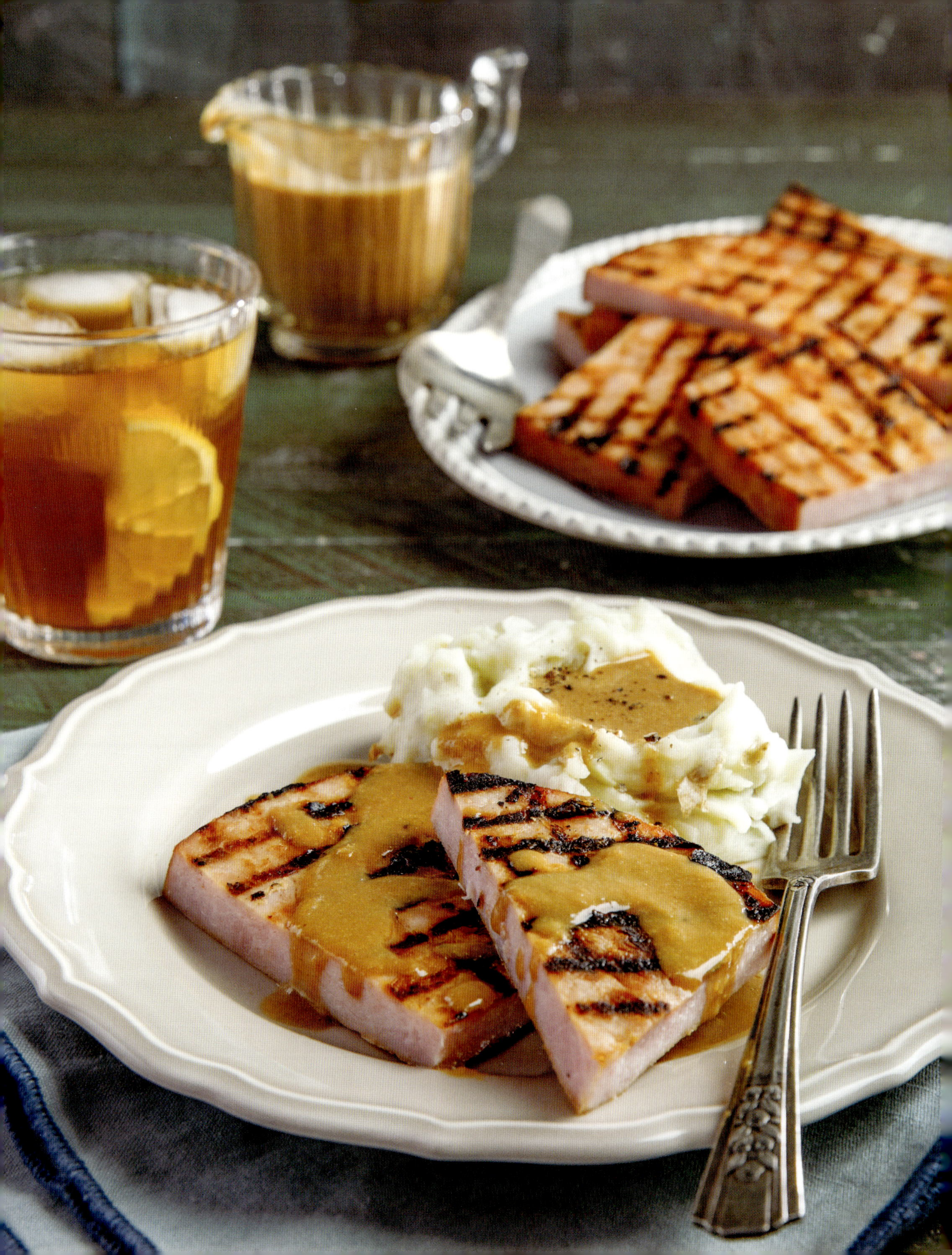

GRILLED PEANUT BUTTER HAM

Oh, my goodness, the flavor the peanut butter adds to this ham recipe is wonderful! A great friend of mine, Ron, gave me this recipe.

Makes 8 to 10 servings

- 1 cup chicken broth
- ½ cup creamy peanut butter
- ¼ cup honey
- 1 small onion, grated
- 1 clove garlic, chopped
- 2 teaspoons soy sauce
- 1 teaspoon browning and seasoning sauce
- ¼ teaspoon ground black pepper
- 2 (1½-inch-thick) slices center-cut ham

1. In the container of a blender, process broth, peanut butter, honey, onion, garlic, soy sauce, browning and seasoning sauce, and pepper.

2. In a shallow glass baking dish, place ham. Pour marinade on top, and refrigerate for 3 to 4 hours.

3. Preheat grill to medium heat (325° to 350°).

4. Remove ham from marinade, reserving marinade. Grill ham until grill marks form, 5 to 6 minutes, turning halfway through grilling.

5. In a small saucepan, heat reserved marinade over medium heat until bubbly. Serve warm over ham.

My boys and me. We worked night and day, seven days a week for so long together. I couldn't have done it all without them!

CHAPTER SIX

TAKING FLIGHT

The Lady & Sons restaurant opened in downtown Savannah on January 8, 1996. Soon after, I got it in my head that I wanted to write a cookbook. Just something simple for my customers who wanted my recipes. I wrote it in no time and took it down the street to a local print shop. When I realized the more copies I ordered, the cheaper they would be, I decided I wanted 5,000. Everyone said I was nuts!

A lot of exciting things were happening in Savannah at that time—the movie adaptation of John Berendt's best-selling book *Midnight in the Garden of Good and Evil* was being filmed in town. Clint Eastwood, the director, was here along with a lot of industry people.

Well, the cookbook had only been printed and for sale in the restaurant for about two weeks when I got a call from an editor with Random House. She said she and her coworkers had been walking downtown when a huge rainstorm started falling on them. They happened to be in front of The Lady & Sons and popped in to have something to eat and wait out the storm.

She asked me, "Did I see a cookbook in your restaurant?" I said, "Oh, honey, you sure did, and it's selling so good!" Really, I'd only sold about 25, but she asked me to mail her two copies of the book. When I told Jamie, I saw all the blood drain from his face. He probably had those books boxed up and shipped off to New York within 15 minutes!

A few days later, Jamie and I were working a private party at the restaurant. I remember everything was so pretty. The sun was setting, the lights were low, the candles were lit, and we just decided to sit down for a minute to catch our breath before everyone arrived. The phone rang, and the voice on the line said, "This is Pamela with Random House. I want to say congratulations, Paula, because we want to purchase your cookbook and reprint it."

I couldn't hang up quick enough to tell Jamie. He and I started dancing all through the restaurant with so much excitement and tears in our eyes. Thank God for that rain! After that, I just couldn't wait to come to work every day to see what was going to happen next.

I had to rewrite the cookbook for Random House, which was so hard. The first round, I just shook all my recipes out of the paper sack I kept them in and put them in a book. Pamela told me I had to assume that whoever read the book had never been in a kitchen before. I had to be clear and specific. Later, I asked Pamela if she could get me on QVC so I could really market the book. She got them to have me on, and, honey, we start selling books like hotcakes on that network! I went on QVC many times after that.

Soon, I got a call from Oprah's team. They were doing a story on women who started businesses out of their homes, and I was one of five selected to appear on that show. After that, my producer, Gordon Elliot, set me up with an agent who started booking me on all kinds of shows and eventually started pitching my own show to Food Network. They weren't quite sure about me at first, but I stayed busy anyway with the restaurant and traveling to promote the book.

Then 9/11 happened. Our country was devastated, and New York City was a ghost town. I was there exactly two months after it happened, and the only place I saw people eating in was a deli that sold comfort foods. My agent went back to Food Network and said, "Listen. This country is scared to death. People need comfort. They need their mother. They need food that reminds them of home and safety. Paula can bring that to them."

At the time, everybody at Food Network was a white coat-type chef. I was just a momma cooking for her family, and the show became a big success.

Opposite page, left to right: The original Lady & Sons staff at our first downtown location. Jamie, me, and Bobby. **This page, top:** Oprah and me. **Middle:** During the early days of my magazine, *Cooking With Paula Deen*, we featured an insider's look into my favorite retreat: my bathroom. Phyllis Hoffman DePiano was directing the shoot—she added so many bubbles to the bath! It was hilarious. **Bottom:** Me standing outside the Lady & Sons with my first and second cookbooks in my arms.

LEMON TART WITH ALMOND CRUST

When I was spending a lot of time at ShopHQ selling products, their wonderful food stylist, Pat Carlson, gave me this amazing recipe. I loved working with her!

Makes 1 (11-inch) tart

CRUST

1½ cups all-purpose flour

½ cup sliced almonds

¼ cup plus 2 tablespoons sugar

¼ teaspoon kosher salt

9 tablespoons cold salted butter, cubed

¾ teaspoon almond extract

3 to 4 tablespoons ice water

FILLING

1½ cups sugar

3 tablespoons lemon zest

1¼ cups fresh lemon juice (about 6 large lemons)

4 large eggs

5 large egg yolks

9 tablespoons salted cold butter, cubed

1. For crust: In the work bowl of a food processor, process flour, almonds, sugar, and salt until almonds are finely chopped and mixture is well combined. Add cold butter and almond extract; pulse until butter is the size of peas. Add 3 to 4 tablespoons ice water, 1 tablespoon at a time, pulsing until dough holds together but is not sticky. Shape into a disk, and wrap in plastic. Refrigerate for 30 minutes.

2. Spray an 11-inch round fluted removable-bottom tart pan with cooking spray.

3. Turn out dough onto a lightly floured surface. Roll into a 15-inch circle, turning every few rolls to keep from sticking. Transfer dough to prepared pan, pressing into bottom and up sides; trim excess dough, and discard. Freeze until firm.

4. Position oven rack in bottom third of oven. Preheat oven to 400°. Bake until golden brown, 15 to 20 minutes. Let cool on wire rack. Reduce oven temperature to 325°.

5. For filling: In a large saucepan, whisk together sugar, lemon zest and juice, eggs, and egg yolks; add cold butter. Cook over medium heat, stirring constantly, until filling thickens slightly but is pourable, 8 to 12 minutes. Strain through a fine-mesh sieve into prepared crust.

6. Bake until filling is set but still jiggly, 15 to 18 minutes. Let cool completely. Serve immediately, or refrigerate until ready to serve.

Pat Carlson and me.

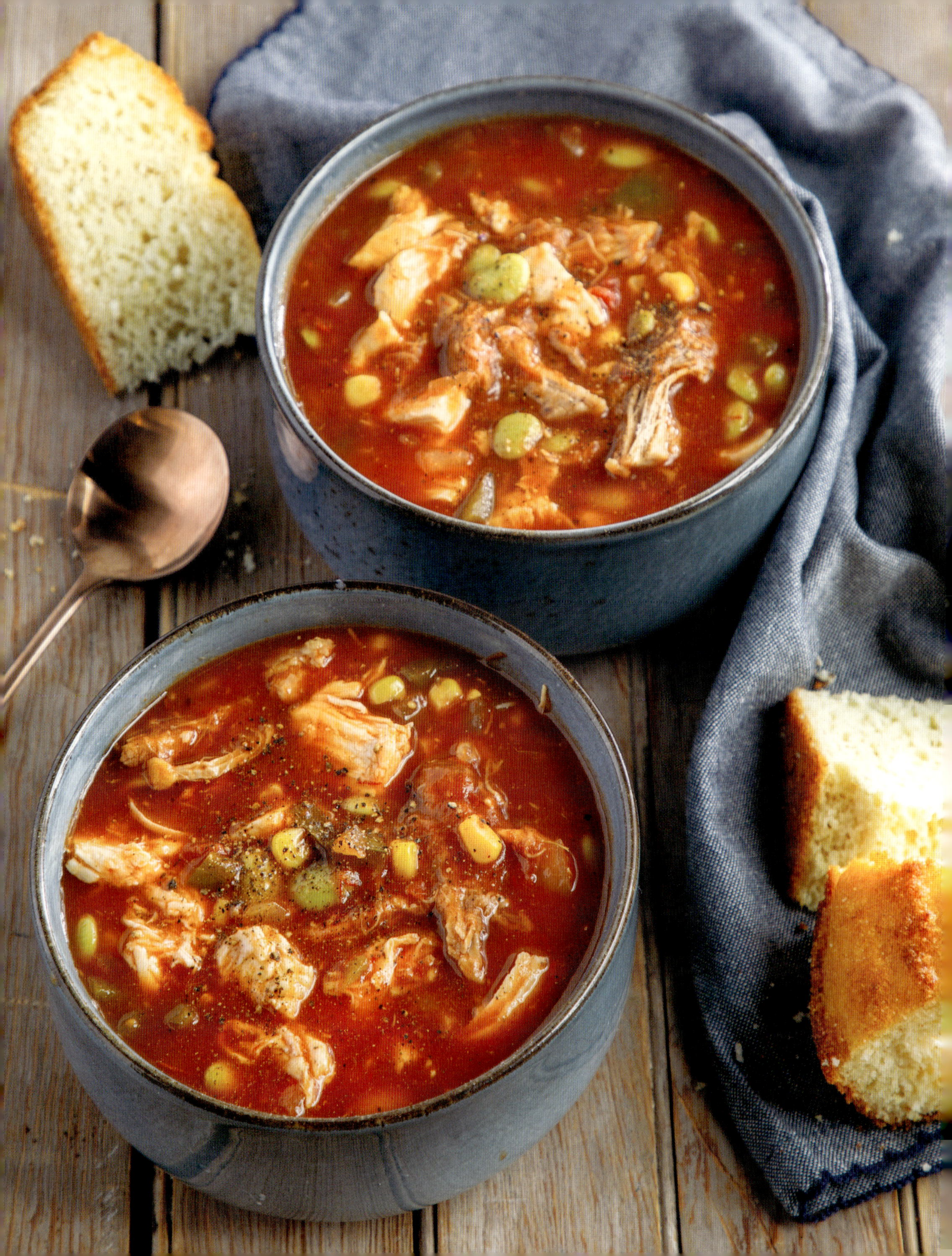

BRUNSWICK STEW

This cozy classic is perfect for chilly weather or anytime you're craving some comfort food. Serve it with your favorite cornbread!

Makes about 5 quarts

- ½ cup salted butter
- 2 cups chopped onion
- 1 green bell pepper, chopped
- 4 cloves garlic, minced
- 2 (32-ounce) cartons chicken broth
- 1 (28-ounce) can crushed tomatoes
- 1 (16-ounce) package frozen corn kernels
- 1 (16-ounce) package frozen lima beans
- 1 (15-ounce) can tomato sauce
- 1½ cups vinegar-based barbecue sauce
- 2 tablespoons Worcestershire sauce
- 1 pound chopped smoked pork
- 3 cups chopped cooked chicken
- 1 teaspoon ground black pepper
- ½ teaspoon salt

1. In a large Dutch oven, melt butter over medium-high heat. Add onion, bell pepper, and garlic; cook, stirring frequently, until just tender, about 8 minutes. Stir in broth, tomatoes, corn, beans, tomato sauce, barbecue sauce, and Worcestershire, and bring to a boil. Reduce heat, and simmer, stirring occasionally, for 30 minute

2. Stir pork, chicken, black pepper, and salt into vegetable mixture, and simmer for 30 minutes.

Corrie and me snuggled up for a slumber party.

TAKING FLIGHT | LOVE AND BEST DISHES

SALMON DIP

One of the best trips I've ever taken was an Alaskan cruise! I remember we had a version of salmon dip one night, and I loved it so much that I started ordering my own salmon from Alaska and created this dip.

Makes 8 to 10 servings

- ¾ pound smoked salmon, chopped
- 1 (8-ounce) package cream cheese, room temperature
- 1 bunch green onions, finely chopped
- 1 cup mayonnaise
- 1 teaspoon Paula Deen Hot Sauce
- 1 teaspoon Worcestershire sauce
- ½ teaspoon garlic powder
- ¼ teaspoon ground black pepper
- Salt, to taste
- ¼ cup sour cream
- Buttery round crackers, to serve
- Garnish: sliced green onion

1. In a large bowl, stir together salmon, cream cheese, chopped green onion, mayonnaise, hot sauce, Worcestershire, garlic powder, black pepper, and salt. Fold in sour cream. Refrigerate for at least 1 hour. Serve with crackers. Garnish with sliced green onion, if desired.

Jamie, me, and Bobby. Look at this feast we had in front of us!

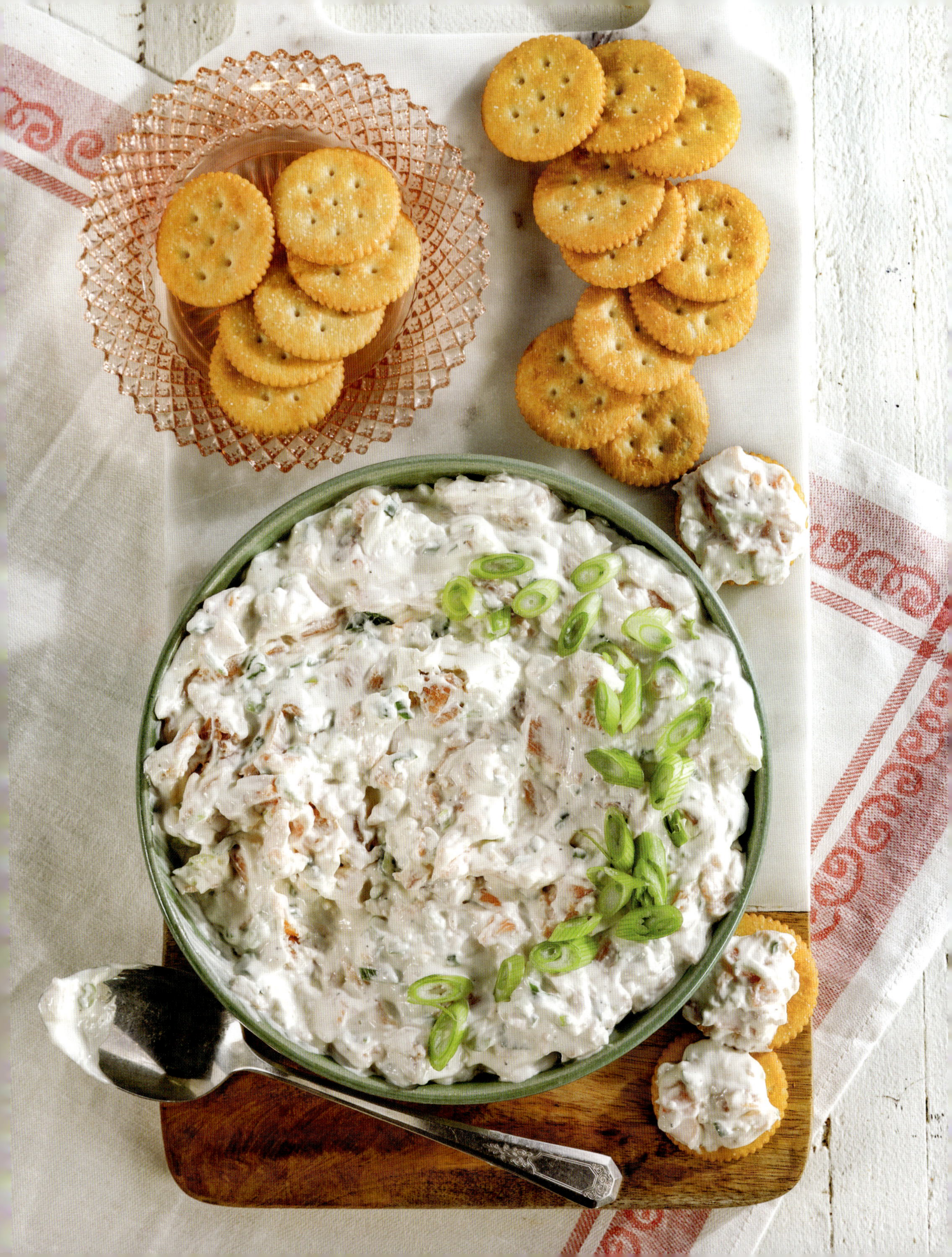

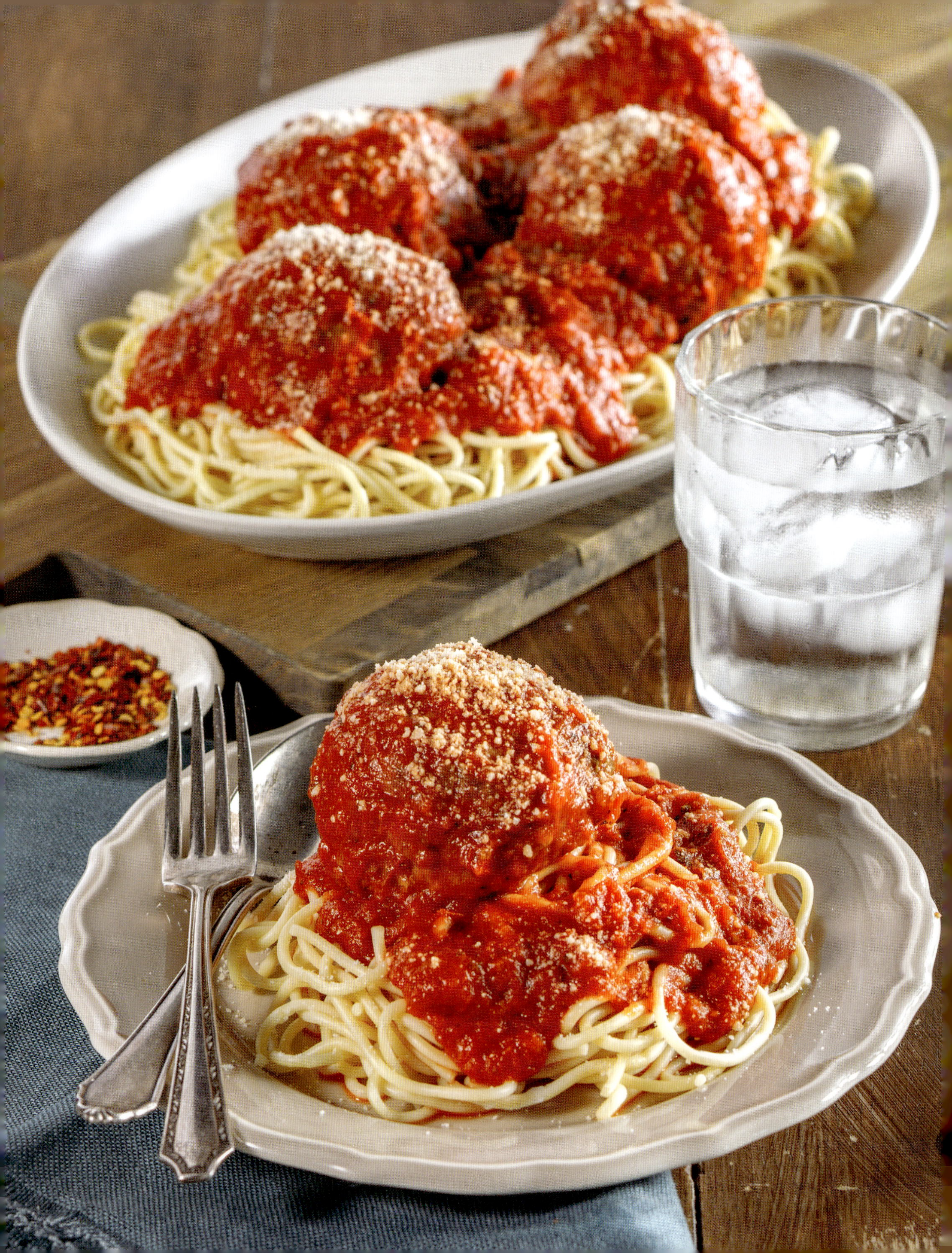

MEATBALLS

When Eddie and I would visit Minneapolis to film with ShopHQ, we'd stay at the same hotel each time. The first thing we'd want to eat was the meatballs at the hotel restaurant! The chef shared his recipe with me and I created my own special version.

Makes 8

- 1 tablespoon olive oil
- 1 medium onion, diced
- 1 clove garlic, sliced
- 1 pound ground ground beef
- 1 pound ground veal
- 1 pound ground pork
- 3 cups diced soft bread (about 4 slices of bread)
- 2 cups grated Parmesan cheese
- 1 cup whole milk
- 4 large eggs, lightly beaten
- 2 tablespoons chopped fresh parsley
- 1 teaspoon fresh lemon juice
- ½ teaspoon salt
- ½ teaspoon crushed red pepper
- ½ teaspoon ground black pepper
- ⅛ teaspoon ground allspice
- ⅛ teaspoon ground nutmeg
- ⅛ teaspoon ground cloves
- All-purpose flour, for rolling
- Vegetable oil, for frying
- Pasta and sauce, to serve

1. In a skillet, heat olive oil over medium heat. Add onion and garlic, and cook, stirring occasionally, until tender, 3 to 4 minutes. Let cool for 10 minutes.

2. In a large bowl, using your hands, gently combine onion mixture, meats, bread, cheese, milk, eggs, parsley, lemon juice, salt, red pepper, black pepper, allspice, nutmeg, and cloves. Shape into ½-cup meatballs. Refrigerate overnight.

3. Reshape meatballs, and roll in flour to coat.

4. In a large skillet, pour vegetable oil to a depth of 1 inch, and heat over medium-high heat.

5. Fry meatballs in batches until browned on all sides.

6. In a large Dutch oven, pour water to a depth of about 3 inches, and heat over medium heat until simmering. Place meatballs, in batches, in water, and gently simmer until an instant-read thermometer inserted in center of a meatball registers 160°. Remove from pot, and set aside. Serve with favorite pasta and sauce.

SCALLOPS CHARLESTON

This recipe is so special to serve up to your loved ones. The scallops are perfectly paired with the mushrooms and Gruyère cheese, and the individual baking dishes will look beautiful on your table.

Makes 4 servings

- 1½ pounds fresh sea scallops
- ¼ cup fresh basil leaves, finely chopped
- ½ teaspoon garlic powder
- ¼ teaspoon salt
- ¼ teaspoon paprika
- ¼ teaspoon ground black pepper
- 6 tablespoons all-purpose flour, divided
- 3 tablespoons olive oil
- 1 (8-ounce) package fresh button mushrooms, cleaned and quartered
- ¾ cup dry sherry or dry white wine
- 1 shallot, finely chopped
- 2 tablespoons salted butter
- 1 cup shredded Gruyère cheese

Garnish: chopped fresh basil

1. Preheat oven to broil.

2. In a large bowl, combine scallops, basil, garlic powder, salt, paprika, and pepper; dust with 3 tablespoons flour.

3. Spray a 12-inch skillet with cooking spray; add oil, and heat over medium-high heat. Add scallops mixture, and cook until scallops are browned, about 2 minutes per side. Remove scallops from skillet.

4. Add mushrooms, sherry or wine, and shallot to skillet; cook over medium-high heat until mushrooms begin to release liquid, 3 to 4 minutes. Remove from heat.

5. In a medium saucepan, melt butter over medium heat. Stir in remaining 3 tablespoons flour, and reduce heat to low; cook, stirring constantly, for 2 minutes. Stir in mushroom mixture and any cooking liquid. Stir in scallops. Transfer to 4 individual broiler-safe baking dishes, and top with cheese.

6. Broil until lightly browned, about 1 minute. Garnish with basil, if desired.

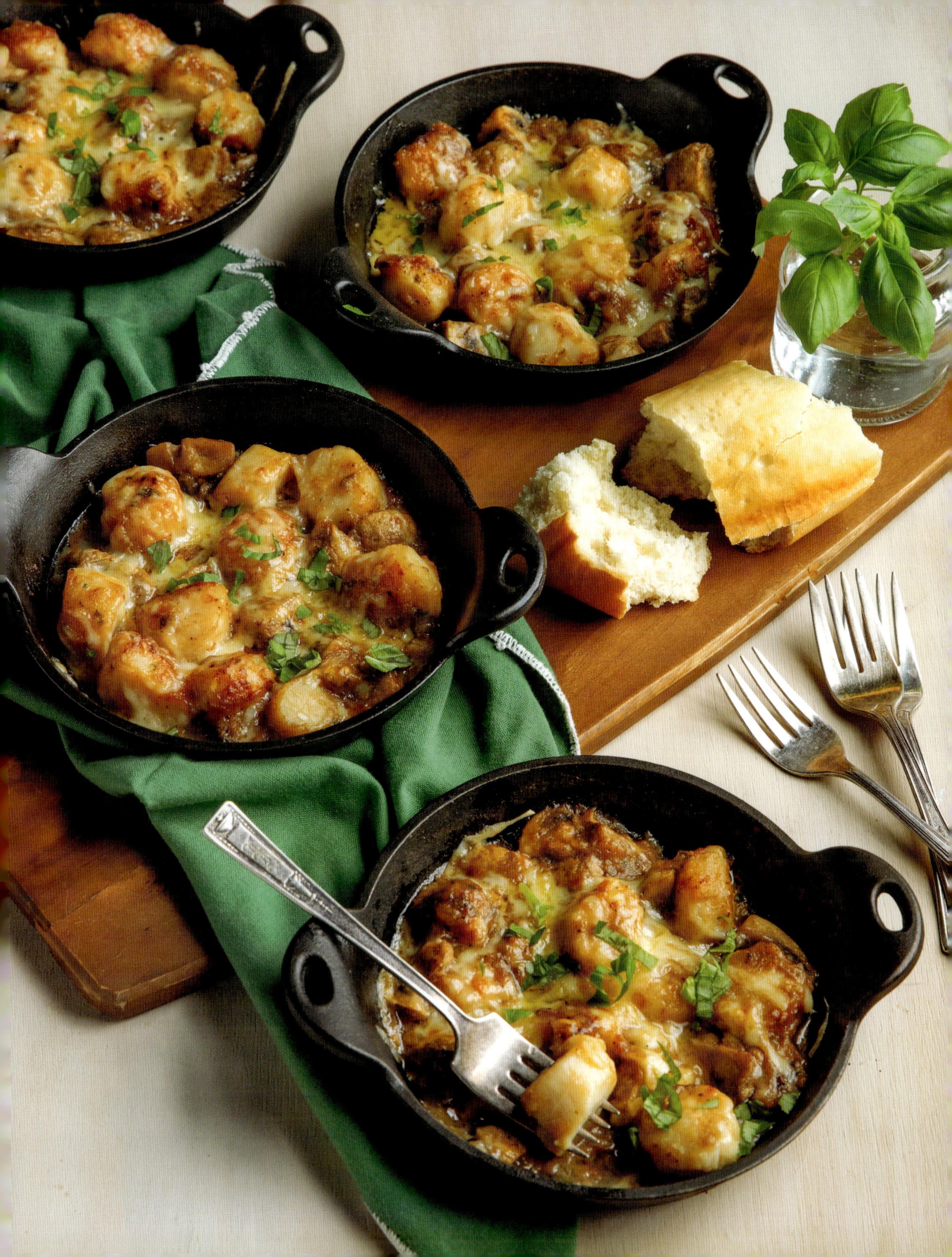

Recipe Tip

For pinker frosting, add 2 to 3 drops of red food coloring to frosting.

There was a wonderful woman in my life named Miss Gloria. She was a character in *Midnight in the Garden of Good and Evil*. John Berendt met her at Joe Odom's house while she worked the catering events there. She was out of work after the movie, so I brought her on to work at the Best Western with me. She became our salad lady, and she would fix up a cart with everything to make a wonderful salad and she'd go tableside with it. When Miss Gloria later had a stroke and was unable to work, I called John Berendt and asked him to come to Savannah and help me raise money for her. Every year for her birthday, she'd ask me to make her this strawberry cake—her absolute favorite. She ended up having another stroke and passing away sometime later, but she was the most beautiful person. I loved her so very much.

STRAWBERRY CAKE

This fluffy, layered cake is absolutely gorgeous and tastes even better! Wow your guests with this beauty in the middle of your table.

Makes 1 (9-inch) cake

- 1 (16.25-ounce) box white cake mix
- 1 (3-ounce) box strawberry gelatin
- 1 (10-ounce) package frozen strawberries in syrup, thawed and puréed
- 4 large eggs
- ½ cup vegetable oil
- ¼ cup water

STRAWBERRY CREAM CHEESE FROSTING

- 1 (8-ounce) package cream cheese, softened
- ¼ cup salted butter, softened
- ¼ cup frozen strawberries in syrup, thawed and puréed
- ½ teaspoon strawberry extract
- 7 cups confectioners' sugar

Garnish: sliced fresh strawberries

1. Preheat oven to 350°. Lightly spray 2 (9-inch) round cake pans with cooking spray.

2. For cake: In a large bowl, combine cake mix and gelatin. Add puréed strawberries, eggs, oil, and ¼ cup water; beat with a mixer at medium speed until smooth. Pour into prepared pans.

3. Bake until a wooden pick inserted in center comes out clean, about 20 minutes. Let cool in pans for 10 minutes. Remove from pans, and let cool completely on wire racks.

4. For frosting: In a large bowl, beat cream cheese and butter with a mixer at medium speed until creamy. Beat in strawberry purée. Beat in strawberry extract. Gradually add confectioners' sugar, beating until smooth.

5. Spread frosting between layers and on top and sides of cake. Garnish with fresh strawberries, if desired. Cover and refrigerate up to 3 days.

LEMON MERINGUE PIE

This cake was the cover star during one of my favorite photoshoots for Cooking with Paula Deen *magazine. It is the most incredible Lemon Meringue Pie I have ever put in my mouth, and it was all I could do to not eat the entire thing that day!*

Makes 1 (9-inch) pie

- 2 cups sugar
- ½ cup cornstarch
- ½ teaspoon salt
- 2 cups cold water
- 8 large egg yolks
- 1 tablespoon lemon zest
- ⅔ cup fresh lemon juice
- 6 tablespoons salted butter, softened
- 2 teaspoons vanilla extract
- 1 (9-inch) frozen pie shell, baked according to package directions

SWISS MERINGUE

- 1½ cups sugar
- 6 large egg whites

Recipe Tip

Resist the urge to use bottled lemon juice for this pie. You need the punch of freshly squeezed lemons.

1. For pie: In a large saucepan, whisk together sugar, cornstarch, and salt. Gradually whisk in 2 cups cold water until smooth. Bring to a boil over medium-high heat; cook, whisking constantly, for 1 minute. Remove from heat.

2. In a medium bowl, whisk egg yolks. Slowly add 1 cup hot sugar mixture, whisking constantly. Whisk egg yolk mixture into remaining hot sugar mixture in saucepan. Cook over medium heat, whisking constantly, until thickened, 2 to 3 minutes. Whisk in lemon zest and juice, butter, and vanilla; cook, whisking constantly, until mixture is thick and smooth, 1 to 2 minutes. Spread mixture into prepared crust. Cover with plastic wrap, pressing wrap directly onto surface of filling to prevent a skin from forming, and refrigerate until cold and set, at least 4 hours or overnight.

3. For meringue: In the top of a double boiler, whisk together sugar and egg whites. Cook over simmering water, whisking constantly, until sugar dissolves and an instant-read thermometer registers 140°, 3 to 4 minutes.

4. Pour mixture into the bowl of a stand mixer fitted with the whisk attachment, and beat at high speed until thick, white, and glossy, about 10 minutes. Spread meringue onto cold pie.

5. If desired, broil meringue until lightly browned, 1 to 2 minutes. Serve immediately, or refrigerate for up to 2 days.

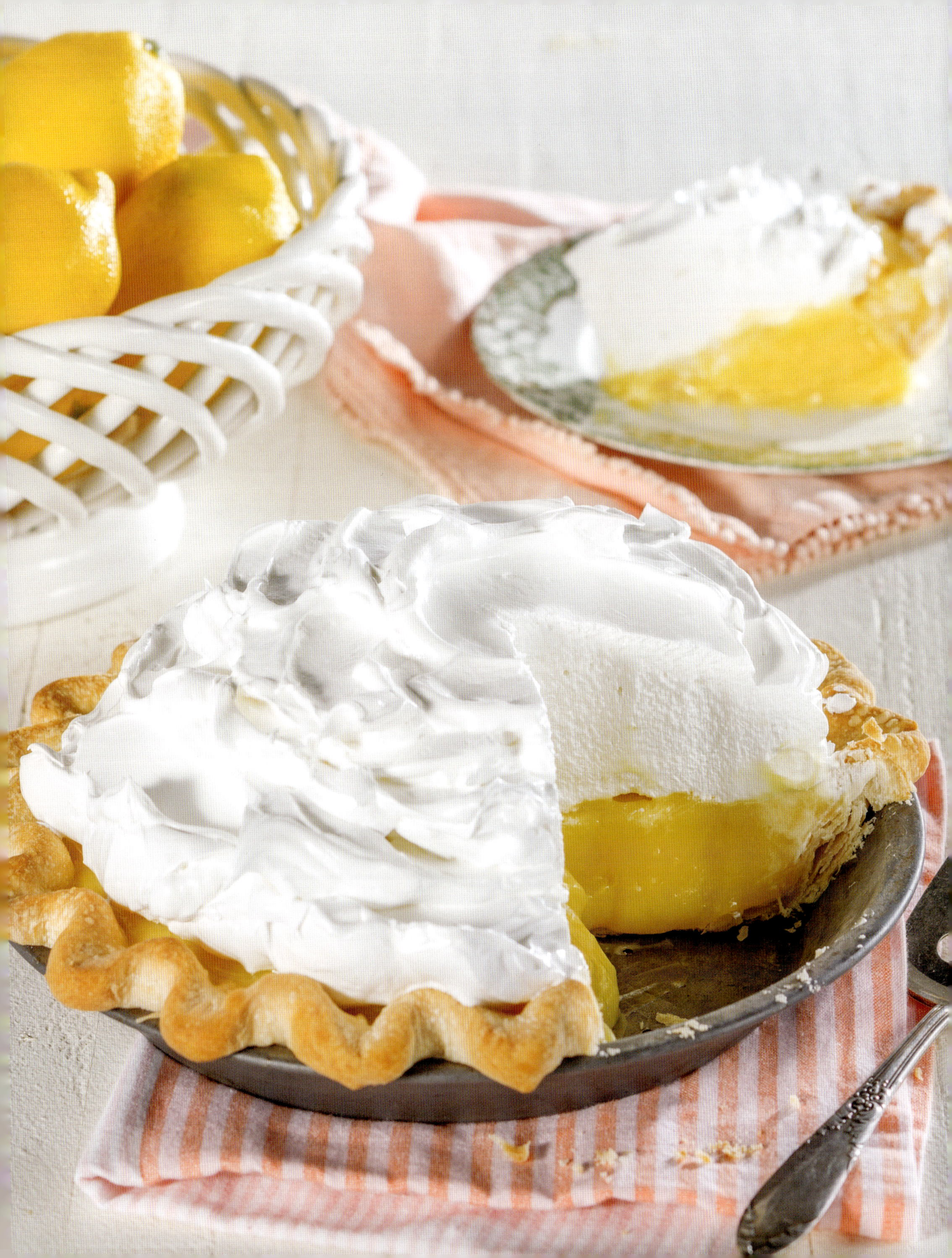

March 6, 2004

CHAPTER SEVEN

FAMILY MATTERS

I had been living downtown in the historic district for a few years when I decided I was ready to leave and live on the water. I'd loved my little house, but I was so lonely there. My business was growing and things were good, but I had no one to share it with. But how was I supposed to meet someone? I spent all my time at the restaurant, so if I didn't meet people in my kitchen, I didn't meet anybody. I decided I was going to start asking God to send me a neighbor. My last words before I went to sleep each night were, "Lord, please send me a neighbor."

After I put my house on the market, I found the perfect spot in a gated community that was modeled after the historic district and the squares. I moved in right after I finished writing *The Lady & Sons: Just Desserts*, and I had taken a hiatus from the restaurant to work on that and test recipes.

I had two little dogs named Otis and Sam that I just adored. One particular day, when I was taking them for a walk, I let them out the back door, and instead of turning to the right like I always did, something got the dogs' attention to the left. I had never been that way, but the dogs were going nuts to get over there. When I found them, I saw a man propped up on his fence talking on the phone.

Right as I made it over to them, Otis started to use the bathroom in the man's yard. I said, "Oh, my gosh, I am so sorry, I'll clean that up!" He said, "No, that's alright. I like animals— it's people I ain't so sure about." This man had shaggy hair and the craziest out-of-control beard and a mustache that covered his mouth—I couldn't even see if he had teeth!

Opposite page, left to right: Me and Michael on our honeymoon in Greece. Me, the blushing bride! The most wonderful day—feeding my new husband wedding cake. **This page, clockwise from left:** Captain Michael on his boat. Michelle, Michael, and Anthony. Our wedding day and my beautiful bouquet. Me and Michael on St. Paddy's Day in our yard.

I scooped up the dogs and apologized again and headed back toward my house when I stopped dead in my tracks. I looked at the sky and said, "Lord, that ain't my neighbor, is it?"

I didn't think about it after that, but two weeks later, Sam and Otis did the same thing. Just like the first time, they found him propped on his fence, talking on the phone. I had three questions I wanted to ask him. "Are you married?" He said, "No." I asked, "Do you have children?" He said, "Yes. I have a teenage daughter and a teenage son." I asked, "You got a job?" He said, "Yes. I'm a harbor pilot on the river." I thought, "Cha-ching! This might be my guy."

So, I said, "Well, I just bought a boat and all I can do is sit in it and play CDs. Do you think you could teach me how to drive it?" And he said, "Oh, yeah, I could." So, we made a date for two days later for him to take me out. I never did learn how to drive that boat because I found my own captain instead.

We've been together ever since. Be careful what you pray for! You might get it.

MICHAEL'S WORLD-FAMOUS TUNA FISH SALAD

It is a running joke in our house that Michael says his tuna salad is world-famous! He made it once on my YouTube channel, and it's one of our highest-viewed videos. This recipe has brought us so many laughs!

Makes about 3 cups

- 2 (6.7-ounce) jars tuna fillets packed in oil, drained
- ½ onion, finely diced (about ½ cup)
- 2 stalks celery, finely diced (about ½ cup)
- 3 hard-cooked eggs, diced
- ⅓ to ½ cup dill pickle relish
- Mayonnaise and ground black pepper, to taste
- Bread and lettuce, to serve

1. In a serving bowl, gently break up tuna fillets. Add onion, celery, eggs, relish, mayonnaise, and pepper, stirring until combined. Serve with bread and lettuce.

Michael and I married in 2004, and we knew blending our families would be challenging. Our children are all wonderful, but it takes time and a lot of memory-making to make things work. You have to develop a history together, and that takes patience. I also believe it's the parents' job to be the bigger person and understand how the kids feel. I was the matriarch of our blended family, so I had to be the one to set the example. It took time, but it was so worth the wait. Michelle and Anthony and their spouses and children have brought so much joy to my life, and I hope I have to theirs, too.

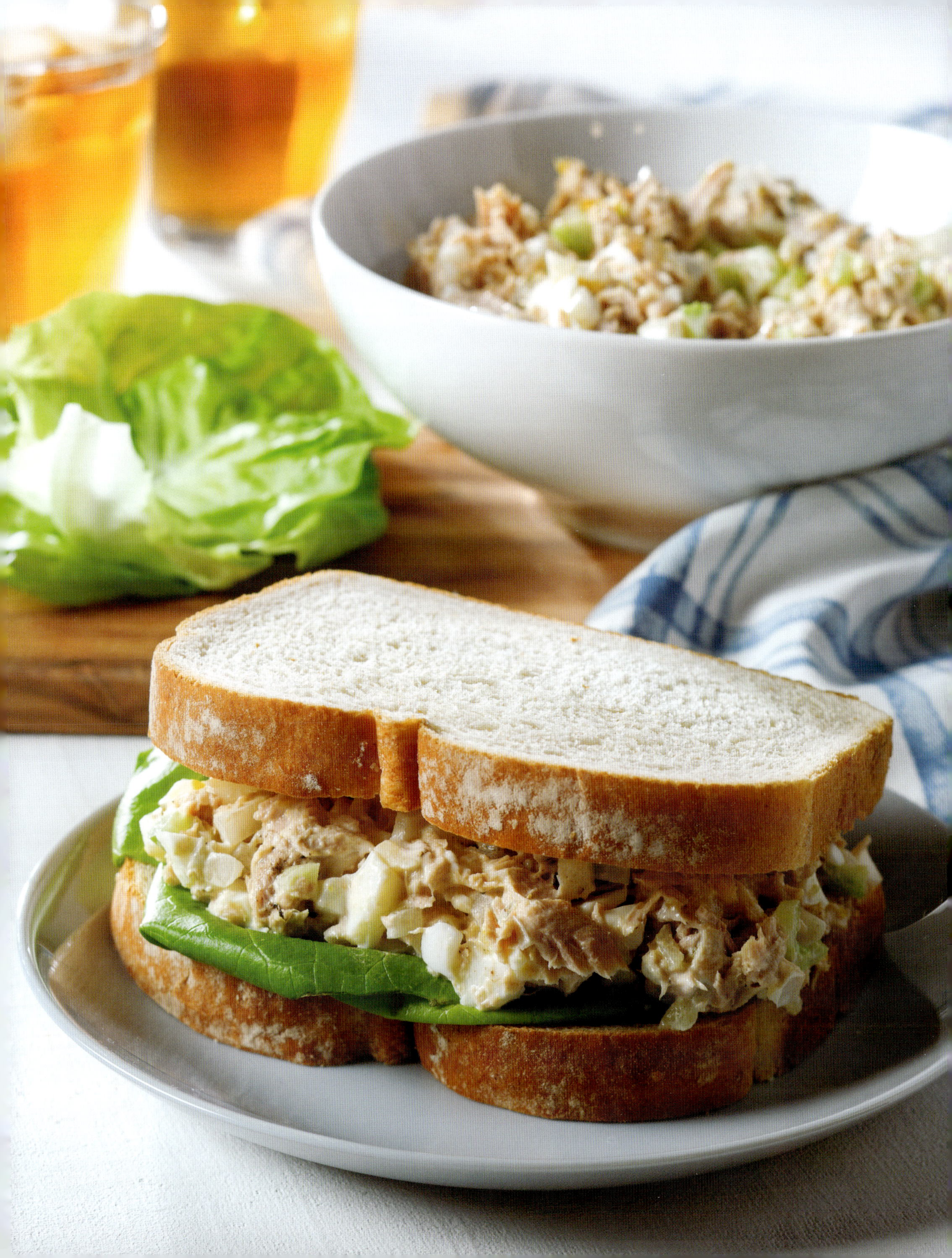

Recipe Tip

In this recipe, I use more nuts than chips because that's the way my family likes them. So, adapt the amount to suit your taste. I also mix the nuts, using pecans, walnuts and macadamias.

THIN AND CRISPY CHOCOLATE CHIP COOKIES

Grandmother Paul always made chocolate chip cookies and stored them in a potato chip tin. Corrie just loved those cookies, and I created my own version for her!

Makes about 24

- 1¼ cups salted butter, room temperature
- 1 cup firmly packed light brown sugar
- ¾ cup granulated sugar
- 1 large egg
- 3 tablespoons water
- 1 tablespoon vanilla extract
- 2 cups all-purpose flour
- 1 teaspoon salt
- ½ teaspoon baking soda
- 2 cup chopped pecans
- 1 cup milk chocolate chips
- ½ cup white chocolate chips

1. Preheat oven to 350°. Line baking sheets with parchment paper.

2. In the bowl of a stand mixer fitted with the paddle attachment, beat butter and sugars at medium speed until fluffy, 2 to 3 minutes, stopping to scrape sides of bowl. Beat in egg, 3 tablespoons water, and vanilla.

3. In a medium bowl, whisk together flour, salt, and baking soda until combined. With mixer on low speed, gradually add flour mixture to butter mixture, beating until combined. Stir in pecans and all chocolate chips.

4. Using about a 2-ounce spring-loaded scoop, scoop dough, and place 2 inches apart on prepared pans (6 cookies per pan). Spray a piece of wax or parchment paper with a cooking spray, and lightly press down on each dough scoop. (This will make for a thinner cookie.)

5. Bake until golden brown, 12 to 15 minutes. Let cool on pans for 2 minutes. Remove from pans, and let cool completely on wire racks.

SAVANNAH RED RICE

Oh, this is such a good side dish! It's flavorful with a spicy kick.

Makes about 6 cups

- 2 tablespoons salted butter
- 1 cup chopped onion
- 1 cup chopped green bell pepper
- 1 cup diced smoked sausage*
- 1 (14.5-ounce) can crushed tomatoes
- 1 cup tomato sauce
- 1 cup water
- 1 tablespoon hot sauce
- 3 chicken bouillon cubes
- Salt and ground black pepper, to taste
- 1 cup long-grain rice

1. Preheat oven to 350°. Spray a 13x9-inch baking dish with cooking spray.

2. In a medium saucepan, melt butter over medium heat. Add onion and bell pepper, and cook until tender, about 5 minutes. Add sausage; cook until mixture is lightly browned. Add tomatoes, tomato sauce, 1 cup water, hot sauce, and bouillon cubes. Season with salt and black pepper. Stir in rice. Pour mixture into prepared pan. Cover with foil.

3. Bake until rice is tender, 45 minutes to 1 hour.

I used Hillshire Farm Sausage.

Michael and I got engaged on Christmas morning! He surprised me by inviting the whole family over.

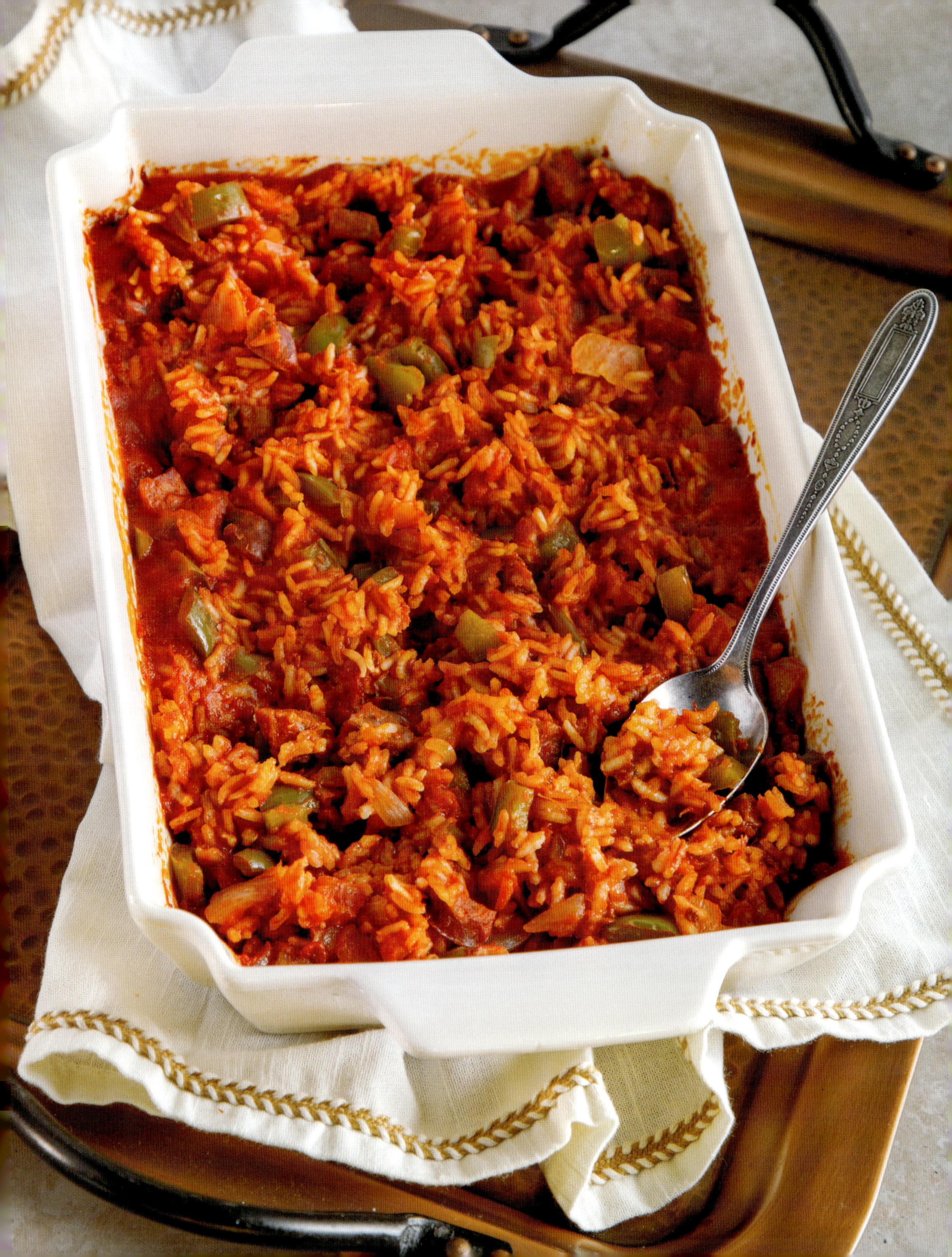

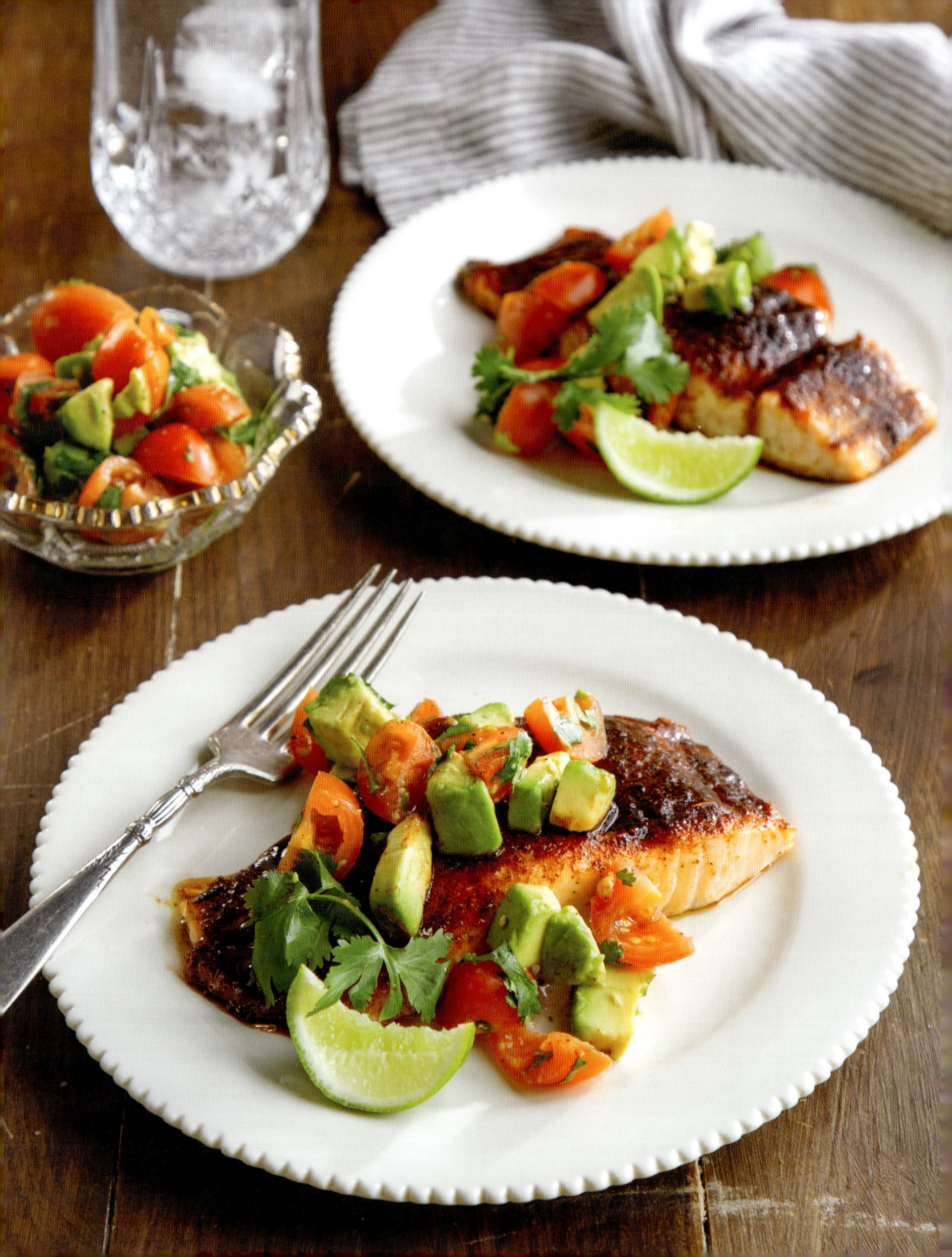

CHILI-RUBBED SALMON TOPPED WITH AVOCADO TOMATO SALSA

This recipe is from our wonderful daughter-in-law Brooke. In our house, we just call it "Brooke's Salmon"—it is so tasty and refreshing.

Makes 4 servings

- 3 tablespoons firmly packed light brown sugar
- 1½ tablespoons chili powder
- 1 teaspoon ground cumin
- 1 teaspoon salt
- 1 teaspoon ground black pepper
- 4 salmon fillets (about 6 ounces each)
- 2 tablespoons olive oil

SALSA

- 2 avocados, diced into ½ inch cubes
- 1 cup cherry tomatoes, quartered
- ¼ cup chopped fresh cilantro leaves
- 1 tablespoon fresh lime juice
- ¼ teaspoon salt
- ¼ teaspoon ground black pepper

Garnish: cilantro, lime wedge

1. Preheat oven to 425°. Line a rimmed baking sheet with parchment paper.

2. For salmon: In small bowl, combine brown sugar, chili powder, cumin, salt, and pepper. Brush salmon lightly with oil. Spread sugar mixture generously on top of salmon. Place on prepared pan.

3. Bake until an instant-read thermometer inserted in center registers 125°, 10 to 12 minutes, or to desired degree of doneness.

4. Meanwhile, for salsa: In a medium bowl, gently stir together avocado, tomatoes, cilantro, and lime juice. Season with salt and pepper.

5. Transfer each salmon fillet to a serving plate, and top with salsa. Garnish with cilantro and lime wedge, if desired.

We all love this dish served over rice, but it's also great on a salad. We called it Brooke's Salmon at Creek House restaurant in Savannah, and it was one of the most popular items on the menu. The sweet from the brown sugar and heat from the chili powder make an excellent combo.

BANANA PANCAKES

Our daughter-in-law Claudia loves to make these pancakes for her children. They are healthy and flavorful and easy to whip up in the morning!

Makes 12

- 2 ripe bananas
- ⅓ baked sweet potato
- ½ cup quick-cooking oats
- ⅓ cup milk
- ¼ cup ground flaxseeds
- 3 large eggs
- Handful raw baby spinach and/or handful raw shredded carrots*
- Peanut butter, maple syrup, and berries, to serve

1. In the container of a blender, process bananas, sweet potato, oats, milk, flaxseeds, and eggs until combined. Stir in spinach and/or carrots.

2. Heat a nonstick pan or griddle over medium-low heat. Spoon batter in small amounts onto pan, and cook top is dry; turn, and cook for about 1 minute. Serve with peanut butter, maple syrup, and berries.

*I do both, but if you only choose one or none, it won't change the texture.

Claudia and Bobby.

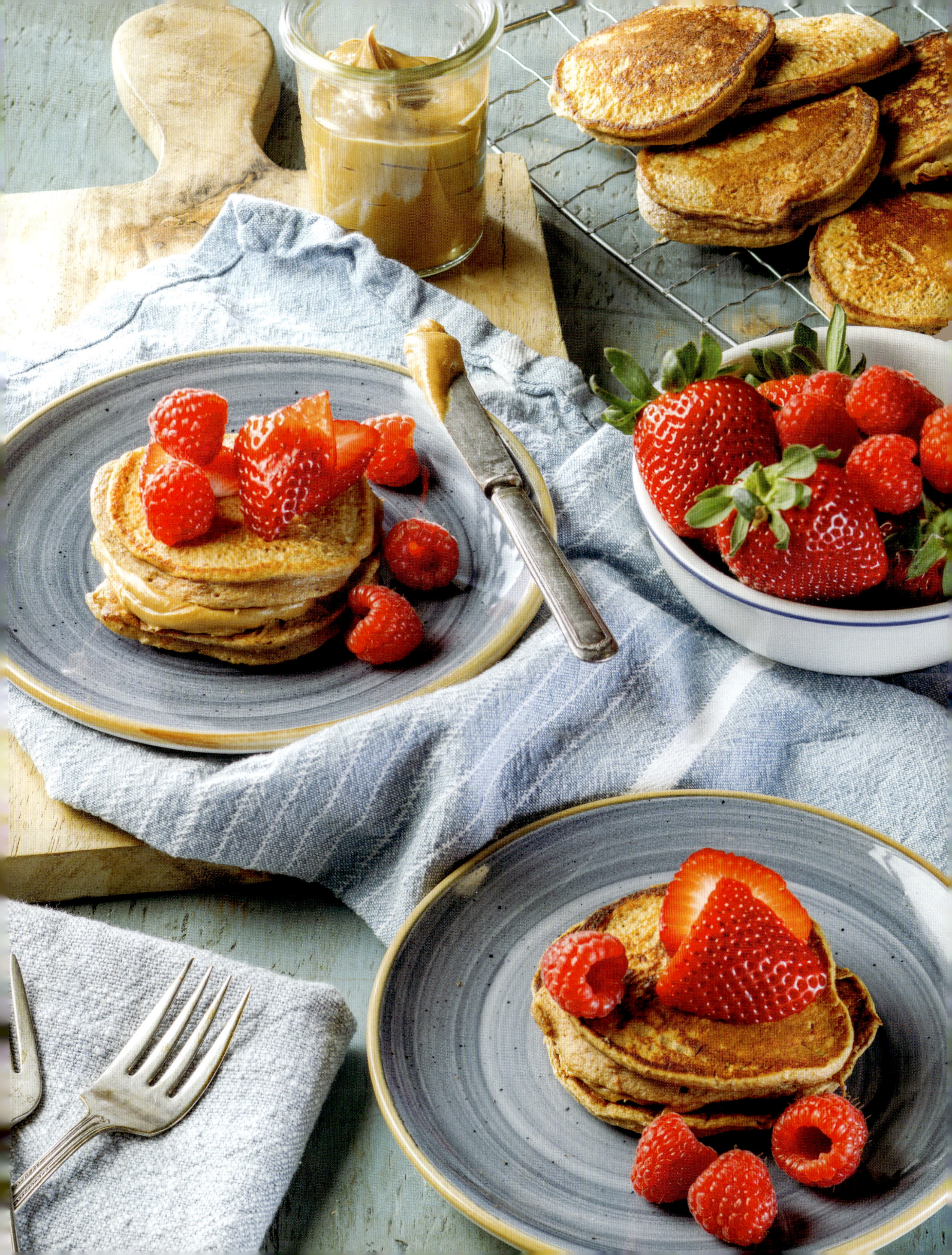

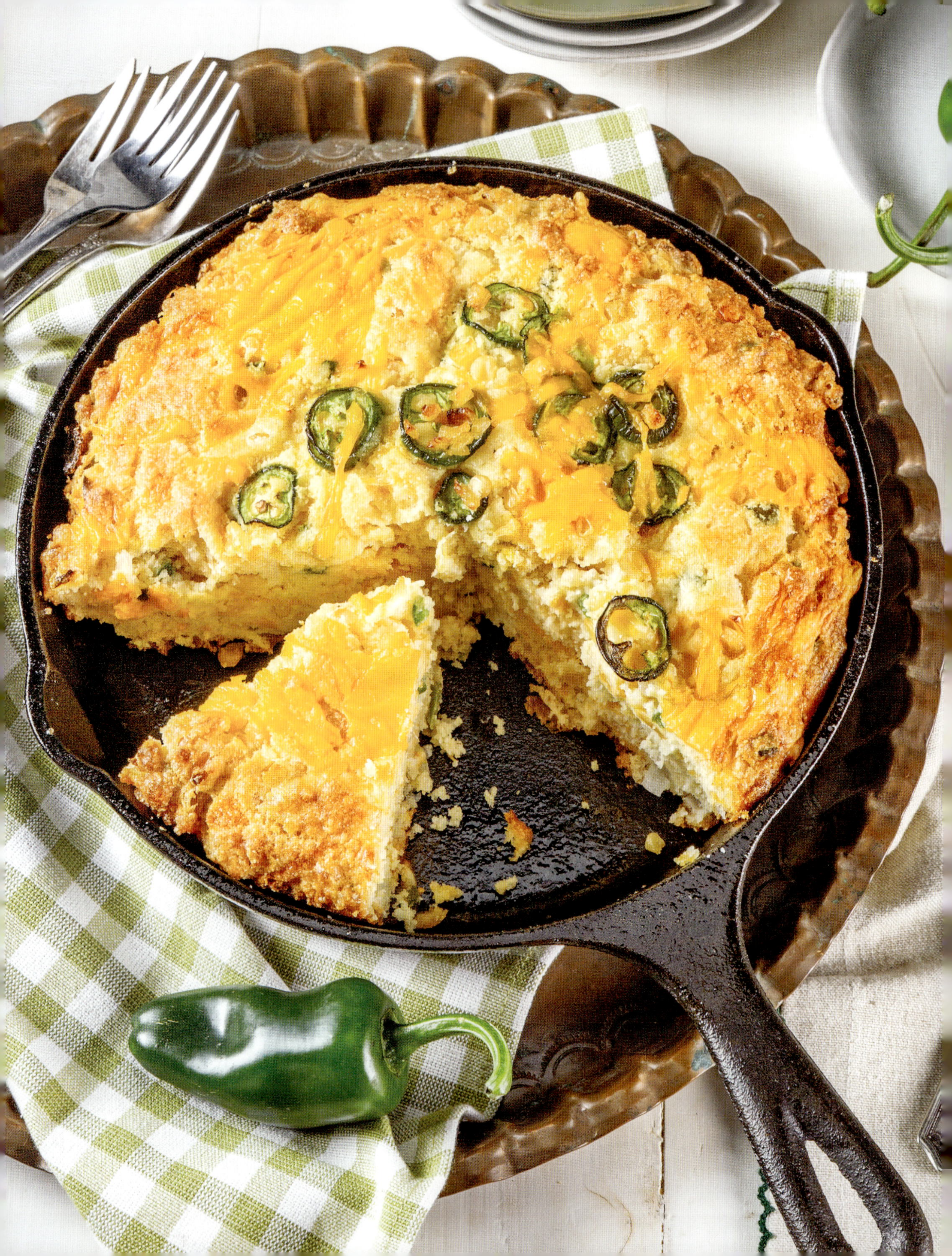

MEXICAN CORNBREAD

Bubba and his partner, Sandy, created this delicious recipe and shared it with me. It is dense and so flavorful!

Makes 1 (10-inch) loaf

- ½ cup vegetable oil, divided
- 1 (15-ounce) can shoepeg corn, drained
- 1½ cups white self-rising cornmeal mix
- 1½ cups sharp Cheddar cheese, grated
- 1 cup all-purpose flour
- 1 cup sour cream
- 3 large eggs, lightly beaten
- 1 large onion, chopped
- ¼ cup plus 2 tablespoons fresh jalapeño*, chopped and divided

1. Preheat oven to 400°.

2. In a 10-inch cast-iron skillet, place 2 tablespoons oil. Place in oven to preheat.

3. In a large bowl, stir together corn, cornmeal, cheese, flour, sour cream, eggs, onion, ¼ cup jalapeño, and remaining 6 tablespoons oil until combined. Remove hot skillet from oven, and pour batter into skillet. Sprinkle with remaining 2 tablespoons jalapeño.

4. Bake until golden brown and a wooden pick inserted in center comes out clean, about 30 minutes.

*For less heat, use a green chile pepper.

Sandy and Bubba.

BEEF RIBS

This recipe from Jamie makes the best beef ribs I have ever put in my mouth! They are out of this world. They take time, but they're worth every moment.

Makes 4 to 6 servings

- ¼ cup salt
- ¼ cup garlic salt
- ¼ cup ground black pepper
- 2 slabs beef ribs, 5 to 7 bones per slab
- Barbecue sauce

1. In a small bowl, stir together salts and pepper.

2. Pat ribs dry. Using a sharp knife, pierce thin membrane on back of ribs; peel off, and discard. Sprinkle both sides of ribs with salt mixture. (You will have leftover salt mixture.) Let ribs stand at room temperature for 30 minutes after seasoning.

3. Soak wood chips in water for at least 30 minutes.

4. Preheat smoker to 225°. Sprinkle soaked wood chips over coals. Place ribs on smoker rack. Cover with smoker lid, and cook for 2 hours.

5. Place a grate inside a roasting pan or disposable foil pan, and fill with water to just under grate. Place ribs on grate, and seal very well with foil. Place back on smoker, and cook for 2 hours.

6. Remove ribs from foil, and place back on smoker grate. Baste with sauce, and cook for 1 hour. Serve with additional sauce.

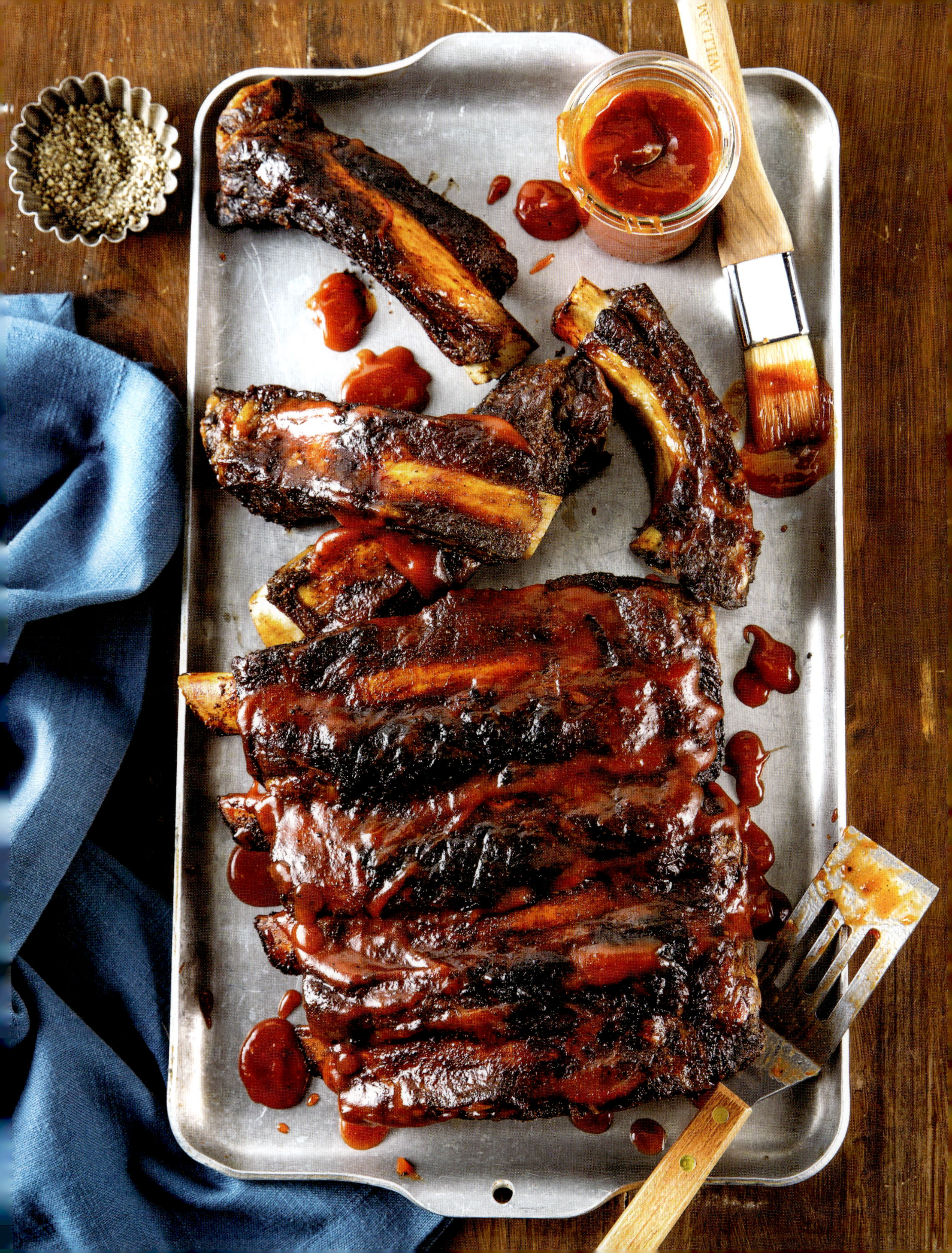

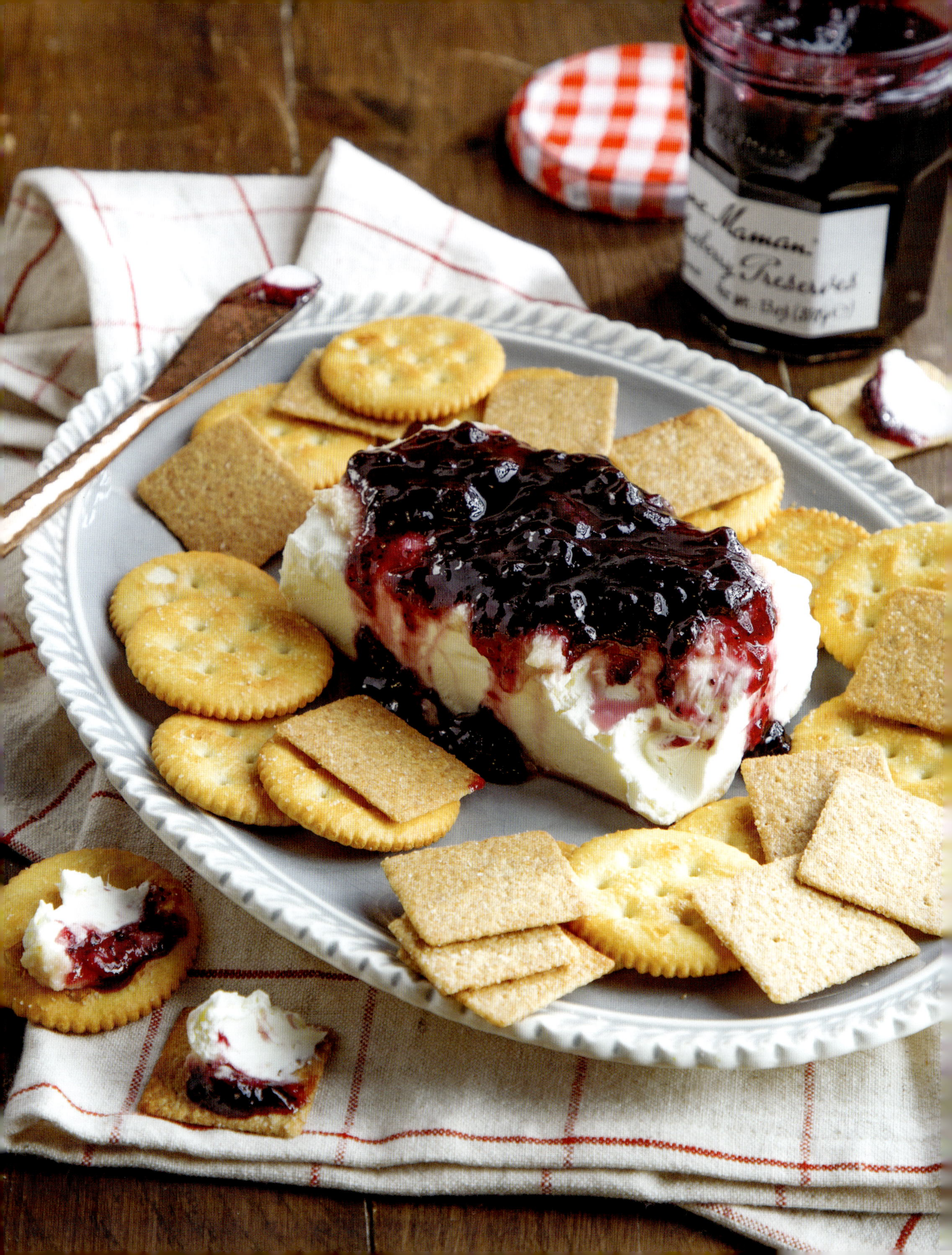
Maman
Preserves

BLUEBERRY CREAM CHEESE SPREAD

Our son Anthony and daughter-in-law Ashley shared this recipe with me. I am so blessed that all of my children love to spend time in the kitchen!

Makes about 4 servings

- 1 (8-ounce) package cream cheese
- ⅓ cup prepared horseradish
- 1 (13-ounce) jar wild blueberry preserves
- Buttery round crackers and wheat thin crackers, to serve

1. On a serving plate, place cream cheese. Spread horseradish on top. Generously layer preserves on top of horseradish. Serve with crackers.

*I used Bonne Maman.

Michael and me sitting with our children Anthony and Ashley and their children, Bennett and Madison.

SODA CRACKER SALAD

*Jamie makes this unique salad that we all just love!
It's fast to make and a big crowd-pleaser.*

Makes 2 cups

---

1   large tomato, finely chopped

1½ cups mayonnaise

1   sleeve saltine crackers, crushed

1   hard-cooked large egg, peeled and finely chopped

3   green onions, finely chopped

1. In a large bowl, stir together all ingredients. Serve immediately.

My dear, sweet Aunt Peggy! When I would get beyond tired from running The Bag Lady, I would call Aunt Peggy and say that I just didn't think I could do it anymore. She'd hop in the car the next day and drive up to help me for a week or two. Those visits and help kept me going! One day, she didn't have a hairnet to wear, so she walked into the kitchen ready to work with a pair of clean underwear on her head.

Recipe Tip

This salad is very good served with fish, especially at an outdoor fish fry.

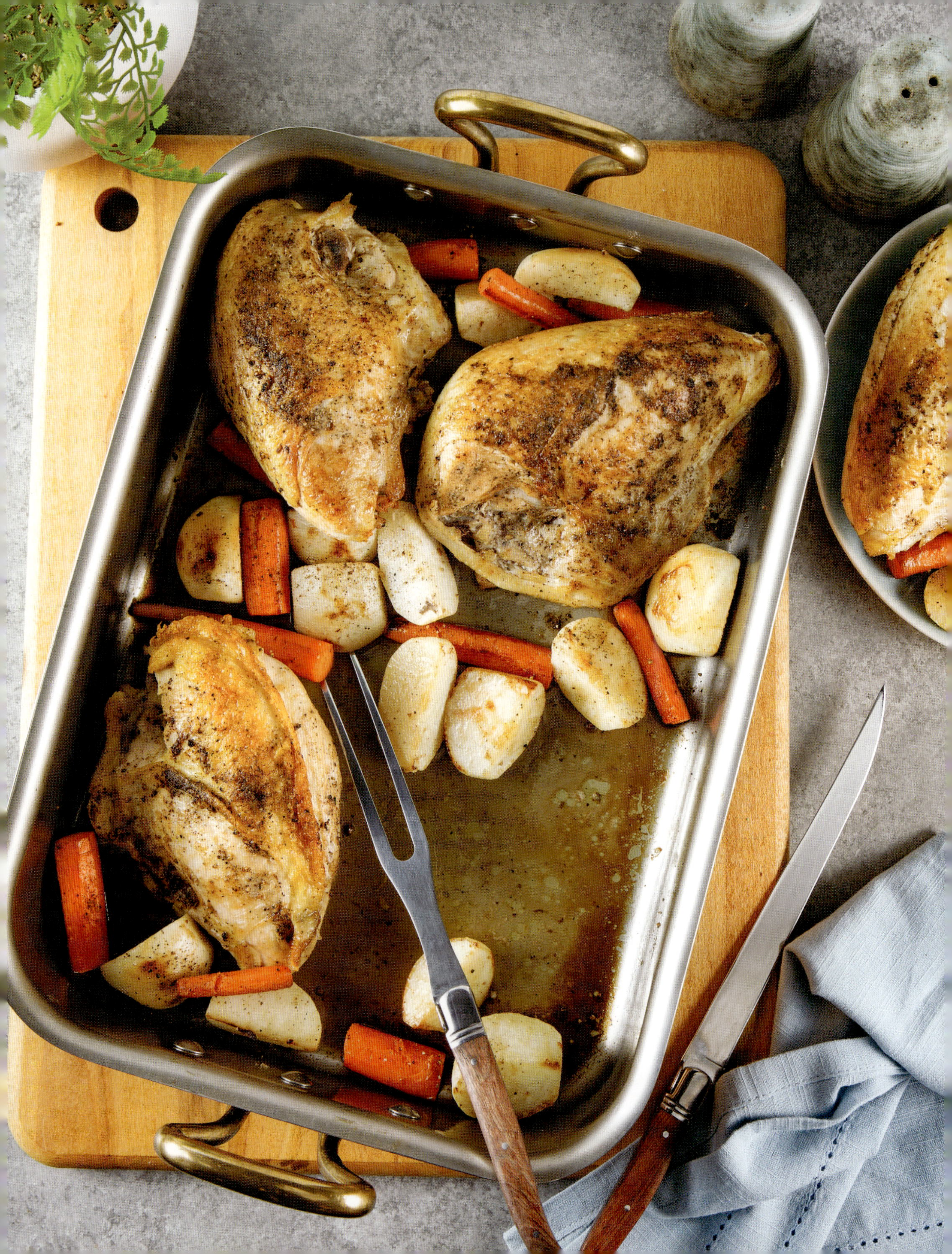

ROASTED CHICKEN

This is Jamie's recipe and a go-to at our house. You may use any cut of chicken you prefer—I like bone-in chicken breast with skin on. Jamie would rather use boneless thighs. That's what makes the world go round, though! Use your favorite.

Makes 4 servings

- 4 bone-in skin-on chicken breasts with rib meat
- Salt, to taste
- Ground black pepper, to taste
- 1 tablespoon salted butter
- 1 tablespoon olive oil
- 4 small carrots, peeled and cut into 2-inch pieces
- 4 medium turnip roots, peeled and quartered

1. In a gallon-size resealable plastic bag, place chicken; season with salt and pepper. Refrigerate for 1 to 3 hours.

2. Preheat oven to 350°.

3. Heat an ovenproof heavy-duty roasting pan over medium-high heat. (Pan will cover two burners.) Add butter and oil, and heat until butter is melted. Add chicken skin side down, and cook until browned, 3 to 4 minutes per side. Add carrots and turnips.

4. Bake until vegetables are tender and an instant-read thermometer inserted in thickest portion of chicken registers 165°, 30 to 45 minutes.

Michael and I dancing while cruising.

CRAB CAKES

Our daughter Michelle loves to make these wonderful crab cakes—especially after a day spent in the marsh with her daddy. We all just love these!

Makes about 6 servings

- 2 pounds lump crabmeat, picked free of shell
- 2⅓ cups panko (Japanese bread crumbs), divided
- ½ cup sliced green onion
- ½ cup mayonnaise
- 2 large eggs, lightly beaten
- ½ teaspoon Old Bay seasoning
- Olive oil, for frying
- Tartar sauce and lemon wedges, to serve
- Garnish: chopped green onion

1. In a large bowl, gently mix together crab, ⅓ cup bread crumbs, green onion, mayonnaise, eggs, and Old Bay until combined. Scoop dough by about ⅓ cupfuls, and shape into patties (about ¾ inch thick).

2. On a rimmed baking sheet, place remaining 2 cups bread crumbs. Dredge patties in bread crumbs to coat.

3. In a large saucepan, pour oil to a depth of ¼ inch, and heat over medium heat. Add patties in batches, and fry until lightly browned, 2 to 3 minutes per side, carefully turning with a spatula. Remove from oil, and let drain on paper towels. Serve with tartar sauce and lemon wedges. Garnish with green onion, if desired.

Michelle and Michael.

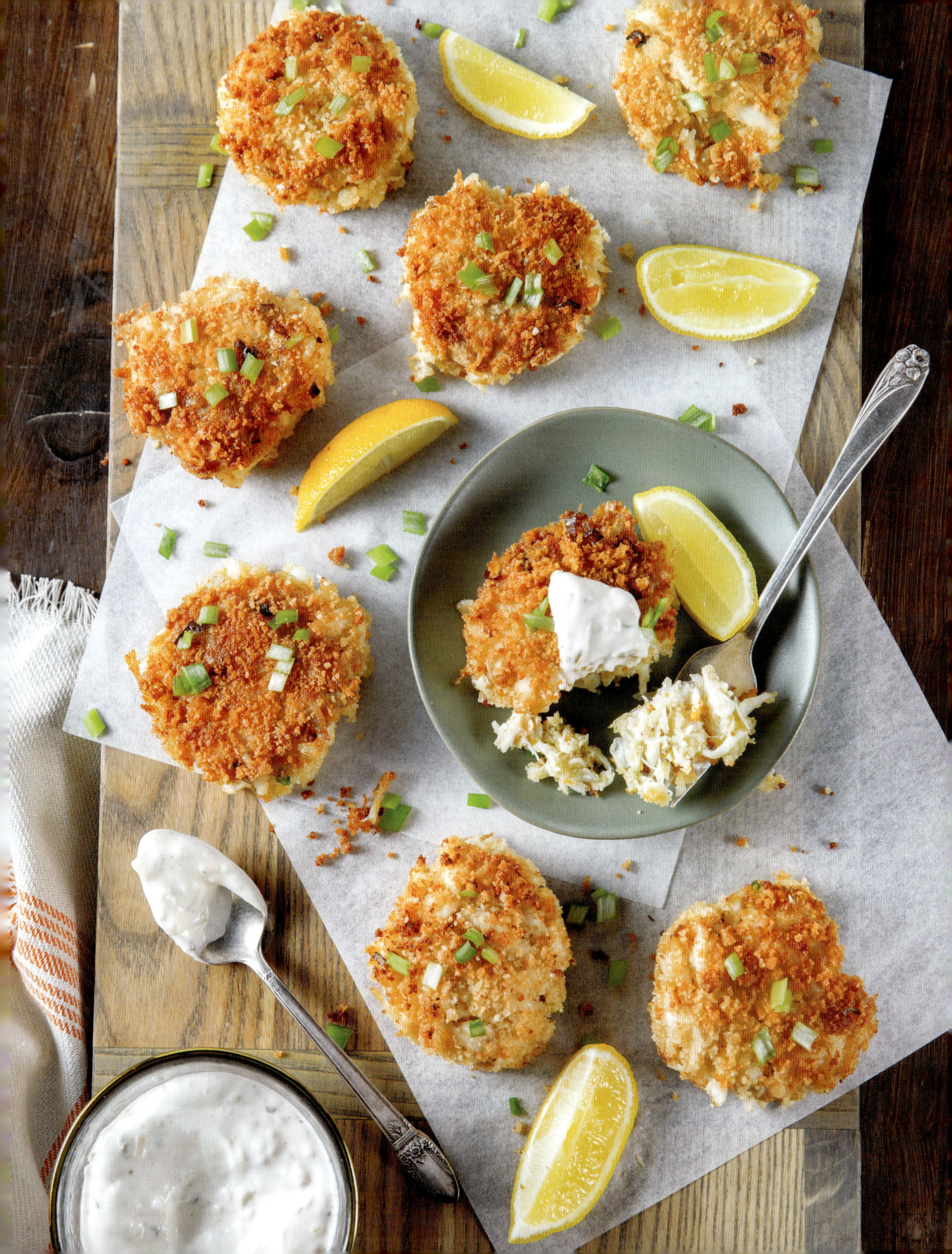

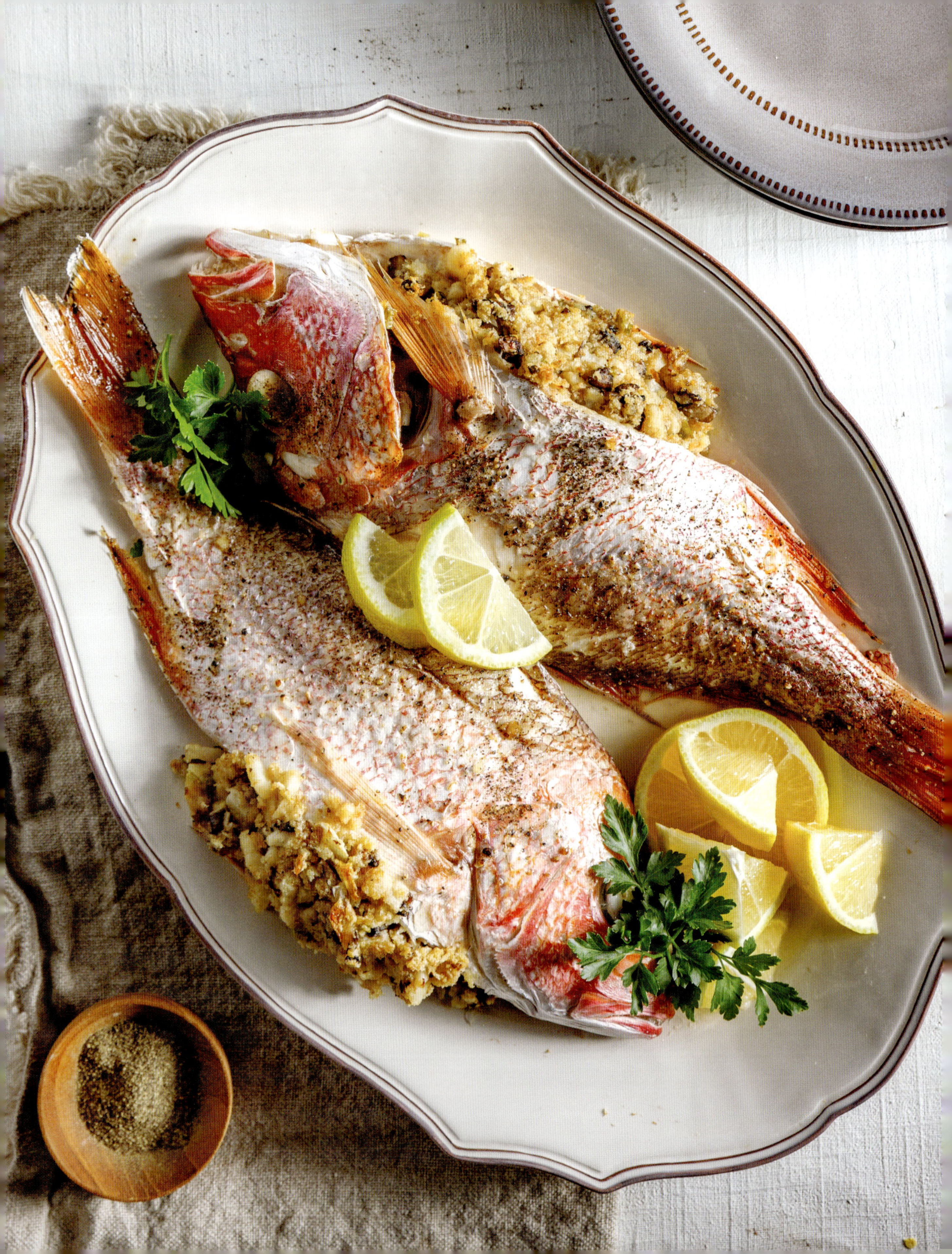

MUSHROOM-STUFFED BAKED RED SNAPPER

This recipe really wows when you're looking to make something a little on the fancy side. If you have access to good red snapper, you should really give this a try.

Makes 6 servings

- ½ pound fresh button mushrooms
- 3 tablespoons salted butter, divided
- ½ cup finely chopped celery
- 5 tablespoons minced onion
- 1 (8-ounce) can water chestnuts, drained and finely chopped
- ½ cup soft bread crumbs
- 1 large egg, lightly beaten
- 1 tablespoon chopped fresh parsley
- 1 tablespoon soy sauce
- Salt and ground black pepper, to taste
- 2 (2½-pound) oven-ready whole red snappers
- ¾ cup water
- ½ cup dry white wine
- Lemon wedges, to serve

1. Preheat oven to 350°.

2. Rinse, pat dry, and finely chop half of mushrooms. Quarter remaining mushrooms.

3. In a small skillet, melt 1 tablespoon butter over medium-high heat. Add mushrooms, celery, and onion. Cook until moisture is absorbed, about 5 minutes.

4. In a large bowl, combine mushroom mixture, water chestnuts, bread crumbs, egg, parsley, soy sauce, salt, and pepper. Spoon mixture into fish cavities. Secure with wooden skewer or wooden picks. Season fish with salt and pepper. Place in a large baking dish; dot with remaining 2 tablespoons butter, and pour in ¾ water and wine.

5. Bake, uncovered, until fish flakes easily with a fork, 45 to 50 minutes, basting occasionally. Serve with lemon wedges, if desired.

PASTA SALAD

This wonderful pasta salad from Jamie is always a hit! Jamie has always been so talented in the kitchen and is known for his salad creations.

Makes 12 cups

DRESSING

- ½ cup vegetable oil
- 1 tablespoon water
- 1 tablespoon mayonnaise
- 1 teaspoon sugar
- 1 (.07-ounce) package dried Italian seasoning

SALAD

- 4 to 6 quarts water
- 1 (16-ounce) package rotini
- 1 cup broccoli florets
- 1 cup chopped carrots
- 2 cups chopped cooked chicken
- 1 cup chopped yellow bell pepper
- 1 cup grape tomatoes, halved
- 1 (8-ounce) package whole-milk mozzarella, cubed
- ¼ cup sliced black olives

Garnish: chopped fresh parsley

1. For dressing: In a bowl or dressing shaker, combine oil, 1 tablespoon water, mayonnaise, sugar, and Italian seasoning.

2. For salad: In a large stockpot, bring 4 to 6 quarts water to a boil over medium-high heat. Add rotini, and cook according to package directions; add broccoli and carrots during final 2 minutes of cooking. Rinse under cold water to stop the cooking process. Drain.

3. Transfer rotini mixture to a large bowl, and add chicken, bell pepper, tomatoes, cheese, and olives; add dressing, and stir until combined. Refrigerate until ready to serve. Garnish with parsley, if desired.

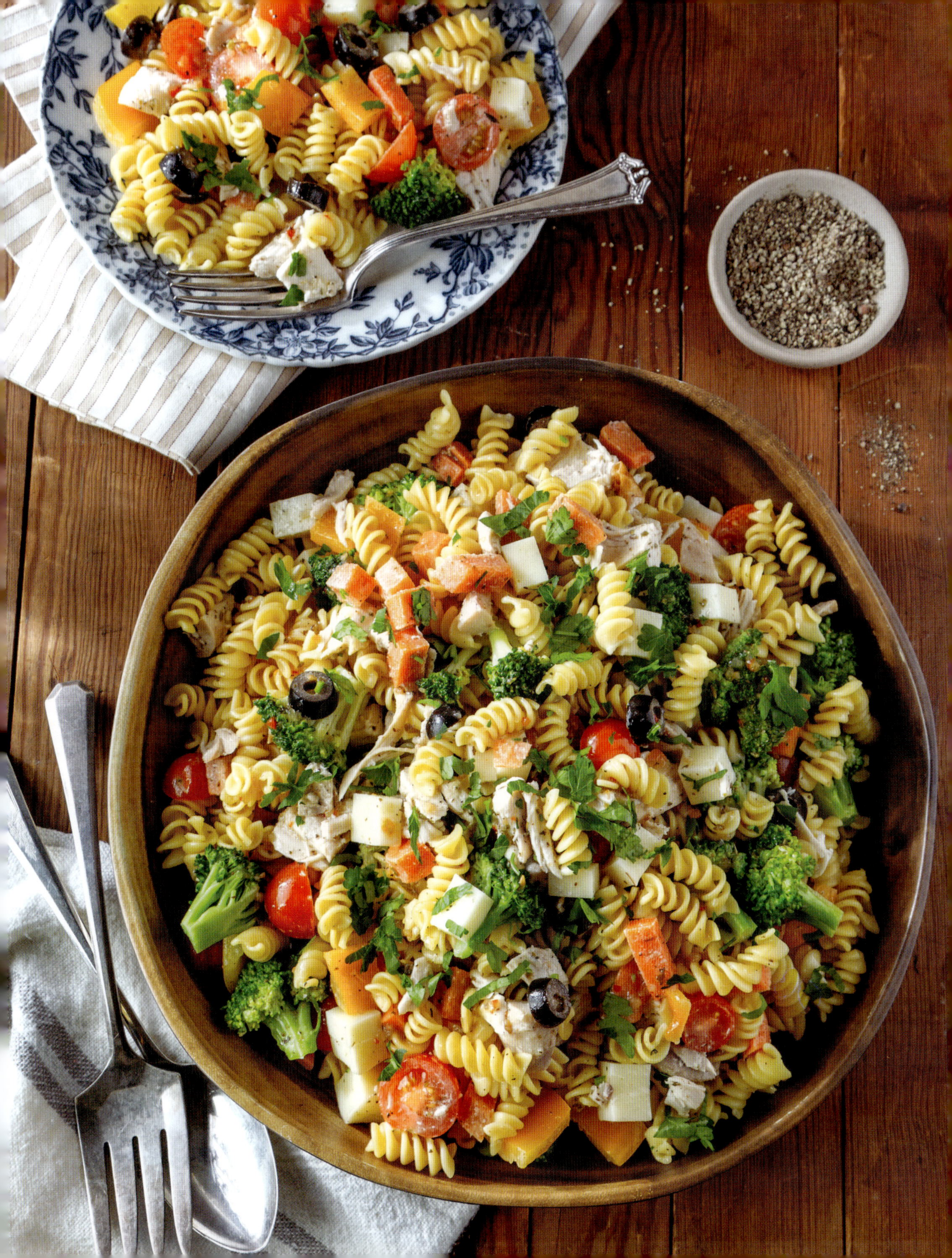

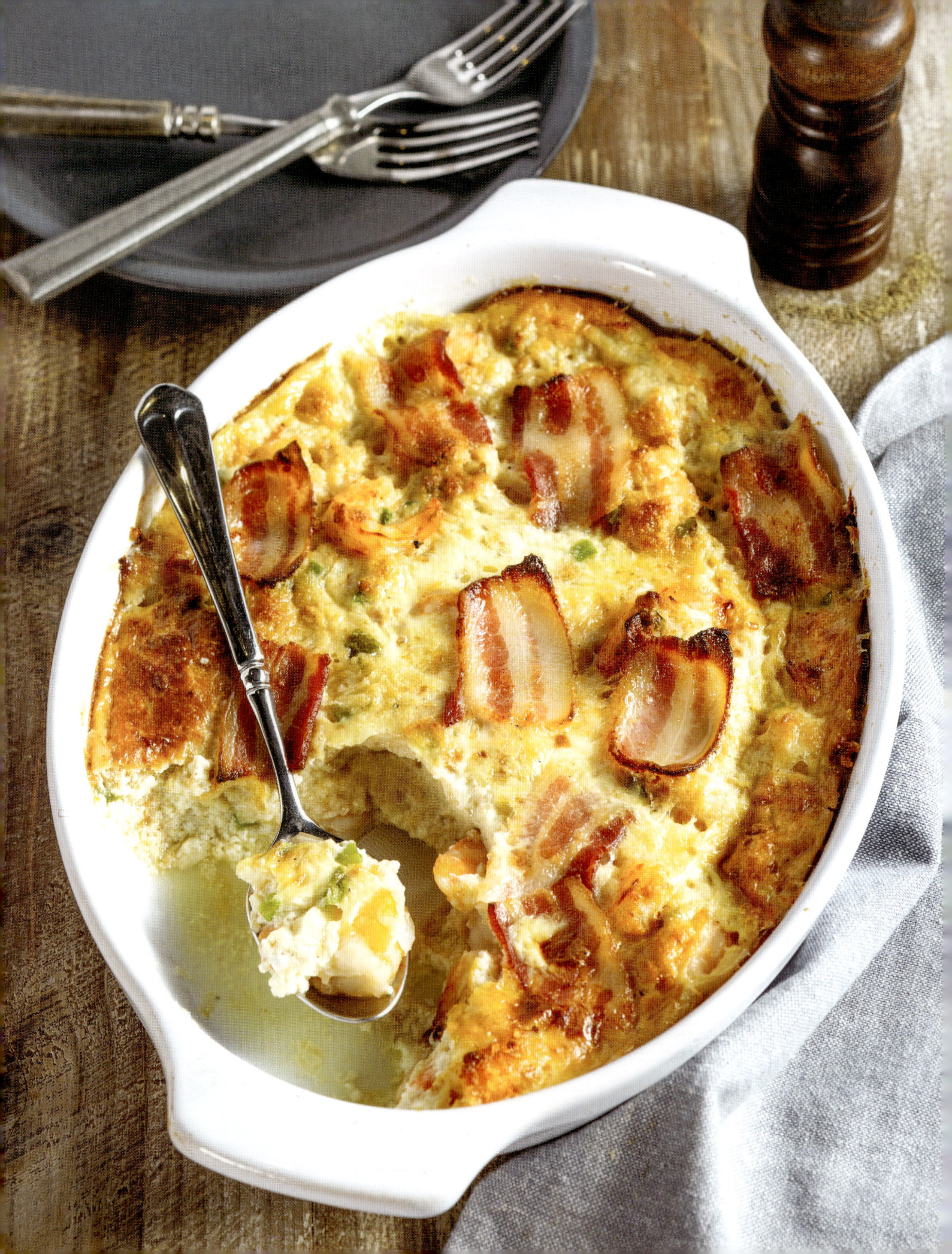

BEAUFORT SHRIMP PIE

In the Carolina Sea Islands, a "pie" does not necessarily have a crust. This shrimp casserole is a superb luncheon dish and is one of these pies.

Makes 6 to 8 servings

- 2 tablespoons salted butter
- ½ cup chopped white onion
- ¼ cup chopped green bell pepper
- 3 cups peeled and deveined large fresh shrimp
- 2 cups soft bread crumbs
- 2 cups whole milk
- 2 large eggs
- ½ teaspoon salt
- ¼ teaspoon ground black pepper
- 3 slices bacon, cut into 4 pieces each

1. Preheat oven to 325°. Spray a 2-quart baking dish with cooking spray.

2. In a medium skillet, melt butter over medium-high heat. Add onion and bell pepper, and cook until soft.

3. In prepared pan, layer shrimp, bread crumbs, and onion mixture.

4. In a medium bowl, whisk together milk, egg, salt, and black pepper, and pour over onion mixture. Lay bacon on top of casserole.

5. Bake until filling is set and bacon is brown, about 45 minutes.

The bread to my butter! I loved these hilarious costumes that Michael and I wore.

FAMILY MATTERS | LOVE AND BEST DISHES

BACON-WRAPPED, SAUSAGE-STUFFED PORK TENDERLOIN

Michael created this wonderful recipe! Now that I have had pork tenderloin prepared like this, I refuse to have it any other way.

Makes 6 servings

- 2 (2-pound) pork tenderloins
- 2 (1-pound) skinless Polska kielbasa sausage
- House Seasoning, to taste (recipe on page 119)
- 16 slices thin-cut bacon

1. Using a long fillet knife, cut an "X" all the way through the center of the tenderloin lengthwise from each side, making sure not to cut to the outside of the tenderloin, and twist the knife, making a tunnel for the sausage to slide in. (You can also ask your butcher to do this part for you.)

2. Slide sausage through tunnel in center of tenderloin until it runs all the way through. Season tenderloin liberally with House Seasoning. Wrap with bacon, securing ends of bacon with wooden picks as needed.

3. Place on a pellet grill or smoker at 225°, and cook until an instant-read thermometer inserted in center registers 145° to 165°, about 3 hours. Once they're cooked through, sear them for a few minutes on a traditional grill until the bacon is crisp. Remove wooden picks before serving.

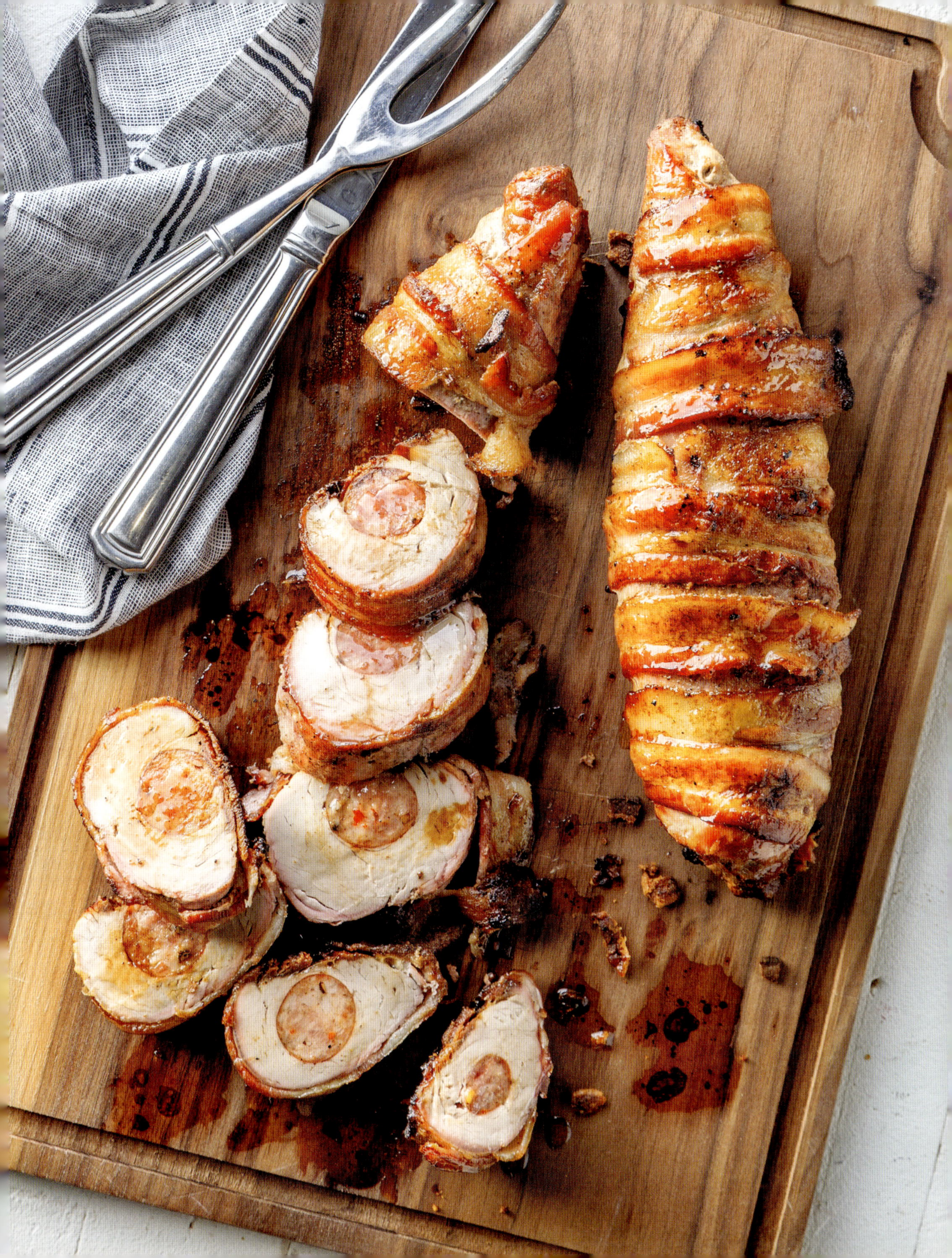

CHAPTER EIGHT

LIFE'S LESSONS

Over the years, I have had to learn some very hard lessons, as we all do in life. Learning and growing can be painful and scary, but it is something we cannot avoid, and we should welcome opportunities for positive change. You cannot enjoy the top of the mountain without being down deep in the valley first. You'll never truly appreciate the good without also enduring the bad. Always choose to take the experiences life throws at you and consider thinking of them as challenges to accept and overcome.

Acceptance has always been hard for me. Starting with the death of my daddy, I never wanted to accept the bad things that were happening. I always fought to avoid them, and I feared them. I had no idea what heartbreaking challenges were ahead of me. My momma's death came shortly after my daddy's. I later grieved the loss of my Uncle George, my grandparents, and more aunts and uncles. Then, the untimely death of my nephew and Corrie's brother, Jay Hiers, was so painful. I have to tell y'all though, even after all that loss, my brother's early death was the one to rip my heart out.

The Serenity Prayer still keeps me going time and time again—it shows me how to take control. I try my best every day to do the right thing. I want to live a life where I give as much love and patience to others as I can and remain positive when times are tough. I want my glass to remain half full rather than half empty.

One thing that fills my glass every single day is my relationship with my fans. I wish more than anything that I could express every ounce of gratitude I feel to each one of them. Their messages, letters, and gifts have gotten me through the hardest times of my life. I remember many days I could not get out of bed without first reading some kind words from my supporters.

Working with my two sons all these years has also been the biggest blessing, but working with family and running a business in your home can be excruciatingly hard. You can't ever get away and turn it off. I know my boys used to wish they could relax and enjoy downtime in the evenings, but they felt so guilty about me staying in the kitchen late into the night. But I chose to do that. It was my choice, not theirs, and we did pay a price in our relationship because of that. It was hard for the boys to say, "That's my momma, but that's also my boss."

When you work with family and you have unconditional love for each other, you don't always remember to respect boundaries. I'm so thankful we survived. Our love for each other was so strong that we turned that $200 into a multimillion-dollar business. We beat the odds together, and I've always found that the harder we worked, the luckier we got.

Opposite page, left to right: Me at The Lady & Sons. My beautiful family. **This page, top to bottom:** Bobby, Bubba, me, and Jamie. Corrie and Jay. Wonderful days working on the set of my TV show. A sweet fan who made her own Paula Deen shirt.

The Serenity Prayer

God, grant me the serenity to accept the things I cannot change, the courage to change the things I can, and the wisdom to know the difference. Amen.

ZUCCHINI-CORN CASSEROLE

This recipe is addictive! I love the flavors of the vegetables and sharp Cheddar cheese together. This is a great way to serve up some veggies with your favorite main.

Makes 8 to 10 servings

- 3 pounds small zucchini, stemmed
- 1 (14.75-ounce) can cream-style corn
- 4 large eggs, lightly beaten
- 2 tablespoons salted butter, melted
- 1 medium onion, chopped
- 1 green bell pepper, chopped
- 1¼ teaspoons salt
- ¼ teaspoon ground black pepper
- 1 cup shredded sharp Cheddar cheese
- Paprika, to taste

1. Preheat oven to 350°. Spray a 2-quart baking dish with cooking spray.

2. Bring a large stockpot of salted water to a boil over medium-high heat; add zucchini, and cook until just tender, about 6 minutes. Drain, and cut into chunks. Transfer to a large bowl, and stir in corn and eggs.

3. Meanwhile, in a large skillet, melt butter over medium-high heat. Add onion and bell pepper, and cook until golden brown, about 5 minutes. Stir into zucchini mixture; stir in salt and black pepper. Pour mixture into prepared pan. Sprinkle cheese on top, and sprinkle with paprika.

4. Bake until lightly browned and bubbly, about 40 minutes.

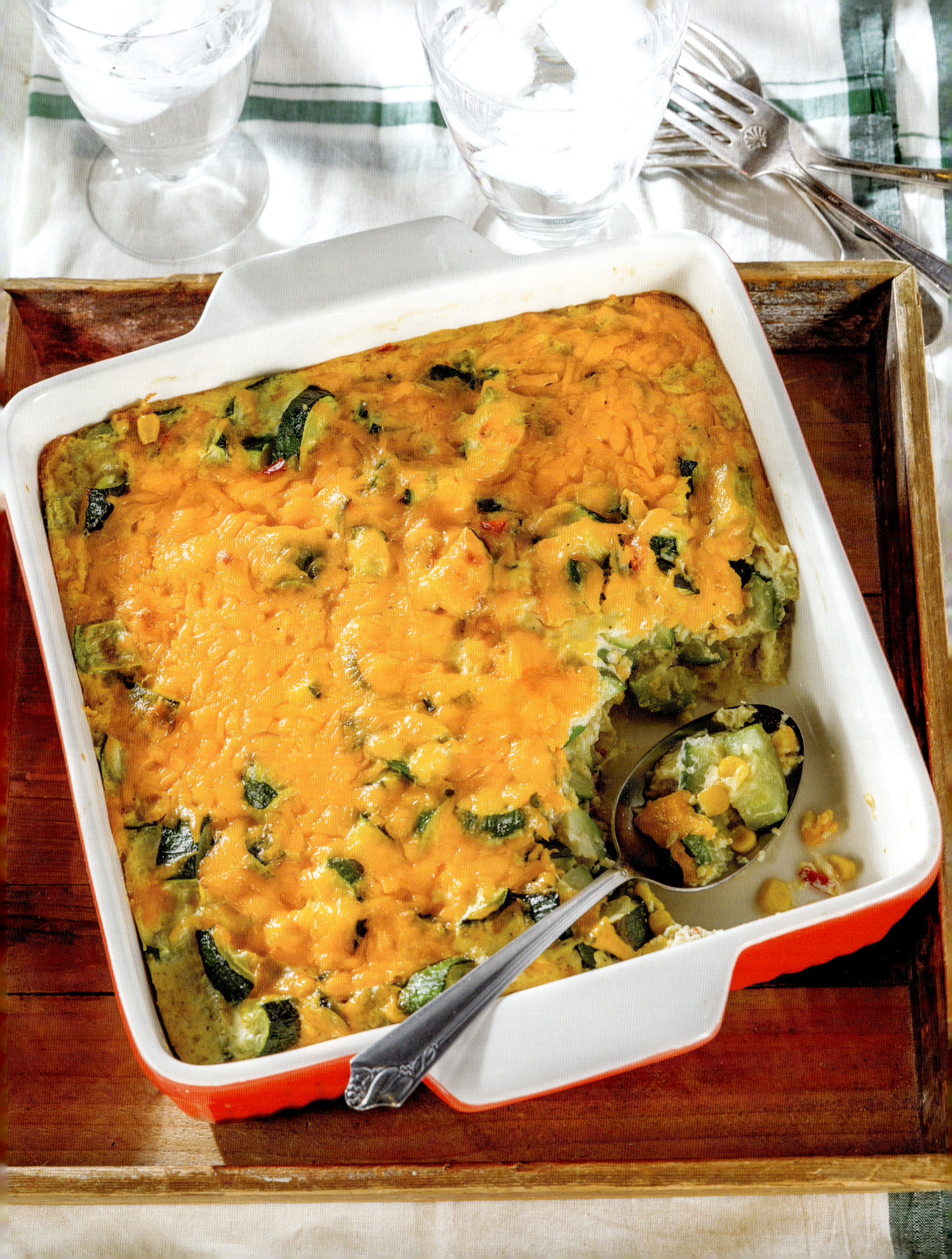

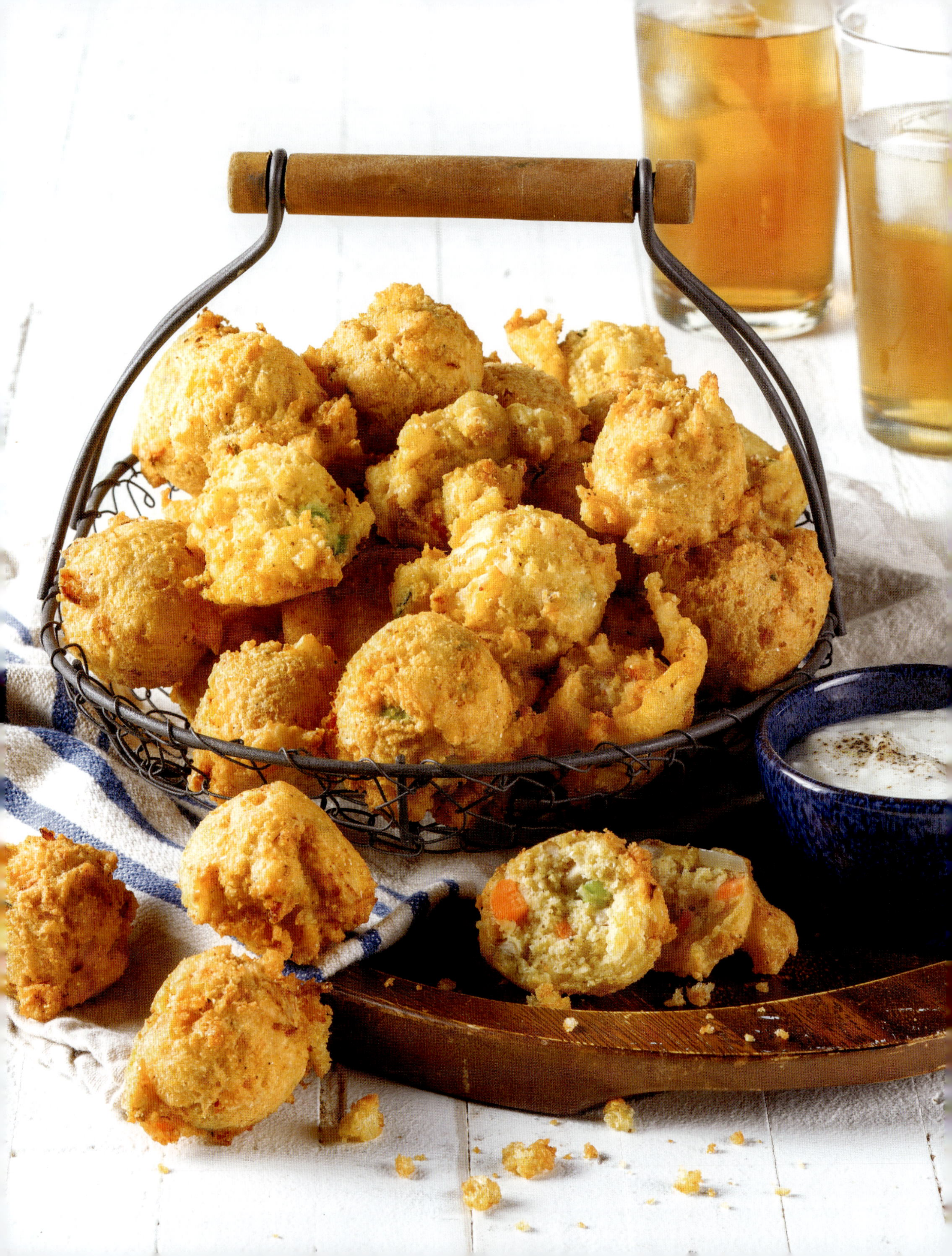

CHICKEN AND DUMPLING FRITTERS WITH SAGE GRAVY

You can't eat just one—get ready for your family to request these again and again.

Makes about 34

FRITTERS

Vegetable oil, for frying
- 2 cups self-rising yellow cornmeal mix
- 1½ cups all-purpose flour
- 1 tablespoon finely chopped fresh sage
- 1 teaspoon baking powder
- 1 chicken bouillon cube, crushed
- ½ teaspoon ground black pepper
- 1¾ cups whole buttermilk
- ¼ cup sour cream
- 2 large eggs
- 8 ounces cooked chicken, shredded and chopped
- ⅓ cup finely chopped carrot
- ⅓ cup finely chopped sweet onion
- ⅓ cup finely chopped celery

GRAVY

- ¼ cup salted butter
- ¼ cup all-purpose flour
- 1 chicken bouillon cube, crushed
- 2 cups whole milk, room temperature
- 1 tablespoon finely chopped fresh sage

1. Line a rimmed baking sheet with paper towels; place a wire rack on top.

2. For fritters: In a large Dutch oven, pour oil to a depth of 4 inches, and heat over medium heat until a deep-fry thermometer registers 350°.

3. In a medium bowl, whisk together cornmeal, flour, sage, baking powder, bouillon, and pepper.

4. In another medium bowl, whisk together buttermilk, sour cream, and eggs. Stir buttermilk mixture, chicken, carrot, onion, and celery into cornmeal mixture until combined. (Batter will be thick.)

5. Working in batches, using a 1½-tablespoon spring-loaded scoop, carefully scoop batter, and drop into hot oil. Fry until golden brown and cooked through, 3 to 4 minutes. Remove from oil using a slotted spoon, and transfer to prepared rack; keep warm in oven until ready to serve.

6. For gravy: In a medium saucepan, melt butter over medium heat. Whisk in flour and bouillon until smooth. Cook, whisking frequently, for 2 minutes. Gradually whisk in milk until smooth. Cook, whisking frequently, until thickened, about 10 minutes. Whisk in sage. Serve immediately with fritters.

MARINATED SHRIMP AND ARTICHOKE HEARTS

This dish is so refreshing and extra special with the artichoke hearts. If you are a shrimp lover, you need to add this one to your list of favorites!

Makes 10 to 12 servings

- 1 cup vegetable oil
- ½ cup red wine vinegar
- ½ cup dry white wine
- 1 tablespoon chopped fresh parsley or 1 teaspoon dried parsley
- 1 teaspoon sugar
- ½ teaspoon salt
- ½ teaspoon paprika
- ¼ teaspoon whole black peppercorns
- 1 clove garlic, minced
- 2 pounds medium fresh shrimp, cooked, peeled, and deveined
- 2 (14-ounce) cans whole artichoke hearts, drained and halved
- 1 (8-ounce) can sliced water chestnuts, drained
- 1 small red onion, thinly sliced into half rings

Garnish: cherry tomato halves

1. In a jar with a tight-fitting lid, combine oil, vinegar, wine, parsley, sugar, salt, paprika, peppercorns, and garlic. Cover and shake well.

2. In a 4-quart food-storage container, combine shrimp, artichoke, water chestnuts, and onion. Pour marinade on top, cover, and shake to coat. Refrigerate overnight, stirring occasionally. Garnish with tomatoes, if desired.

Bubba in front of his restaurant, Uncle Bubba's Oyster House.

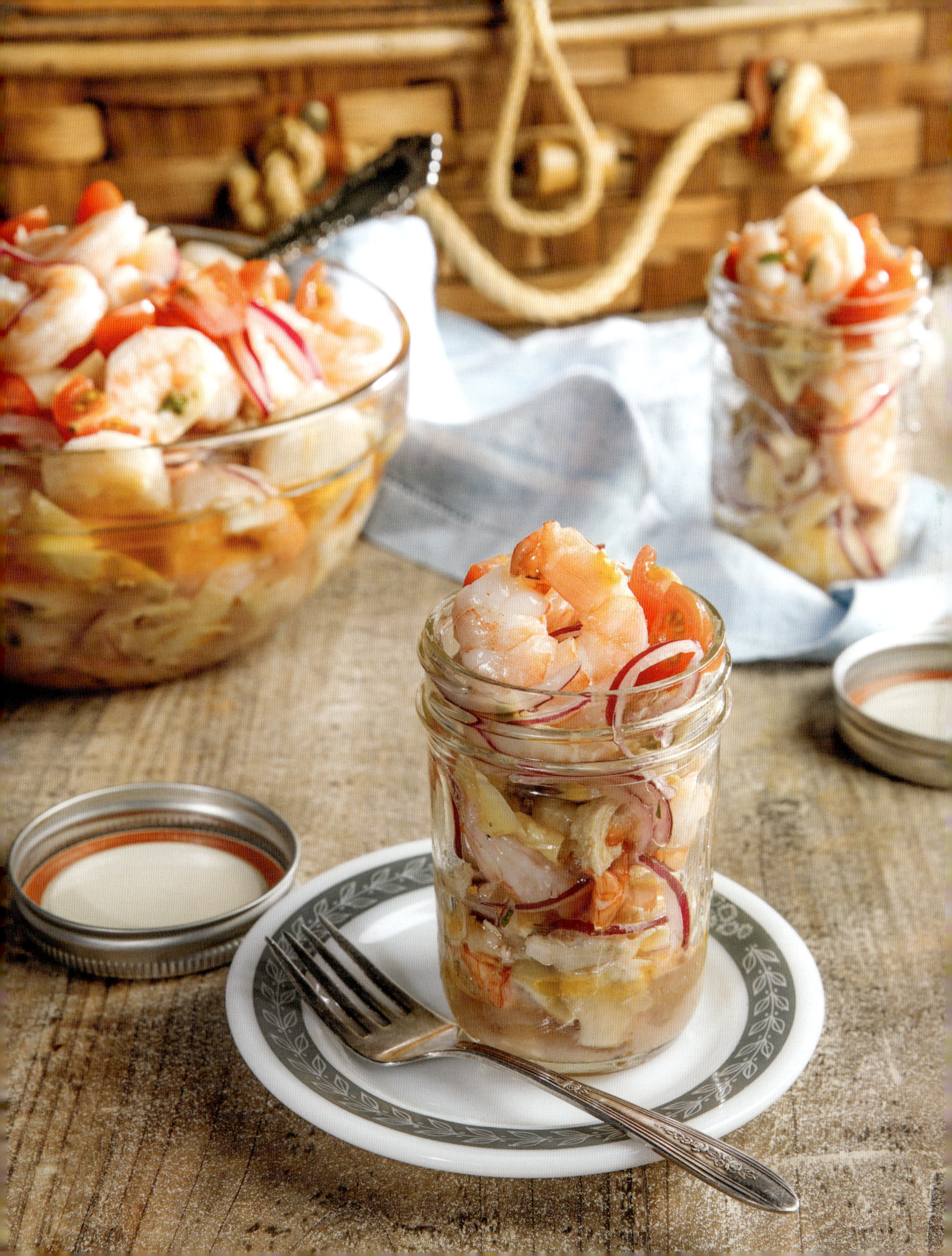

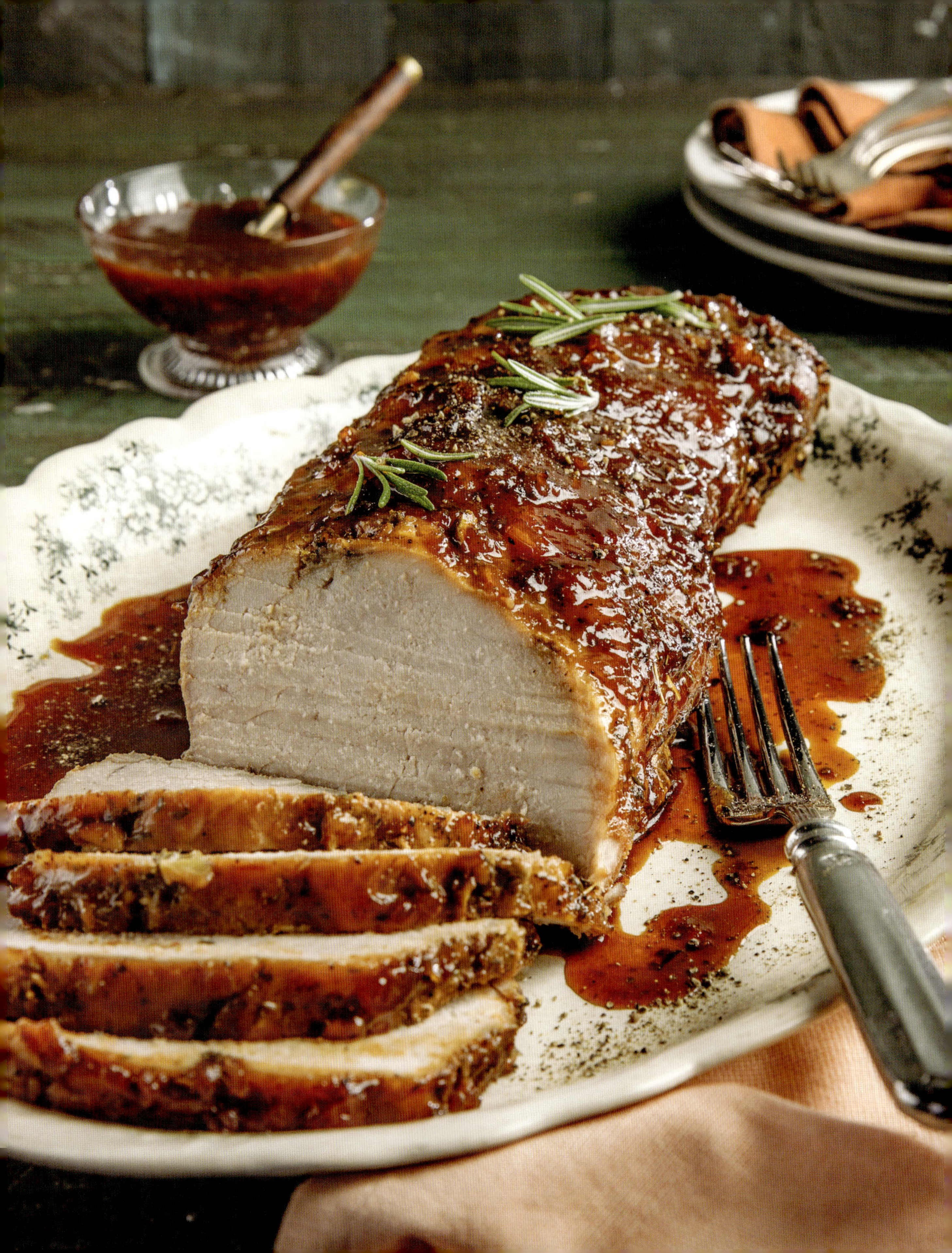

ROAST PORK WITH PLUM SAUCE

This pork would be perfect to serve for a special occasion and looks so beautiful with the plum sauce drizzled on top.

Makes 10 servings

SAUCE

- 2 tablespoons salted butter
- ¾ cup chopped onion
- 1 cup plum preserves
- ½ cup firmly packed light brown sugar
- ½ cup water
- ½ cup chili sauce
- ¼ cup soy sauce
- 2 tablespoons mustard
- 2 tablespoons fresh lemon juice
- 3 drops hot sauce
- Garlic salt, to taste

ROAST

- 2 cloves garlic, slivered
- 2 teaspoons salt
- 2 teaspoons dried or fresh rosemary
- 1½ teaspoons dried oregano
- 1½ teaspoons dried thyme
- 1½ teaspoons rubbed sage
- ¼ teaspoon freshly grated nutmeg
- ¼ teaspoon ground black pepper
- 1 (5-pound) pork loin roast

Garnish: fresh rosemary

1. For sauce: In a medium saucepan, melt butter over medium heat; add onion, and cook until tender. Add preserves, brown sugar, ½ cup water, chili sauce, soy sauce, mustard, lemon juice, hot sauce, and garlic salt, stirring until combined; simmer, stirring occasionally, for 15 minutes. Remove from heat and reserve ½ cup sauce.

2. Preheat oven to 325°.

3. For roast: In a small bowl, stir together garlic, salt, rosemary, oregano, thyme, sage, nutmeg, and pepper.

4. Moisten roast with a damp paper towel. Using a sharp knife, make 8 (½-inch-deep) slits in top of roast. Press garlic mixture into slits, and rub remaining mixture over entire roast. Place in a roasting pan, and pour half of sauce on top. Cover with foil.

5. Bake for 2 hours. Uncover and baste with sauce; bake until nicely browned, about 30 minutes more, basting every 10 minutes. Place on a serving platter, and drizzle with pan drippings. Garnish with rosemary, if desired. Serve with reserved sauce.

VEGETABLE PANCAKES

These pancakes are delicious with a dollop of sour cream.

Makes 8 servings

- ½ cup all-purpose flour
- ½ teaspoon baking powder
- ½ teaspoon salt
- ¼ teaspoon ground black pepper
- 1 cup grated carrots (about 2 carrots), patted dry
- 1 cup grated zucchini (1 medium zucchini), patted dry
- 2 green onions, sliced
- ¼ cup whole milk
- 1 large egg
- 2 tablespoons vegetable oil

Sour cream, to serve

1. In a large bowl, stir together flour, baking powder, salt, and pepper.

2. In a medium bowl, whisk together carrots, zucchini, green onion, milk, and egg. Add carrot mixture to flour mixture, and stir until just combined.

3. In a large skillet, heat 1 tablespoon oil over medium heat. Pour batter by tablespoonfuls 1 inch apart into skillet. Cook until golden, about 2 minutes per side. Add remaining 1 tablespoon oil to skillet as needed. Serve immediately. Serve with sour cream.

> **When I think about my legacy,** I think about the long line of strong women I came from. My momma raised two children while running a business and keeping her family safe. My Aunt Peggy has been my biggest cheerleader and kept me going when no one else could. I will always idolize my two grandmothers who each were exactly what I hope to live long enough to become—a woman of substance.

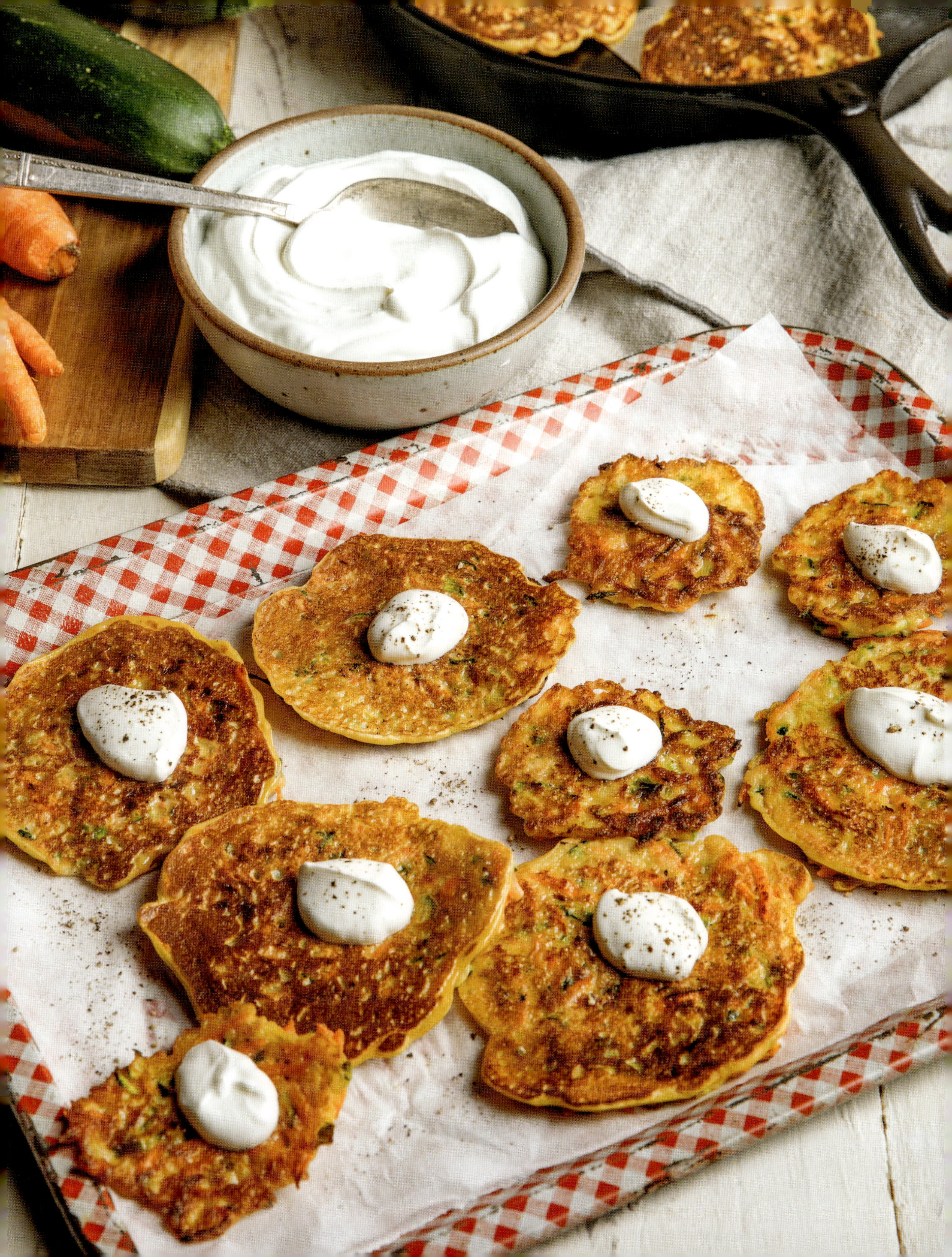

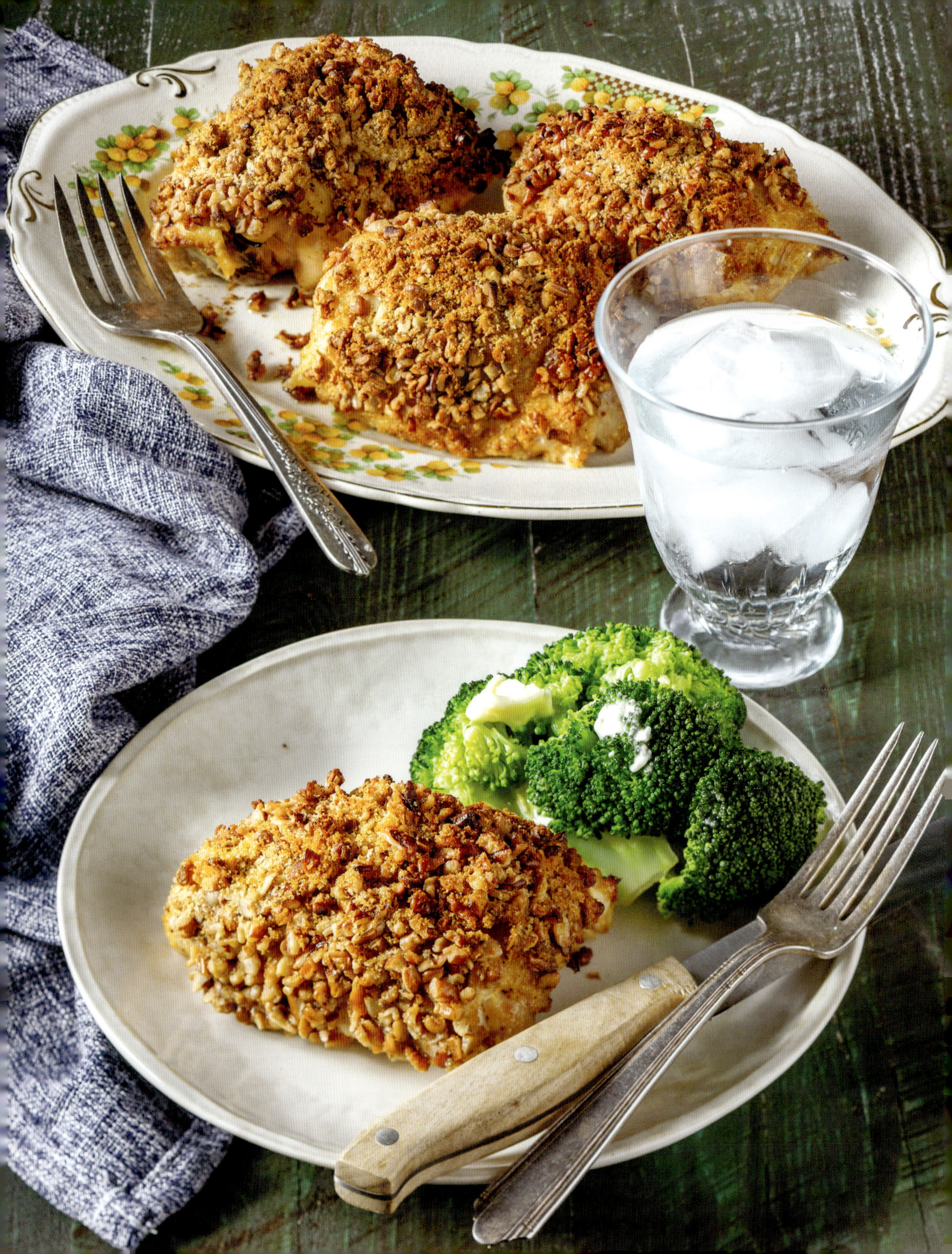

PECAN-CRUSTED CHICKEN THIGHS

The crunch of the pecan coating on these chicken thighs makes them irresistible! I love to serve mine with broccoli or other greens.

Makes 4 servings

- ½ cup finely chopped pecans
- 3 tablespoons plain bread crumbs
- ¾ teaspoon salt
- ½ teaspoon chili powder
- ½ teaspoon dried thyme
- 1 large egg white
- 1 teaspoon water
- 4 bone-in skin-on chicken thighs, patted dry
- 2 tablespoons olive oil

1. Preheat oven to 400°. Lightly spray a rimmed baking sheet with cooking spray.

2. In a small bowl, stir together pecans, bread crumbs, salt, chili powder, and thyme.

3. In a shallow dish, whisk together egg white and 1 teaspoon water. Dip each chicken thigh into egg white mixture, letting any excess drip off. Dip into pecan mixture, turning to coat. Place on prepared pan, and drizzle with oil.

4. Bake until coating is golden and an instant-read thermometer inserted in thickest portion of chicken registers 165°, 25 to 30 minutes.

From left: Brooke, Ashley, Corrie, Aunt Peggy, Sandy, Claudia, me, Susan/Bubbles, and Michelle.

POTATO CAKES

Fry up these cakes and get ready to go back for more!

Makes 8

- ½ cup vegetable oil
- 2 cups leftover mashed potatoes
- ½ cup all-purpose flour, divided
- 1 large egg, lightly beaten
- ½ teaspoon salt
- ¼ teaspoon ground black pepper
- ½ cup panko (Japanese bread crumbs)

1. In a large skillet, heat oil over medium-high heat. In a medium bowl, stir together potatoes, ¼ cup flour, egg, salt, and pepper. Shape mixture into 8 patties.

2. In a small bowl, whisk together bread crumbs and remaining ¼ cup flour. Dredge patties in bread crumb mixture to coat.

3. Fry patties until golden brown, 1 to 1½ minutes per side. Serve immediately.

CREAMY SWEET ONION POTATO SAUCE

We do not serve potatoes in my house unless this sauce is also on the menu.

Makes about 2 cups

- 1 cup diced sweet onion
- 1 cup mayonnaise
- ¼ cup sour cream
- Salt, to taste
- Baked potatoes, to serve
- Garnish: chopped parsley

1. In a small bowl, stir together onion, mayonnaise, sour cream, and salt, and refrigerate until ready to use. Serve over baked potatoes. Garnish with parsley, if desired.

CHAPTER NINE

GUINNY & HER LOVES

Oh my gosh, honey! I didn't think I was ever going to be a grandmother. I used to jokingly tell my kids, "Listen, if you can't find the woman you want to spend the rest of your life with, that's fine, but at least bring me a grandbaby!" I also always told them that I would love whoever they loved, and it's worked out so beautifully. I have two wonderful daughters-in-law from my boys and my wonderful children by marriage. They are all such blessings to me, and I cannot express enough what amazing parents they are.

I was talking to Bobby's wife, Claudia, recently, and I told her, "You know, Claudia, when I go to bed at night, there's one thing that I never have and never will worry about, and that's my grandchildren being taken care of." All my children take the best care of their babies.

All my girls are incredible mothers. All my guys are incredible fathers. I could not say one bad thing about any of them. They will do anything to take care of their children. I hear about many grandmommas out there—in their later years when they should be concentrating on themselves and enjoying that time in life—and they're having to raise grandchildren instead. Bless them for taking care of their own. I admire that so much—I just can't imagine because when I'm with my younger grandchildren, they wear me out!

I got my grandmother name, Guinny, when my very first grandbaby, Jack, was little. He is 17 now, but back then, Jamie and Brooke were trying to teach him to say "Granny."

Opposite page, left to right: Me, Henry, and Michael. Matthew and me. Sweet Sullivan. **This page, top row from left to right:** Henry, Michael, John, Davis, Jack, and Matthew. **Bottom row from left to right:** Madison, Linton, me, Amelia, Olivia, and Bennett. **Below:** Young Jack when he would cook for me in his own "restaurant" that he called Rooster's Restaurant. **Bottom:** Amelia and me.

I'd loved that name because that's what I'd called Grandmother Paul. Well, the little fella just couldn't say it. It came out "Guinny." I said, "Well, that is perfect because I am your guinny pig, angel. Now and forever." I couldn't have picked out a better name myself.

I feel most fortunate that I am blessed with grounded children who do the right thing and raise their children to do the same. I know how lucky I am. All 11 of my grandchildren are kind and thoughtful. There's not a mean-spirited one in the bunch. Jamie and Brooke, Bobby and Claudia, Ashley and Anthony, Michelle and Daniel, and Corrie and Brian have dedicated so much time to raising their children to be good people.

And I ain't bragging—that's just a fact, jack!

APPLE BACON STICKY BISCUITS

These sticky biscuits are an easy sweet treat that's perfect for fall!

Makes 12

- 1¼ cups prepared classic caramel dip
- ½ cup chopped pecans
- 3½ cups all-purpose baking mix
- 1 cup whole milk
- 3 tablespoons firmly packed light brown sugar
- ½ teaspoon apple pie spice
- 1 cup chopped peeled apples
- 3 slices bacon, cooked until crisp and crumbled

1. Preheat oven to 425°. Spray a 12-cup muffin pan with baking spray with flour.

2. In a small bowl, stir together caramel dip and pecans. Divide among prepared muffin cups.

3. In a large bowl, stir together baking mix, milk, brown sugar, and pie spice just until ingredients are moistened. Fold in apples and bacon. Divide mixture among prepared muffin cups.

4. Bake until wooden pick inserted in center comes out clean, about 10 minutes. Let cool in pan for 2 minutes. Place a rimmed baking sheet on pan; invert biscuits onto baking sheet. Transfer to a wire rack lined with parchment paper. Serve warm.

My grandchildren are the light of my life. Spending time with them fills my cup every time! This is Jack and me playing at his "restaurant."

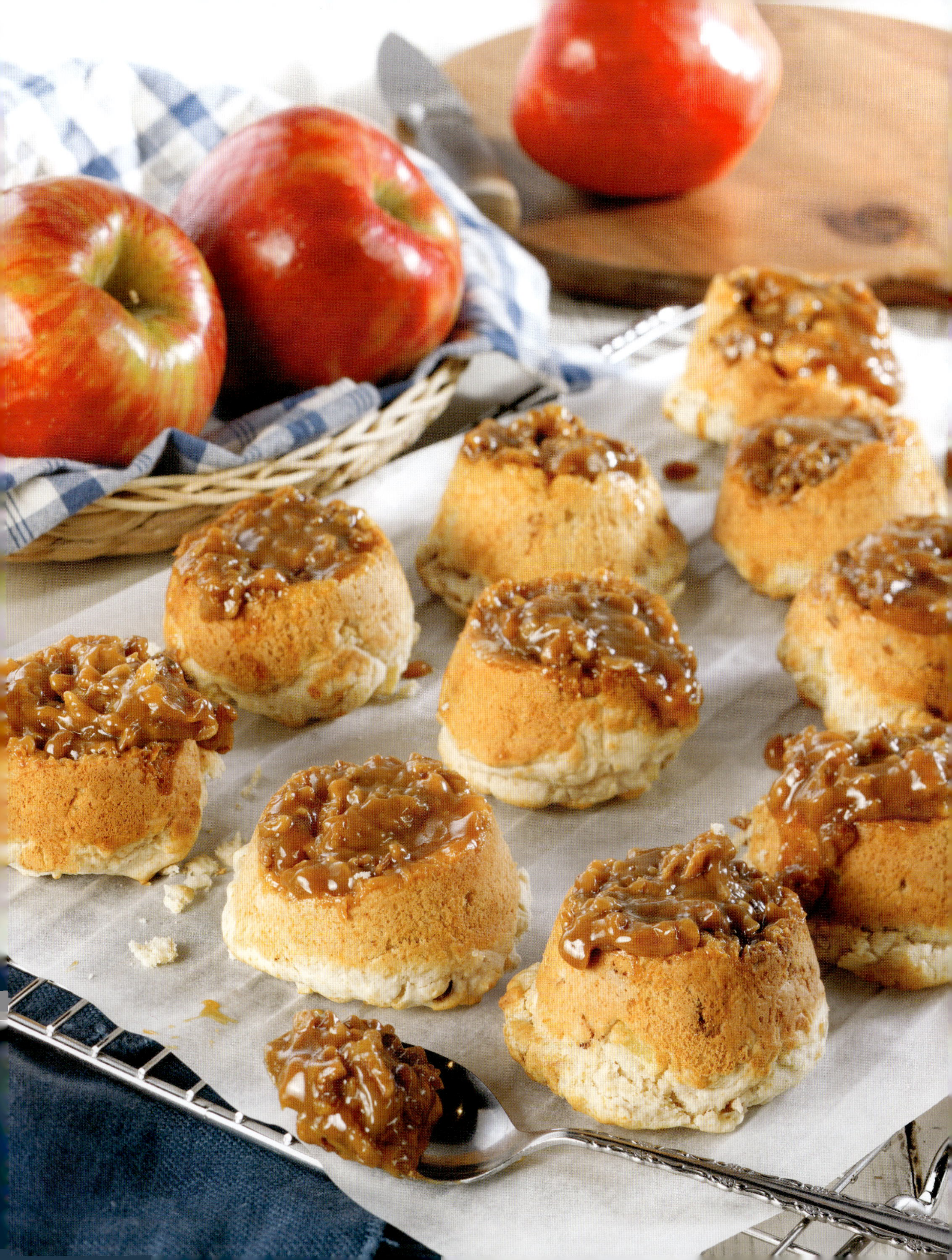

Recipe Tip

For a richer soup, add two diced 6-ounce filet mignons to the broth after adding the thyme and bay leaf.

FRENCH ONION SOUP

My grandson Jack's absolute favorite food is French onion soup! Anytime we go out to eat together, he orders it and we rate it. This is my version that he loves.

Makes 8 servings

- ⅓ cup olive oil
- 8 sweet onions, sliced (about 12 cups)
- 2 cloves garlic, minced
- 2 tablespoons all-purpose flour
- 8 cups beef stock
- ¼ cup dry white wine
- ½ teaspoon dried thyme or 1 tablespoon chopped fresh thyme
- 1 dried bay leaf
- Salt and ground black pepper, to taste
- 8 ¾-inch slices French bread
- ⅓ cup butter, room temperature
- 1 cup grated Gruyère cheese

Garnish: fresh thyme

1. In a Dutch oven, heat oil over medium-low heat. Add onions and garlic, and cook, stirring occasionally, until onions are tender and golden yellow, 30 to 40 minutes.

2. Sprinkle flour onto onion mixture, and cook, stirring constantly, until flour is well browned, 3 to 5 minutes. Stir in stock and wine, and bring to a boil over medium-high heat. Add thyme and bay leaf. Reduce heat, cover, and simmer for about 20 minutes. Season to taste with salt and pepper. Discard bay leaf.

3. Preheat oven to 350°.

4. Spread butter onto cut sides of bread. Place on a large rimmed baking sheet.

5. Bake until lightly browned, 6 to 8 minutes, turning slices halfway through baking. Leave oven on.

6. Preheat broiler. Ladle soup into broiler-safe bowls. Place toasted bread on top, and cover with cheese. Place ovenproof bowls on a foil-lined rimmed baking sheet.

7. Broil on middle oven rack until cheese is melted, about 2 to 3 minutes. Garnish with thyme, if desired.

GLAZED HONEY BARS

These sweet treats are an easy dessert that everyone adores! The mayonnaise in the glaze gives it its signature tang that will have people coming back for seconds!

Makes about 24

- 1 cup sugar
- ¾ cup vegetable oil
- ¼ cup honey
- 1 large egg
- 2 cups self-rising flour
- 1 teaspoon ground cinnamon
- 1 cup chopped walnuts
- 1 cup confectioners' sugar
- 1 tablespoon mayonnaise
- 1 tablespoon milk
- 1 teaspoon vanilla extract

1. Preheat oven to 350°. Lightly spray a 13x9-inch baking pan with cooking spray.

2. In a large bowl, beat sugar, oil, honey, and egg with a mixer at medium speed until combined.

3. In a medium bowl, whisk together flour and cinnamon. Add flour mixture to sugar mixture, and beat at low speed until combined. Stir in walnuts. Spread batter into prepared pan.

4. Bake until set, about 30 minutes. Let cool in pan for 30 minutes. Remove from pan, and let stand.

5. In small bowl, whisk together confectioners' sugar, mayonnaise, milk, and vanilla. Drizzle glaze over warm cake, and let cool completely. Cut into bars.

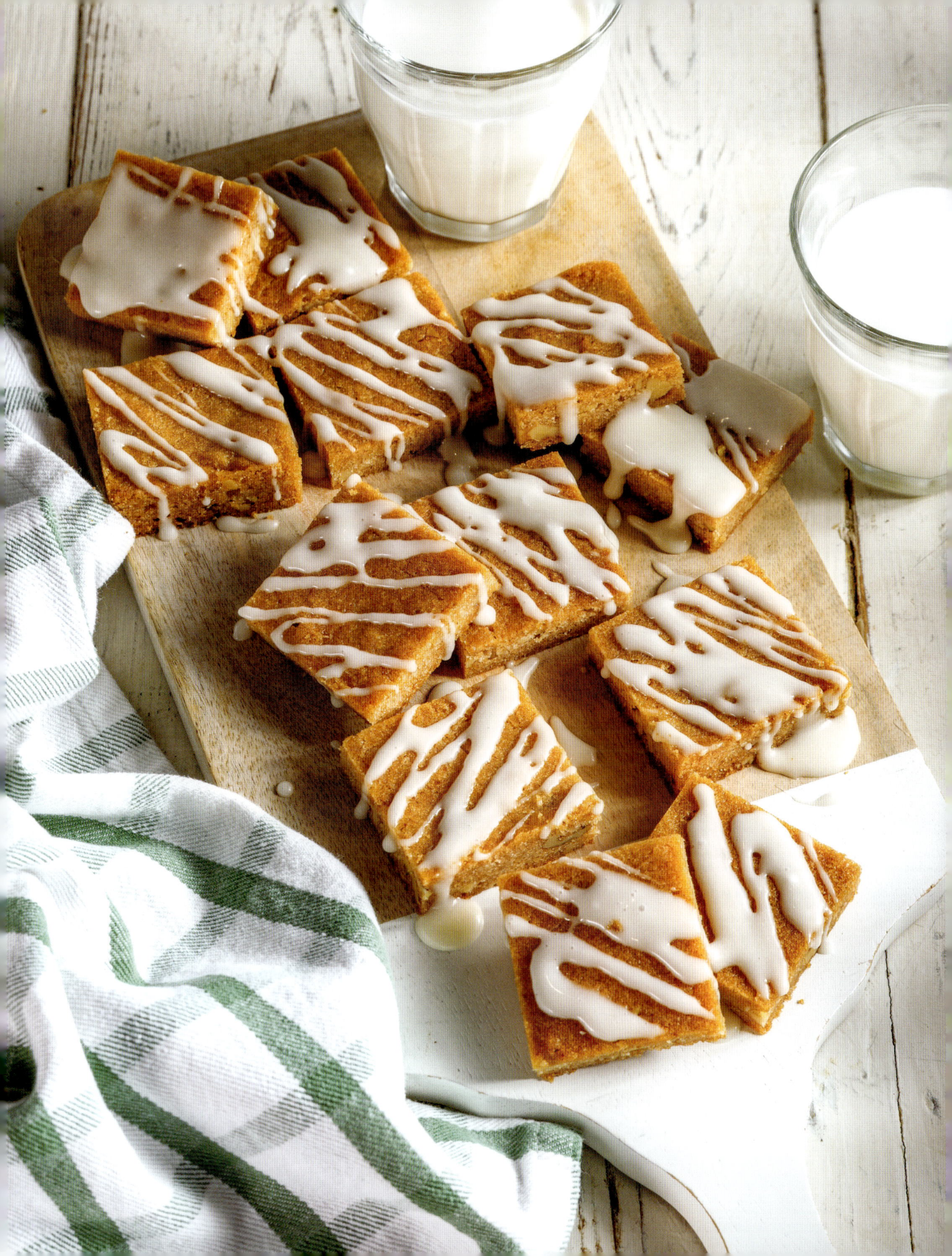

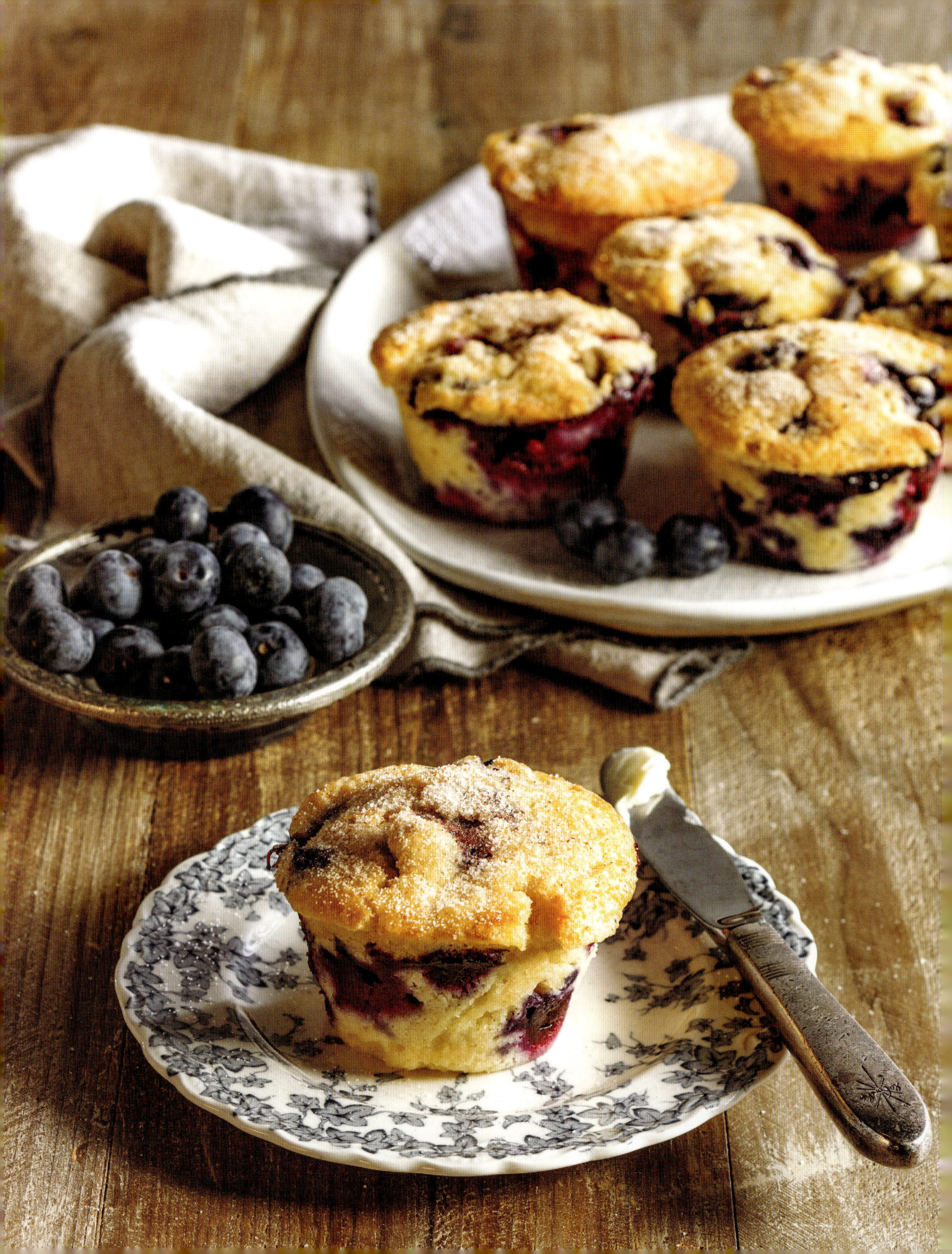

BLUEBERRY MUFFINS

There is something hard to beat about a classic, simple muffin to start your day.

Makes 12

- 2 cups all-purpose flour
- 1 cup sugar
- 2 teaspoons baking powder
- ¼ teaspoon salt
- 2½ cups fresh blueberries
- 1 cup whole milk, room temperature
- ½ cup salted butter, melted
- 2 large eggs, room temperature
- 1 teaspoon vanilla extract

TOPPING

- 2 tablespoons sugar
- ½ teaspoon nutmeg

1. Preheat oven to 375°. Lightly spray a 12-cup muffin pan with cooking spray.

2. For muffins: In a large bowl, whisk together flour, sugar, baking powder, and salt. Stir in blueberries.

3. In a medium bowl, whisk together milk, melted butter, eggs, and vanilla. Add milk mixture to flour mixture, and stir just until moistened. Divide batter among prepared muffin cups.

4. For topping: In a small bowl, whisk together sugar and nutmeg. Sprinkle over batter in pan.

5. Bake until wooden pick inserted in center comes out clean, 20 to 25 minutes.

Brooke and Matthew.

LADY BIRD CAKE

I created this recipe in honor of my beloved pet macaw, Lady Bird. She passed away at 29 years old and was my cherished companion for so long.

Makes 1 (8-inch) cake

- 1 cup salted butter, softened
- 2 cups sugar
- 4 large eggs
- 2 cups mashed ripe bananas
- 1 (12-ounce) jar pineapple preserves
- 2½ cups all-purpose flour
- 2 teaspoons baking soda
- ½ cup whole buttermilk
- 1 cup chopped dates

FROSTING

- 1 cup salted butter, softened
- 1 (8-ounce) package cream cheese, softened
- ¼ cup pineapple preserves
- 1 (2-pound) package confectioners' sugar

Garnish: pecan halves, chopped pecans

1. Preheat oven to 350°. Spray 3 (8-inch) round cake pans with baking spray with flour.

2. For cake: In a large bowl, beat butter and sugar with a mixer at medium speed until fluffy, 3 to 4 minutes, stopping to scrape sides of bowl. Add eggs, one at a time, beating well after each addition. Beat in mashed banana and preserves until combined.

3. In a medium bowl, whisk together flour and baking soda. Gradually add flour mixture to butter mixture alternately with buttermilk, beginning and ending with flour mixture, beating at low speed just until combined after each addition. Stir in dates. Pour batter into prepared pans.

4. Bake until a wooden pick inserted in center comes out clean, 30 to 35 minutes. Let cool in pans for 10 minutes. Remove from pans, and let cool completely on wire racks.

5. For frosting: In a large bowl, beat butter and cream cheese with a mixer at medium speed until creamy. Beat in preserves. Gradually beat in enough confectioners' sugar until desired consistency is reached. Spread frosting between layers and on top and sides of cake. Garnish with pecans, if desired. Cover and refrigerate for up to 3 days.

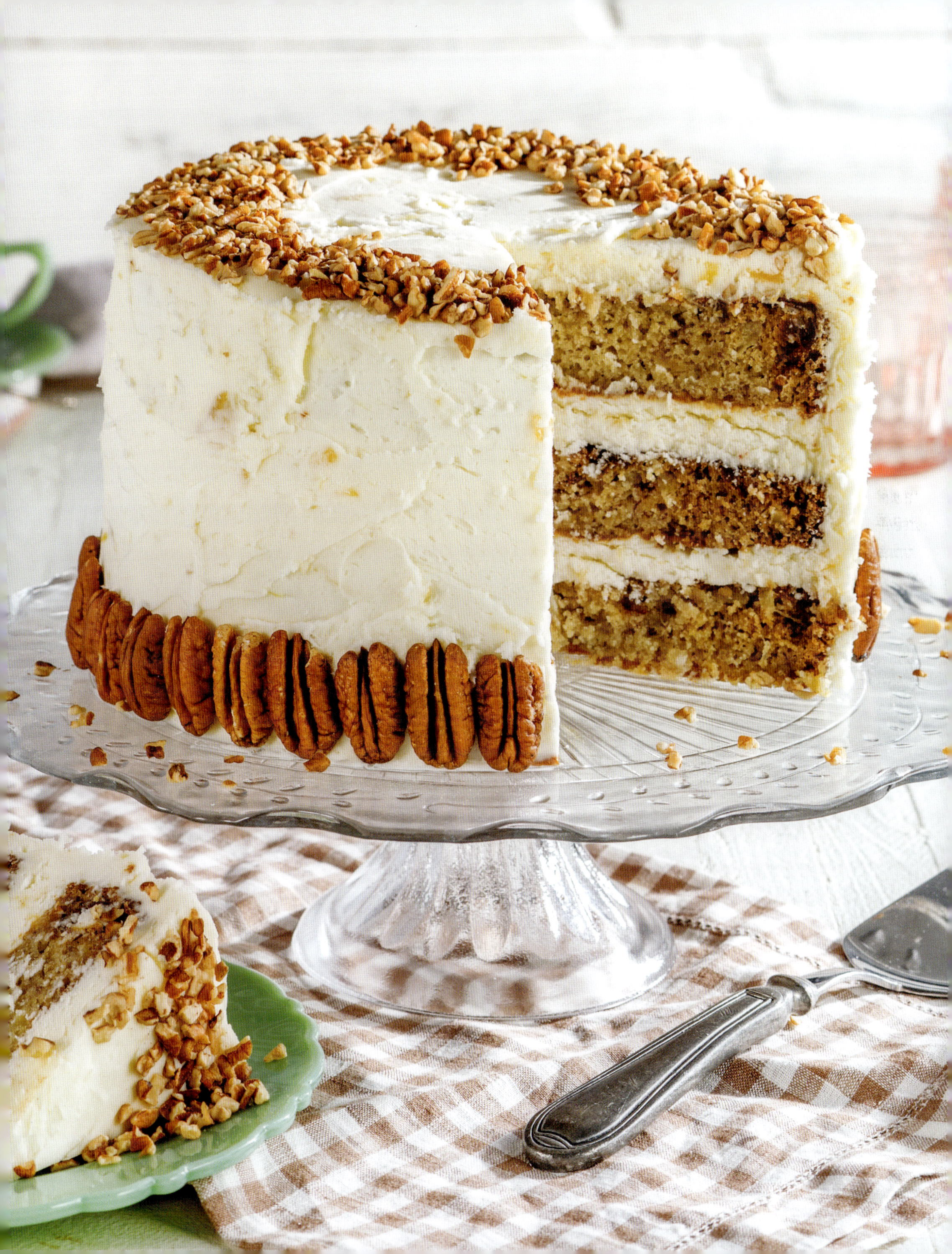

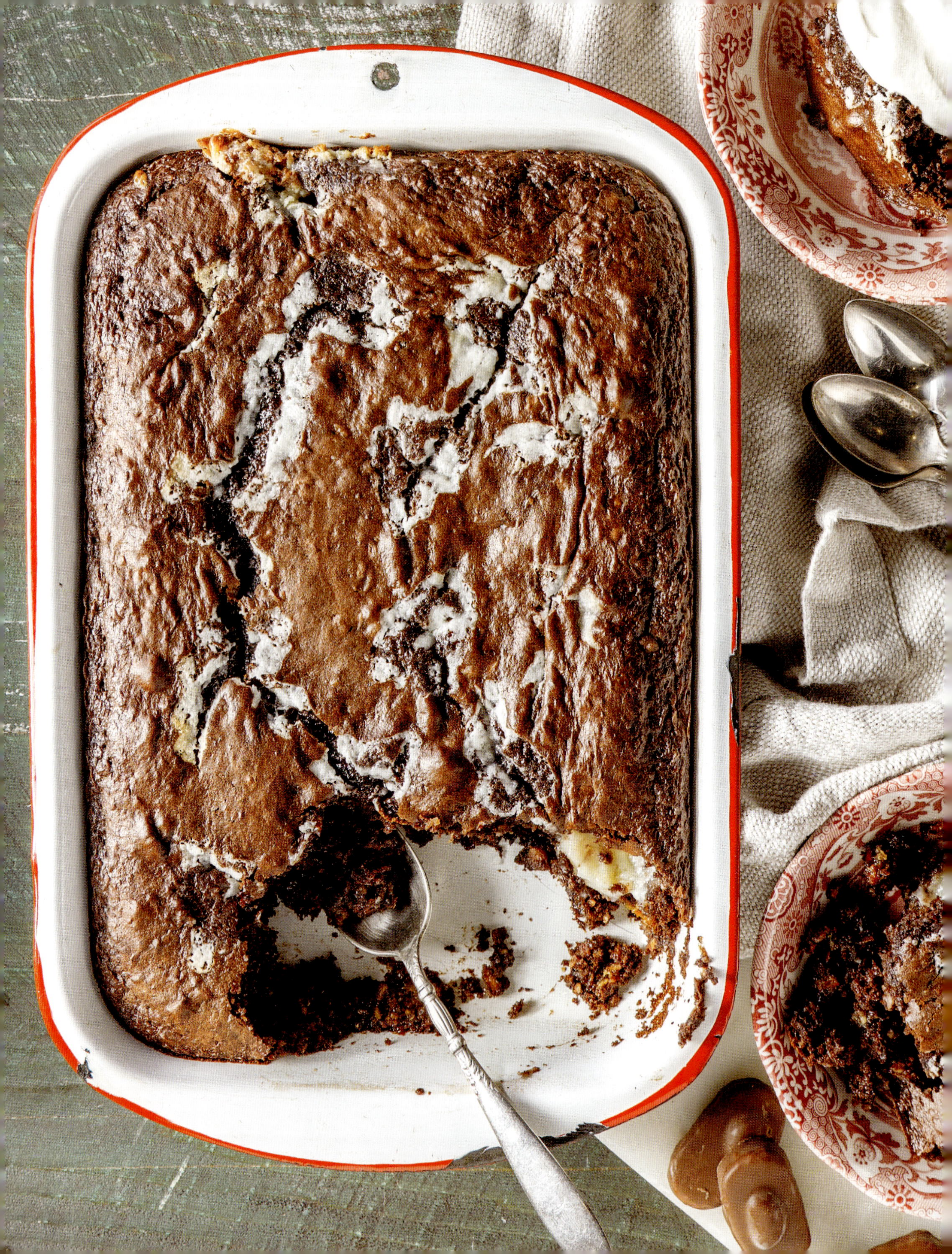

VOLCANO CAKE

You can mix and match your favorite cake mix flavors, candy bars, and nuts. It's always good.

Makes 1 (13x9-inch) cake

- 1 cup sweetened flaked coconut
- 1 cup chopped walnuts or pecans
- 1 (15.25-ounce) box German chocolate cake mix
- 10 bite-size/fun-size chocolate-coated coconut-almond candy bars, chopped
- 2 cups confectioners' sugar
- 1 (8-ounce) package cream cheese, room temperature
- ½ cup salted butter, softened

QUICK CHOCOLATE FROSTING

- 1 cup sugar
- ⅓ cup cocoa
- ½ cup whole milk
- 4½ tablespoons butter, cut into small pieces
- 2 tablespoons light corn syrup
- 4 cups confectioners' sugar
- 2 tablespoons vanilla

Sweetened whipped cream, to serve

1. Preheat oven to 350°. Spray 13x9-inch baking pan with baking spray with flour.

2. For cake: In a small bowl, combine coconut and nuts; spread in bottom of prepared pan.

3. Prepare cake mix according to package directions; stir in chopped candy bars. Spread batter onto coconut mixture in pan.

4. In a medium bowl, whisk together confectioners' sugar, cream cheese, and butter until smooth. Dollop tablespoonfuls of mixture onto batter in pan; do not spread together.

5. Bake until cake pulls away from sides of pan, 40 to 50 minutes.

6. Meanwhile, for frosting: In a large saucepan, whisk together sugar and cocoa. Whisk in milk, and stir in butter and corn syrup. Bring to a boil over medium-high heat, whisking constantly. Remove from heat, and stir in confectioners' sugar and vanilla. Pour icing over hot cake. Serve warm or at room temperature with sweetened whipped cream.

PECAN CRISPS

With their sweet, buttery crunch, these treats will disappear from the cookie jar before it's even filled!

Makes about 30

- 1½ cups all-purpose flour, sifted
- 1 cup sugar, plus more for dipping
- ¾ teaspoon salt
- ½ cup all-vegetable shortening
- 1 large egg, separated
- 3 tablespoons whole milk
- 1 teaspoon vanilla extract
- 1 cup finely chopped pecans

1. In a large bowl, whisk together flour, sugar, and salt. Using a fork, stir in shortening, egg yolk, milk, and vanilla. Cover and refrigerate for 30 minutes.

2. Preheat oven to 375°.

3. Shape dough into 1-inch balls. Place 3 inches apart on ungreased baking sheets. Using the bottom of a glass dipped in sugar, press dough balls flat. (Dough must be pressed very thin so cookie is wafer-like; otherwise, it will be too chewy.)

4. In a small bowl, whisk egg white. Brush egg white on top of dough disks. Sprinkle with pecans.

5. Bake until golden, 8 to 10 minutes. (Don't overbake.)

Me and Jack playing at Rooster's Restaurant!

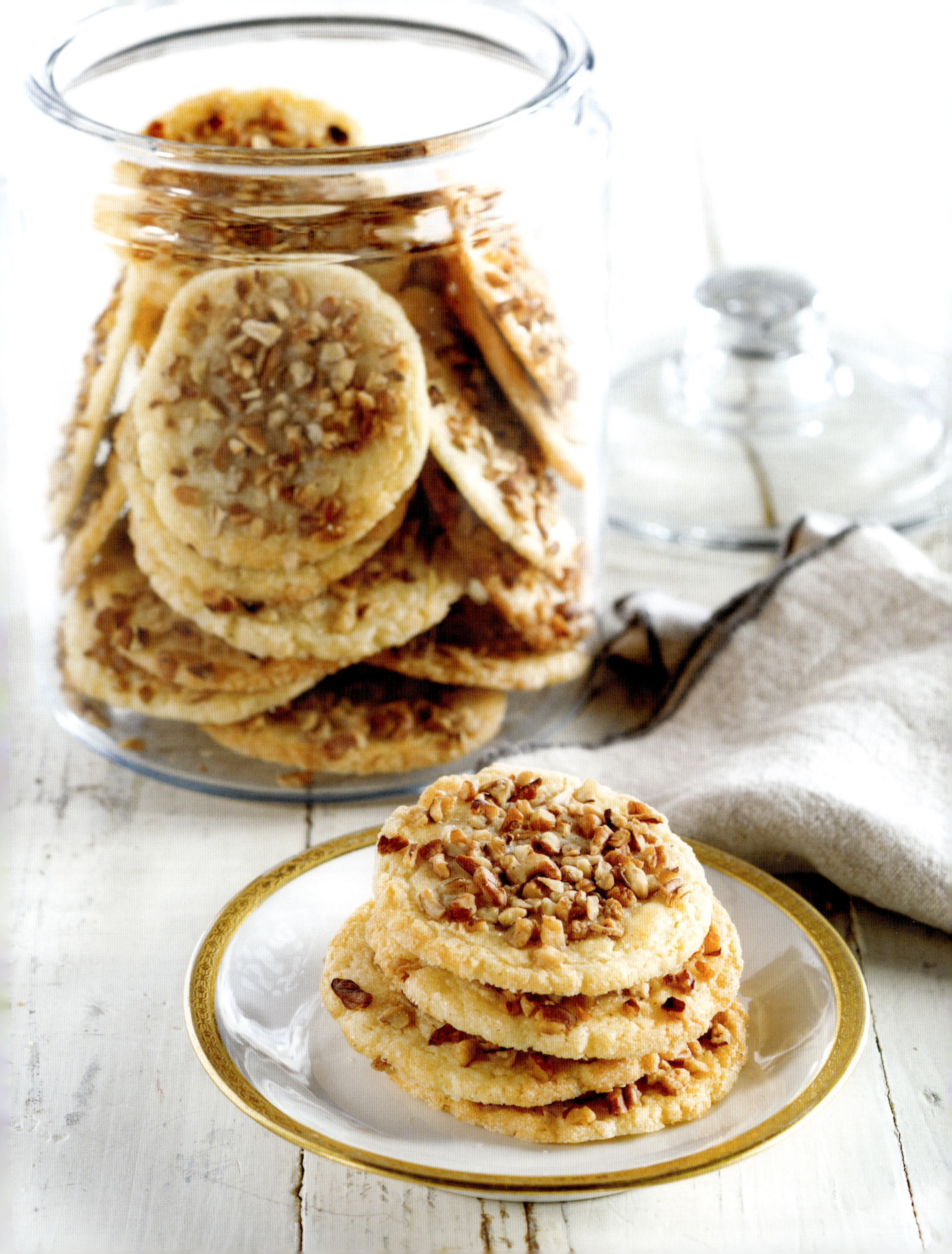

CHAPTER TEN

STAYING PRESENT

Today, something that brings me so much joy is spending time with and giving back to my supporters. When we were all ordered to stay at home during the COVID-19 pandemic, I was very concerned about women who were maybe quarantined by themselves who couldn't get to their family. I know that would have absolutely terrified me. I was trying to think of what I could do. I told Bobby, "I wish there was a way I could reach my followers who are quarantined." He said, "Well, Momma, just get on YouTube and shoot a show." I said, "I can do that?" So, we did.

My personal assistant, Eddie, and I started Quarantined Cooking. I got a lot of positive feedback and people would tell me it felt so good to laugh and smile again. I felt it was worth the effort it took to make it happen. It's been three years and we're still going.

We don't call it Quarantined Cooking anymore, but I told my subscribers that as long as I had breath in me, I'd keep doing it. It's called Paula Deen's Love and Best Dishes. I ask my fans to send me requests for dishes to make and share their favorite recipes from their families. I like to read the letters I get from them and then tell everyone who sent it in and a little history about the recipe. I am beyond grateful for these people I have never even met. They give me validation that I am worth it and that I'm doing something positive.

I also find joy in spending time with my dearest friends. I am blessed to have some of the best—old and new. My friend Susan, whom we all know as Bubbles, and I knew each other from growing up in Albany, but we reconnected and grew close after I moved to Savannah. I treasure her friendship, and we even refer to each other as "sissy" because she is an only child and I never had a sister. My friend Donna is someone I met later in life and was my closest friend in town while she lived here. She is a fabulous cook, and I love to visit with her and her family whenever I can. Great friends are so important to have in your corner. They are the ones who will be there when life gets truly difficult.

At the end of the day, all I can say is how blessed I am to be able to share these recipes and these stories. I believe that we all have a story to tell, and I know not everyone is fortunate enough to be able to share theirs.

I am so grateful that I have gotten to share mine.

Opposite page, left to right: Me and Alveda King. Me. Me and my wonderful personal assistant, Eddie. **This page, clockwise from top left:** Me with my friends Susan and Phil Greene. My dear friend Donna and me. Me and my dear friend Kim Pelote. Aunt Peggy and me.

AVOCADO TOAST

Our daughter-in-law Claudia always shares healthy recipes with the family, and I love making this with her. There are so many ways you can make this breakfast.

Makes 2

- 2 tablespoons salted butter, room temperature
- 2 slices multigrain bread
- 1 ripe avocado, halved and pitted
- ⅛ teaspoon salt

1. Heat a large skillet over medium heat.

2. Spread butter evenly on both sides of bread. Place bread in skillet, and cook until golden brown, 2 to 3 minutes per side.

3. Slice or mash avocado, and sprinkle with salt. Divide avocado between bread slices. Top with desired topping option. (See notes.)

FRIED EGG

- 2 fried eggs
- Hot sauce, to serve
- Garnish: black pepper

1. Top each slice of avocado toast with 1 fried egg. Serve with hot sauce. Garnish with black pepper, if desired.

SMOKED SALMON

- 4 slices smoked salmon
- Everything bagel seasoning

1. Top each slice of avocado toast with 2 slices smoked salmon. Sprinkle with everything bagel seasoning.

TOMATO-RADISH

- ¼ cup halved cherry tomatoes
- ¼ cup sliced radish
- Garnish: fresh cilantro leaves

1. Top each slice of avocado toast with tomatoes and radish. Garnish with cilantro, if desired.

BACON CHOWCHOW

- 4 slices cooked bacon, crumbled
- 2 tablespoons chowchow

1. Top each slice of avocado toast with 2 slices bacon and 1 tablespoon chowchow.

SMOKED SALMON

FRIED EGG

BACON CHOWCHOW

TOMATO-RADISH

Recipe Tip

These delicious shrimp have even more flavor if you cook them unpeeled and with the tails on.

BARBECUE SHRIMP

Michael and I love visiting New Orleans. The food and the music make us feel right at home. We found a restaurant, Deanie's Seafood, during one of our visits. They serve the most succulent barbecue shrimp we've ever had. It has a buttery consistency that I just had to re-create!

Makes 6 to 8 servings

- 1 cup salted butter
- ½ cup ketchup
- ½ cup Worcestershire sauce
- ¼ cup fresh lemon juice
- 2 lemons, halved and thinly sliced
- 4 cloves garlic, minced
- 1 tablespoon hot sauce
- 1 teaspoon dried rosemary
- 1 teaspoon dried thyme
- 2 dried bay leaves
- 4 pounds large fresh shrimp, peeled and deveined (tails left on)

French bread, to serve

Garnish: lemon wedges

1. In a large skillet, melt butter over medium heat; stir in ketchup, Worcestershire, lemon juice, lemon slices, garlic, hot sauce, rosemary, thyme, and bay leaves. Bring to a boil; reduce heat, and simmer, stirring occasionally, for 15 minutes. Add shrimp, and cook, stirring occasionally, until shrimp are just pink, 2 to 3 minutes. Remove from heat, and serve immediately. Garnish with lemon wedges, if desired.

Captain Michael hard at work!

BEAN DIP

Carol, Eddie's mother, sent me this handwritten recipe a few years ago. It's inspired by the famous dip from the former New Hampshire restaurant The Chateau. I love that it uses ingredients I always have on hand and comes together with a simple stir.

Makes 4½ cups

- 1 (8-ounce) container sweet pepper relish
- 2 (15.5-ounce) cans dark red kidney beans, drained
- 1 (8-ounce) container sour cream
- 1 small onion, finely chopped
- 1 cup mayonnaise
- ½ teaspoon salt
- ¼ teaspoon garlic powder
- ¼ teaspoon ground black pepper
- Butter crackers, to serve

1. Reserve 2 tablespoons relish.

2. In a large bowl, stir together remaining relish, beans, sour cream, onion, and mayonnaise. Stir in salt, garlic powder, and pepper until combined. Top with reserved 2 tablespoons relish. Refrigerate for at least 2 hours. Serve with crackers.

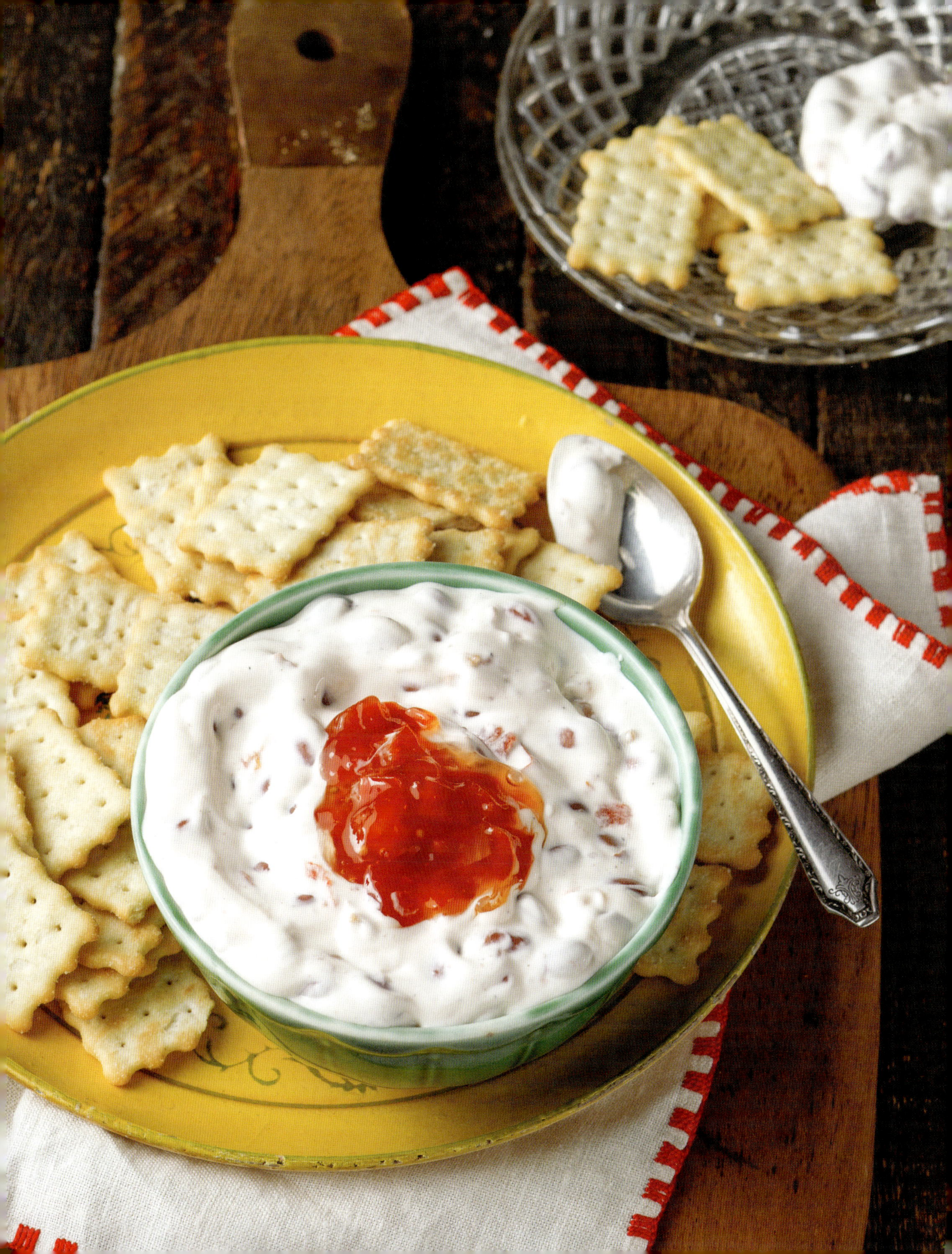

DILL PICKLES

Eddie gave me this recipe from his father, Stan. Stan had his own little vegetable garden where he grew his pickling cucumbers.

Makes 12 servings

- 8 cups cold water
- 1¼ cups distilled white vinegar
- ¼ cup salt
- 12 pickling cucumbers, sliced
- 3 cloves garlic, chopped
- 1 (0.5-ounce) package fresh dill or fresh from the garden

1. In a crock or large glass bowl, stir together 8 cups water, vinegar, and salt until dissolved. Add cucumbers, garlic, and dill. Place a heavy plate directly on top to submerge cucumbers under liquid. Place a weight such as a can or two of vegetables on plate. Let stand at room temperature 48 hours.

2. Place pickles in clean jars; cover with vinegar mixture. Refrigerate pickles up to 2 weeks.

> Six years ago, I was blessed with one of the most special people who has ever come into my life, my personal assistant, Eddie. He is the most loyal, trustworthy, and even-tempered person I know.

My Dear Eddie,

I don't know what I would do without you. You have filled such a void in my life. You are a constant friend and companion. I'm lucky you agreed to live here on our property with us, and I cannot say enough good things about you. Thank you for your support.

Much Love,
Paula

Eddie with the pups—Max, Lulu, and Gus.

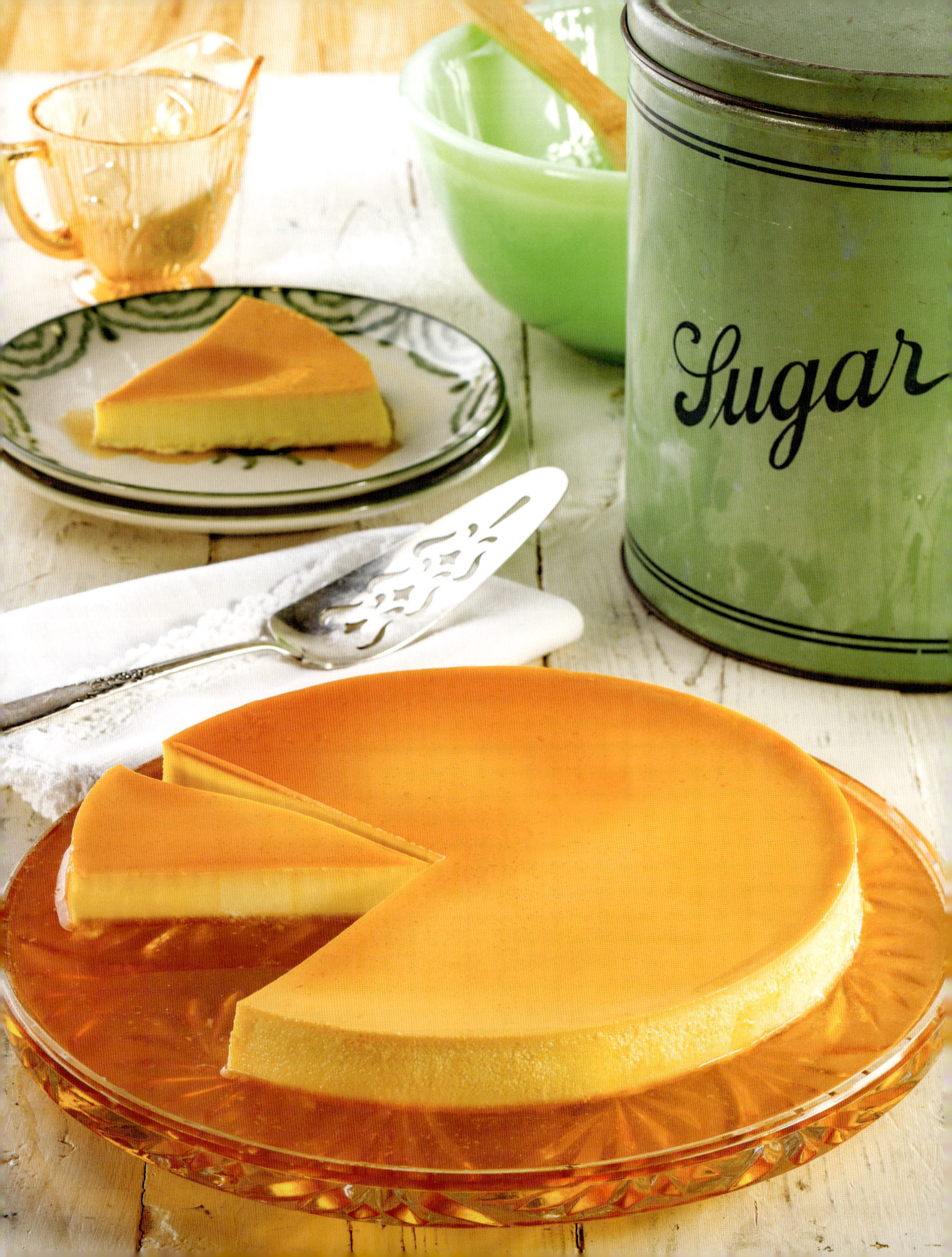
Sugar

CARAMEL CUSTARD

This custard is a dinner party favorite. Make it ahead and let it chill overnight. Guests are always impressed with how the shiny caramel highlights the creamy texture.

Makes 8 servings

- 1 cup sugar, divided
- ¼ cup hot water
- 4 large eggs
- 4 large egg yolks
- ⅛ teaspoon salt
- 2½ cups whole milk
- 1 cup heavy whipping cream
- ½ teaspoon vanilla extract

1. Preheat oven to 325°.

2. In a small heavy-bottomed skillet, heat ⅔ cup sugar over low heat, stirring frequently, until sugar is melted and a golden caramel color. (Do not burn.) Remove from heat; add ¼ cup hot water. Return to heat, and stir until caramel dissolves and mixture is slightly thickened. Pour into a 9-inch round cake pan. Place pan in cold water to harden caramel.

3. In a large bowl, whisk together eggs and egg yolks until frothy. Whisk in salt and remaining ⅓ cup sugar.

4. In a small saucepan, heat milk and cream over medium heat just until bubbles form around sides of pan. (Do not boil.) Slowly add hot milk mixture to egg mixture, whisking until sugar dissolves. Stir in vanilla. Strain through a fine-mesh sieve into caramel-coated pan. Place cake pan in a shallow baking pan, and pour hot water into baking pan to come 1 inch up sides. Cover baking pan with foil.

5. Bake until a knife inserted near edge comes out clean, 45 to 50 minutes. Let cool completely on a wire rack. Refrigerate until ready to serve. Run a thin knife around edges to loosen, and invert onto serving platter.

Aunt Peggy and me.

EVERYTHING SEASONING-ROASTED CAULIFLOWER

Cauliflower is one of my favorite substitutes for potatoes, and I love experimenting with fun ways to cook it. My favorite part is the mayonnaise spread over the steamed cauliflower; it helps give it a crispy edge while packing in a ton of flavor.

Makes 4 to 6 servings

- 2 teaspoons salt
- 1 large head cauliflower
- 2 tablespoons salted butter, melted
- ¼ teaspoon garlic powder
- ½ cup mayonnaise
- 3 tablespoons everything bagel seasoning
- ½ teaspoon crushed red pepper

1. In an 8- to 10-inch cast-iron skillet, pour water to a depth of ½ inch; add salt, and bring to a boil over medium-high heat. Add cauliflower, stem side down; cover skillet with foil. Cook until cauliflower is just tender, about 8 minutes. Remove cauliflower, and let drain, stem side down, on a wire rack for 15 minutes. Wipe skillet dry.

2. Preheat oven to 425°.

3. In same skillet, place cauliflower stem side down.

4. In a small bowl, stir together melted butter and garlic powder. Slowly drizzle butter mixture into center of cauliflower. Spread mayonnaise all over cauliflower; sprinkle everything seasoning and red pepper all over cauliflower.

5. Bake for 25 to 30 minutes. Rotate skillet; bake until golden brown and a knife inserted in center of cauliflower comes out easily, 5 to 8 minutes more.

Recipe Tip

Not all everything bagel seasonings are created equal. Some contain a ton of salt, while others have none! With your seasoning in mind, play around with the spice mixture until it's to the saltiness you like.

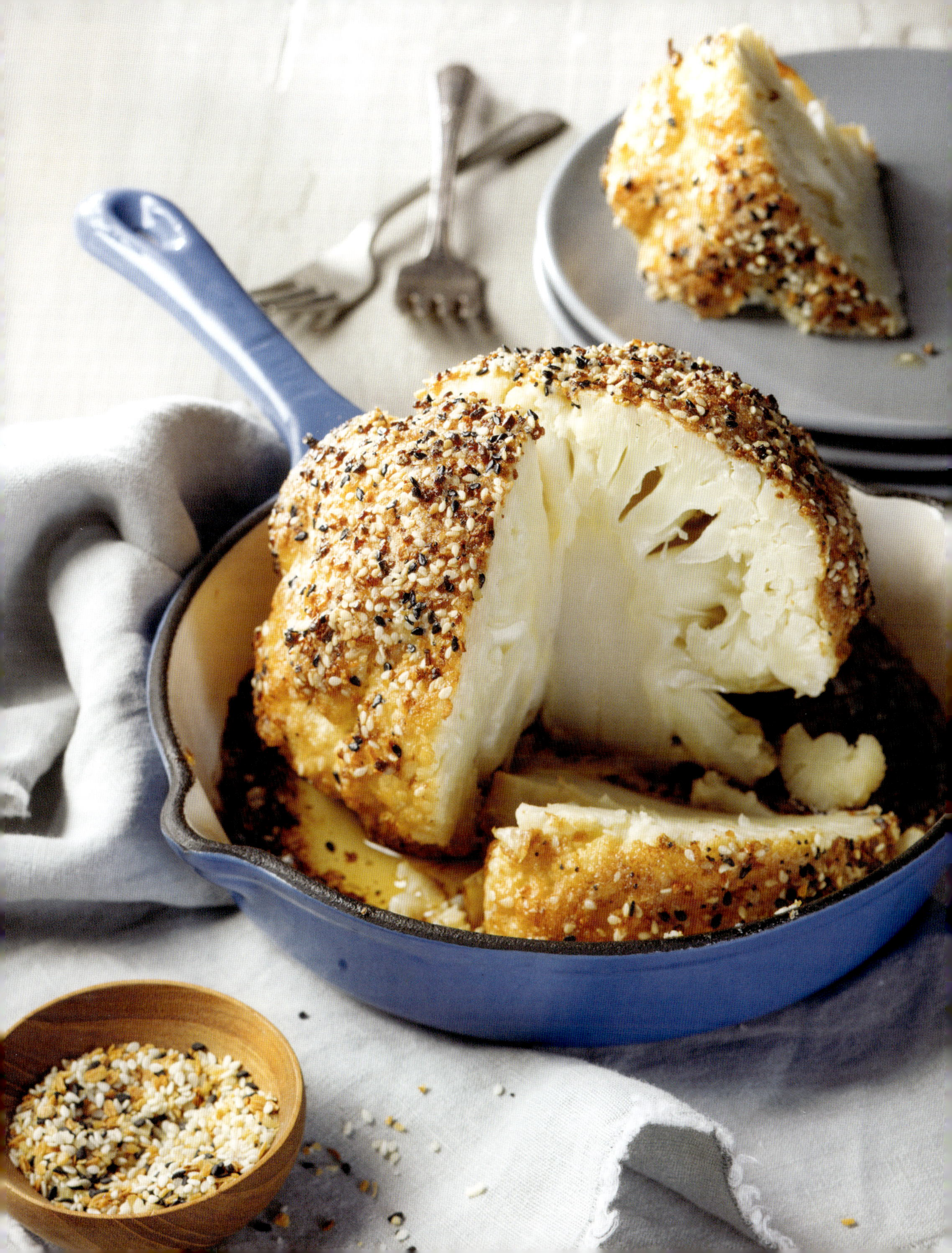

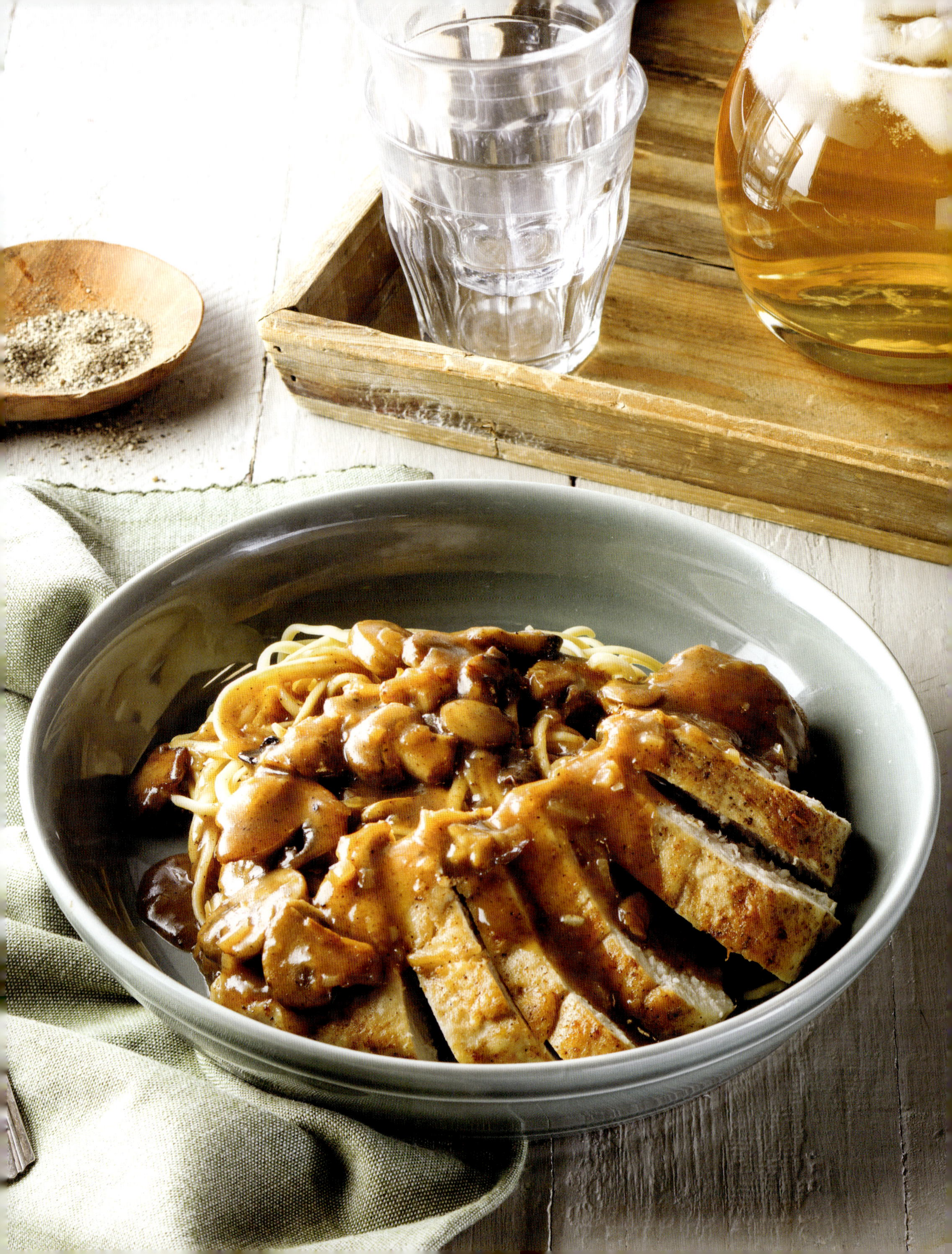

CHICKEN MARSALA

This favorite dish is full of succulent flavors that are perfect for a cozy fall dinner. It pairs well with a variety of sides. I like to eat mine over pasta or mashed cauliflower.

Makes 4 to 6 servings

- ¼ cup olive oil
- 4 (9-ounce) boneless skinless chicken breasts
- 1½ teaspoons salt, divided
- ½ teaspoon ground black pepper
- 1 (8-ounce) package sliced fresh baby portobello mushrooms
- 1 shallot, chopped
- 1 cup Marsala wine
- 1 cup chicken broth
- 1 tablespoon cornstarch
- 1 tablespoon water
- Hot cooked pasta, to serve

1. In a large skillet, heat oil over medium heat.

2. Sprinkle chicken with 1 teaspoon salt and pepper. Add chicken to skillet, and cook until browned and an instant-read thermometer inserted in thickest portion registers 165°, 6 to 8 minutes per side. Transfer chicken to a plate, and keep warm.

3. Add mushrooms, shallot, and remaining ½ teaspoon salt to skillet; cook over medium heat until softened, about 4 minutes. Add wine and broth, and bring to a boil; reduce heat, and simmer.

4. In a small bowl, stir together cornstarch and 1 tablespoon water; whisk into sauce, and simmer, whisking constantly, until thickened, about 1 minute.

5. Slice chicken, and top with sauce. Serve immediately over pasta.

Something that brings me great joy is my work with two organizations that are very close to my heart. In 2012, I started The Bag Lady Foundation to provide food, education, and support for women and families in need. I am also involved with Lee and Kim Greenwood and the wonderful Helping a Hero organization that provides specially adapted homes to injured veterans.

CLAM CHOWDER

Based on traditional New England clam chowder, this recipe uses both clam broth and seafood stock to help elevate the sweet saltiness of the clams. The rich flavor is perfect to warm you up during cold winter nights.

Makes 10 cups

- 4 tablespoons salted butter
- ¾ cup finely chopped yellow onion
- ⅓ cup finely chopped celery
- 2 (6.5-ounce) cans clams in broth, drained, minced, and broth reserved
- 7 cups diced peeled russet potatoes
- 2 (8-ounce) bottles clam juice
- 2 cups seafood stock
- 1 teaspoon salt
- ¼ teaspoon garlic powder
- ¼ teaspoon ground white pepper
- ½ cup heavy whipping cream

French bread, to serve

Garnish: crumbled cooked bacon, minced fresh parsley

1. In a large saucepan, melt butter over medium-high heat. Reduce heat to medium-low, and add onion and celery; cook, stirring occassionally, until tender, about 10 minutes. Add reserved clam broth. Stir in potatoes, clam juice, stock, salt, garlic powder, and white pepper. Bring to a boil; reduce heat, and simmer until potatoes are very tender, about 15 minutes. Add cream, stirring well.

2. Using a handheld immersion blender in a deep bowl, or using a regular blender, purée 2 cups soup. Return purée to pot, stirring until combined. Add minced clams, and cook until heated through. Serve with French bread. Garnish with bacon and parsley, if desired.

Recipe Tip

Clams, oysters, and scallops can be used interchangeably in recipes. Try this chowder with oysters or scallops for a new twist on a classic.

Whoopie!

Eggless chocolate cake is made even better when topped with a frosting like this!

GRAMMY LANGLEY'S CHOCOLATE CAKE

When Eddie moved down here with us, he brought with him a whole lot of his family recipes. This is by far my favorite. The first time I tried it, it made my tongue want to slap my brains out. It was so good!

Makes 1 (9-inch) cake

- 3 cups all-purpose flour
- 2 cups sugar
- ⅔ cup unsweetened cocoa powder
- 2 teaspoons baking soda
- 1 teaspoon salt
- 2 cups cold water
- ⅔ cup vegetable oil
- 2 teaspoons vanilla extract
- 2 teaspoons vinegar

FROSTING

- 1 cup salted butter, softened
- 4 tablespoons shortening
- 2½ cups confectioners' sugar
- 1 (16-ounce) container marshmallow crème
- 4 teaspoons vanilla extract

Garnish: unsweetened cocoa powder

1. Preheat oven to 350°. Spray 2 (9-inch) round cake pans with baking spray with flour.

2. In a large bowl, whisk together flour, sugar, cocoa, baking soda, and salt. Add 2 cups cold water, oil, vanilla, and vinegar. Beat with a mixer at low speed just until smooth. Divide batter between prepared pans.

3. Bake until a wooden pick inserted in center comes out clean, 25 to 30 minutes. Let cool in pans for 10 minutes. Remove from pans, and let cool completely on wire rack.

4. For frosting: In a large bowl, beat butter and shortening with a mixer at medium speed until combined. Slowly beat in confectioners' sugar. Beat in marshmallow crème and vanilla until well combined. Spread frosting between cake layers and on top and sides of cake. Garnish with cocoa, if desired.

SQUASH CROQUETTES

Most people know about salmon croquettes as the famous Southern staple, but I prefer this version. These fried Squash Croquettes deserve the same level of popularity; they're that good, y'all!

Makes 40

Vegetable oil, for frying
2   cups yellow cornmeal mix
1½ cups all-purpose flour
2   tablespoons baking powder
1   tablespoon chopped fresh thyme
1   teaspoon salt
1   teaspoon ground black pepper
1¾ cups whole buttermilk
1   cup grated yellow squash
1   cup grated zucchini
⅓   cup finely chopped onion
⅓   cup sour cream
2   large eggs, lightly beaten

1. In a large skillet, pour oil to a depth of 1 inch, and heat over medium-high heat.

2. In a large bowl, whisk together cornmeal, flour, baking powder, thyme, salt, and pepper.

3. In a medium bowl, whisk together buttermilk, squash, zucchini, onion, sour cream, and eggs. Add to cornmeal mixture, and whisk until just combined.

4. Working in batches, using a 1½-tablespoon spring-loaded scoop, carefully scoop batter into hot oil. Fry until golden brown and cooked through, 3 to 4 minutes. Remove from oil using a slotted spoon, and transfer to wire rack to cool.

Me with President Jimmy Carter. I attended the 75th anniversary party for him and his wife, Rosalynn.

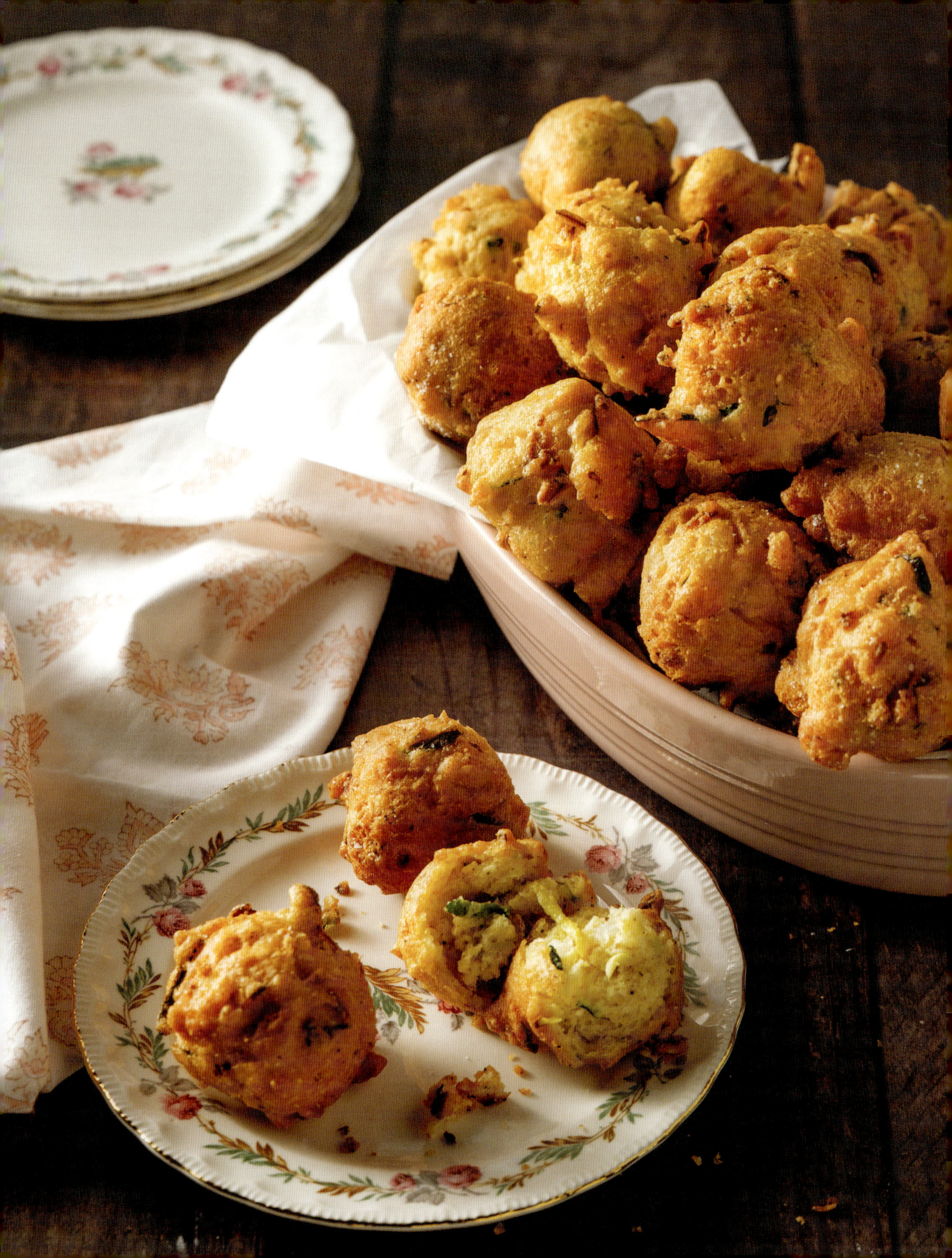

Me with Quinetta Hall in her kitchen.

Q'S CAKES SQUASH CASSEROLE

I met Quinetta Hall—owner of Q's Cakes in Albany, Georgia—through my best friend, Bubbles. Q is a remarkable woman who has rebuilt a life with food after facing some dark times. We share a deep love of cooking, and she was nice enough to share some of her favorite recipes with me. To learn more about Q and her journey, check out her book, Naughti But Neccessari: A Story of Growth. *I have great admiration for this woman.*

Makes 1 (13x9-inch) casserole

- 10 cups water
- 3 tablespoons plus 2 teaspoons salt, divided
- 2½ pounds yellow squash, cut into ⅛-inch slices
- 1 cup diced white onion
- 3 cups buttery round crackers, divided
- 2 cups sour cream
- 2 cups shredded Parmesan cheese, divided
- 2 cups shredded Gouda cheese, divided
- 1 cups heavy whipping cream
- ¾ cup unsalted butter, melted and divided
- 4 large eggs, lightly beaten
- 2 teaspoons ground black pepper

1. In a large stockpot, bring 10 cups water and 3 tablespoons salt to a boil over medium-high heat. Add squash and onion, and cook until just tender, about 5 minutes. Drain.

2. Preheat oven to 350°. Lightly spray a 13x9-inch baking dish with cooking spray

3. In a large bowl, stir together squash mixture, 1½ cups crackers, sour cream, 1 cup Parmesan, 1 cup Gouda, heavy cream, ½ cup melted butter, eggs, pepper, and remaining 2 teaspoons salt. Pour into prepared pan.

4. In a medium bowl, stir together remaining 1½ cups crackers, remaining 1 cup Parmesan, remaining 1 cup Gouda, and remaining ¼ cup melted butter. Sprinkle on top of squash mixture.

5. Bake until golden brown and set in center, 30 to 35 minutes. Let cool for 10 minutes before serving.

PECAN PIE MINI MUFFINS

Eddie, Sandy, and I once went to a murder mystery event together with Jimmy and Rosalynn Carter in Plains, Georgia. We rode a train to an old hotel to have lunch, and everyone's meal came with two little muffins. We all kept asking for more! We loved those muffins so much I recreated them once we got home to Savannah.

Makes 24

- 1 cup firmly packed light brown sugar
- 1 cup chopped pecans
- ½ cup all-purpose flour
- ⅔ cup salted butter, melted
- 2 large eggs, lightly beaten

1. Preheat oven to 350°. Spray a 24-cup mini muffin pan with baking spray with flour.

2. In a large bowl, stir together brown sugar, pecans, and flour.

3. In a small bowl, whisk together melted butter and eggs. Stir butter mixture into sugar mixture. Divide batter among prepared muffin cups.

4. Bake until tops begin to brown, about 10 minutes. Remove from pans, and let cool completely on wire racks.

As I was writing this book, I got a package from a fan. I get the most wonderful homemade gifts from my fans—I have a storage unit full of them from over the years! Something I joke about a lot on my YouTube channel is when Eddie is filming me, I always say, "No butt shots, Eddie," as I bend down to take something out of the oven. A wonderful woman made me this "backward apron" to wear while I film. Have I mentioned how much I adore my fans?

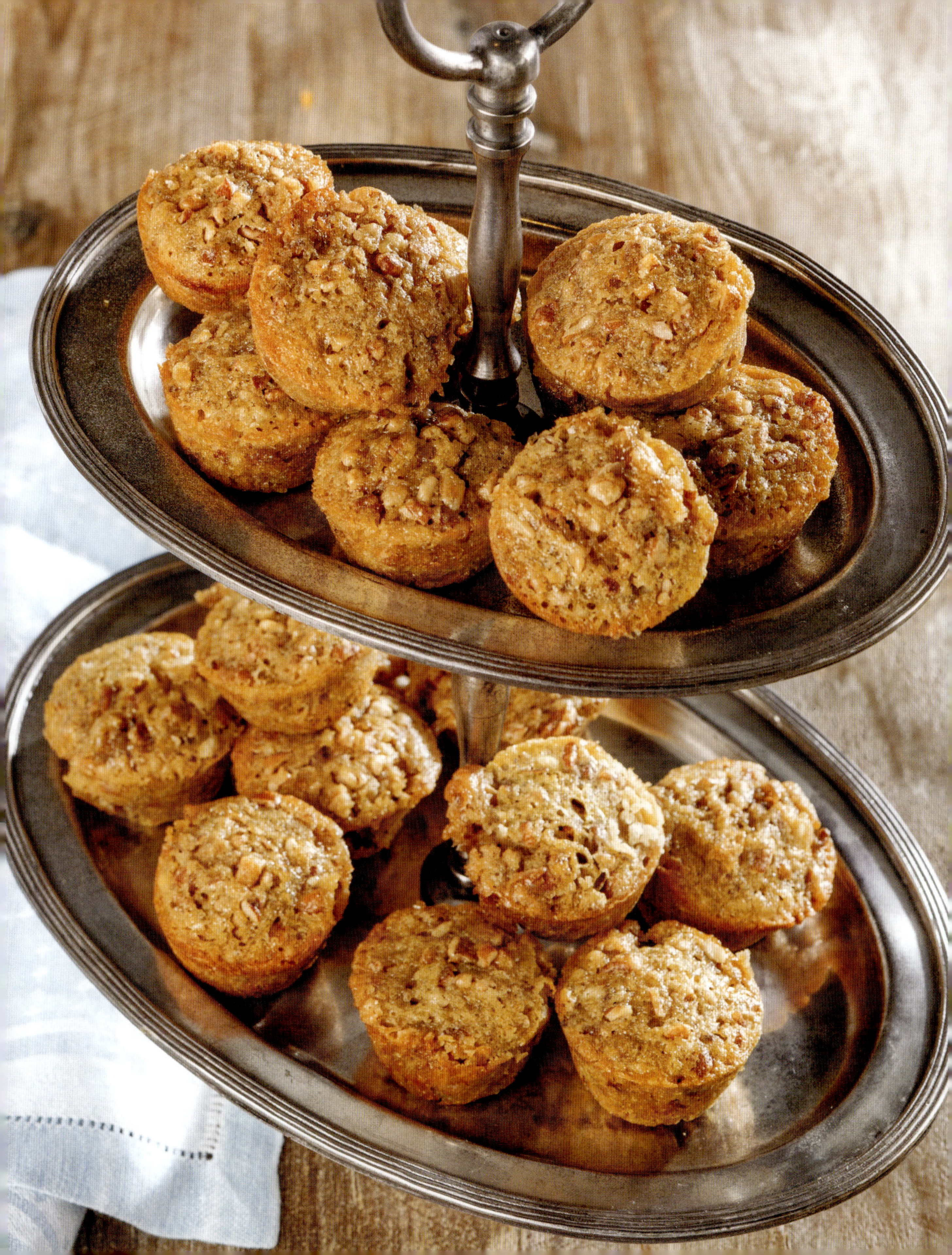

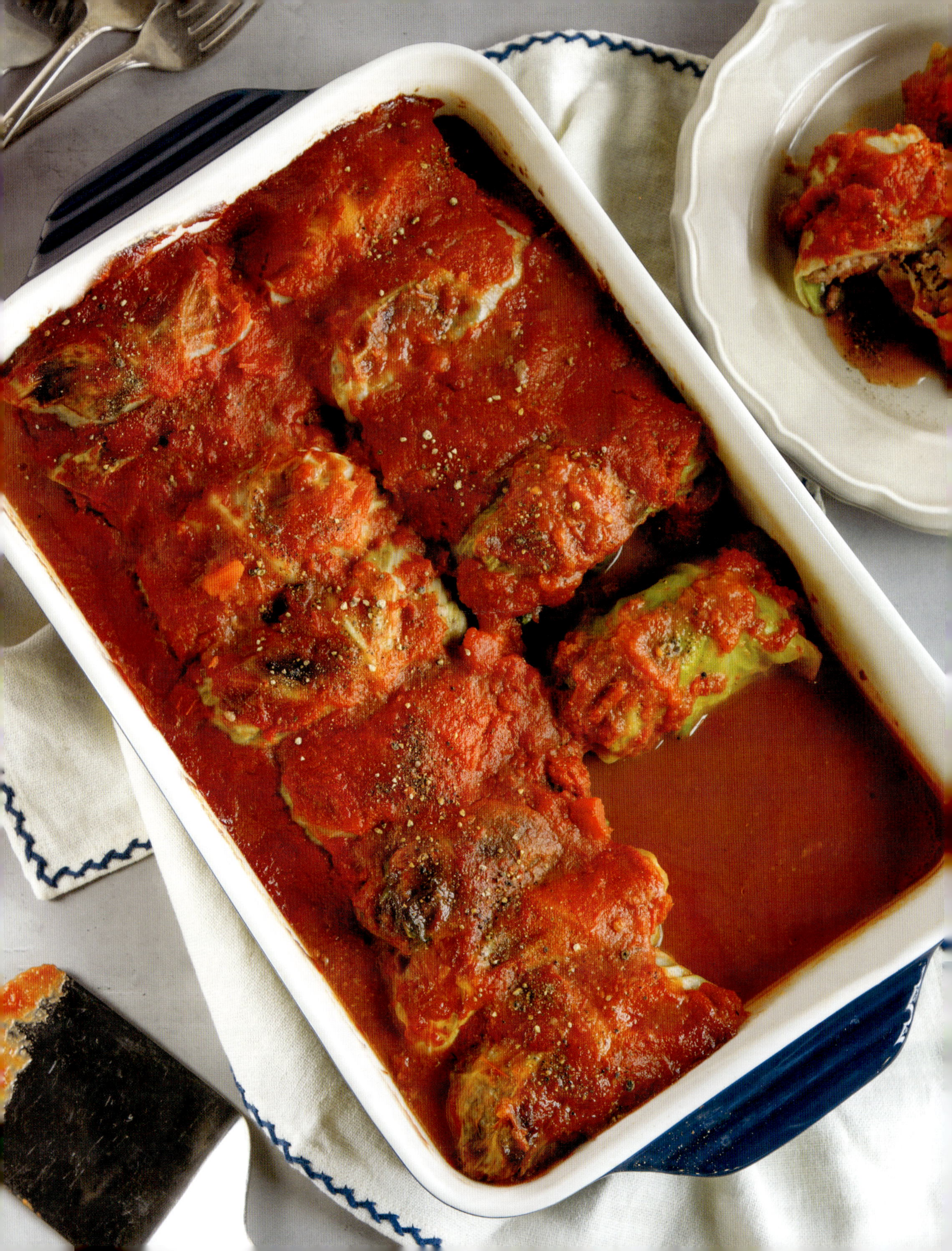

STUFFED CABBAGE ROLLS

This is another recipe from Eddie's father, Stan, whose family came from Poland. This will become your new favorite way to cook cabbage!

Makes about 8 servings

- 1 large head green cabbage, cored
- 2 teaspoons salt, divided
- ¼ cup finely chopped onion
- 2 slices bacon, chopped
- 1 pound lean ground beef
- 1 pound lean ground pork
- 1 cup cooked long-grain rice
- 1 large egg
- ¾ teaspoon garlic powder
- ¾ teaspoon ground black pepper
- 1 (28-ounce) can crushed tomatoes
- 2 tablespoons firmly packed light brown sugar
- 2 cups tomato juice

1. Preheat oven to 350°. Spray a 13x9-inch baking dish with cooking spray.

2. In a large stockpot, add cabbage, 1 teaspoon salt, and enough water to cover. Cook over medium heat until leaves are softened enough to separate, one at a time, with tongs. Drain leaves well. Reserve 16 large leaves. Trim veins from each leaf.

3. In a small saucepan, cook onion and bacon over medium heat, stirring occasionally, until onion is tender and bacon is crispy, about 8 minutes. Remove from heat.

4. In a large bowl, mix together onion mixture, beef, pork, rice, egg, garlic powder, pepper, and remaining 1 teaspoon salt. Pack a small amount of mixture (¼ to ⅓ cup) in center of each leaf. (Do not overstuff.) Fold long sides of leaves over filling; starting at stem end, roll up leaves. Place, seam side down, in prepared pan.

5. In a small bowl, stir together tomatoes and brown sugar until combined. Pour mixture over cabbage rolls. Pour tomato juice to cover rolls. Loosely cover with foil.

6. Bake for 30 minutes. Uncover and bake until an instant-read thermometer inserted in meat registers 160° and cabbage is tender, 30 to 45 minutes more.

SWEET-AND-SPICY HAM-AND-TURKEY SLIDERS

During football season, everyone loves a simple recipe to enjoy while watching the game. These sandwiches are perfect for your next tailgate for an easy grab-and-go treat for your family and friends!

Makes 12

- ¼ cup salted butter
- 1 tablespoon grated onion
- ½ teaspoon sugar
- ½ teaspoon Worcestershire sauce
- 1½ teaspoons sesame seeds
- 1 (12-ounce) package Hawaiian rolls, halved horizontally
- ½ cup red pepper jelly
- 3 tablespoons stone-ground mustard
- ⅓ pound thinly sliced smoked ham
- ⅓ pound thinly sliced smoked turkey
- 6 slices Swiss cheese

1. Preheat oven to 350°.

2. In a small saucepan, cook butter, onion, sugar, and Worcestershire over medium heat, stirring frequently, until butter is melted and onion is translucent, about 5 minutes. Remove from heat, and stir in sesame seeds.

3. Brush ½ butter mixture onto cut sides of rolls, and place bottom half of rolls in a 13x9-inch baking dish. Brush cut side of bottom half with jelly; brush cut side of top half with mustard. Layer bottom half with ham, turkey, cheese, and top half of rolls; brush with remaining butter mixture. Cover with foil.

4. Bake until cheese is melted, about 15 minutes. Cut into sandwiches, and serve immediately.

Recipe Tip

If you can't find pepper jelly, grab a jar of apricot preserves, and heat it up on the stove. Add in some chili powder until it reaches a spice level you enjoy. This makeshift version adds the spicy sweetness found in traditional pepper jelly.

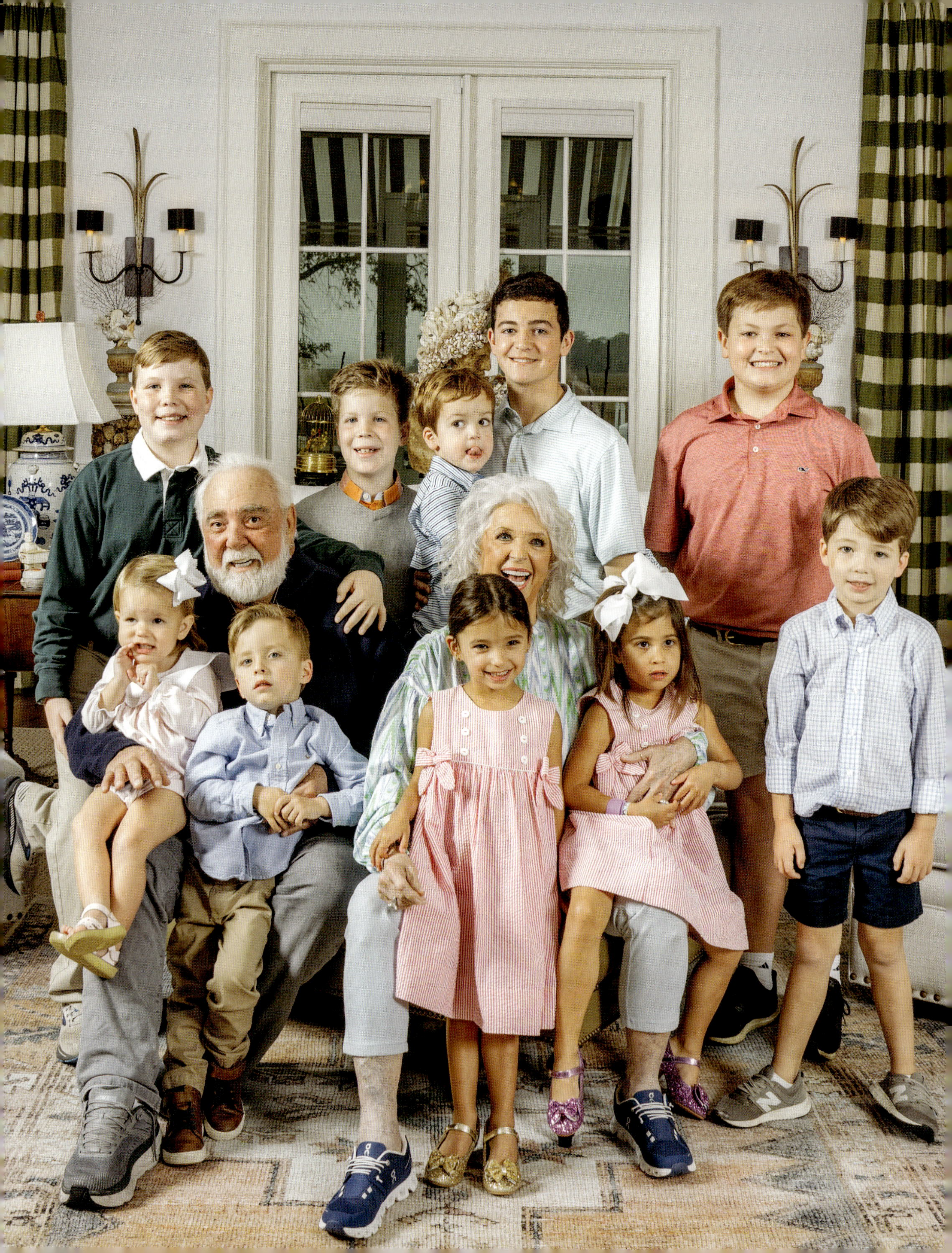

To my precious grandbabies,

In my wildest dreams, I could not have imagined that I'd ever become a grandmother to 11 amazing grandchildren. You are my biggest joy—my heart and soul. When I lay my head down at night, I am at peace because I know how much your parents love you and that you will all continue to grow into wonderful, kind, and smart young people. I am forever in your corner and always your biggest fan!

Love,
Ginny

RECIPE INDEX

APPETIZERS AND DIPS
Bean Dip 226
Blueberry Cream Cheese Spread 173
Cheese Appetizers 108
Chicken and Dumpling Fritters with Sage Gravy 193
Crab Cakes 178
Green Onion Mini Quiches 72
Layered Shrimp Dip 95
Okra Hoecakes 21
Pimento Cheese 100
Salmon Dip 146
Shrimp Puffs 52

BREAKFASTS AND BREADS
Apple Bacon Sticky Buns 206
Avocado Toast 222
    Bacon Chowchow 222
    Fried Egg 222
    Smoked Salmon 222
    Tomato-Radish 222
Banana Pancakes 166
Blueberry Muffins 213
Bubba's Beer Biscuits 30
Mexican Cornbread 169
Pecan Pie Mini Muffins 244
South Georgia Icebox Rolls 65
Sweet Potato Biscuits 69
Vegetable Pancakes 198

CAKES AND COOKIES
Aunt Glennis's Pound Cake 66
Aunt Trina's Fruitcake Cookies 47
Butter Nut Cake 26
Cherry Christmas Cookies 61
Chocolate Pound Cake 55
Coconut Cream Cake 79
Elvis Presley Cake 40
Grammy Langley's Chocolate Cake 239
Johnny Appleseed Cake 39
Lace Cookies 99
Lady Bird Cake 214
Old-Fashioned Tea Cakes 18
Pecan Crisps 218
Red Velvet Cake 29
Strawberry Cake 153
Thin and Crispy Chocolate Chip Cookies 161
Volcano Cake 217

CASSEROLES AND BAKES
Bayou Casserole 44
Corn Casserole 76
Deviled Seafood Casserole 117
Luncheon Seafood Bake 35
Pimento Cheese Tomato Bake 87
Q's Cakes Squash Casserole 243
Savannah Breakfast Casserole 96
Zucchini-Corn Casserole 190

MAINS
Bacon-Wrapped, Sausage-Stuffed Pork Tenderloin 186
Barbecue Shrimp 225
Beaufort Shrimp Pie 185
Beef Ribs 170
Cheeseburger Meat Loaf with Cheese Sauce 120
Chicken-Fried Pork Chops with Gravy 123
Chicken-Fried Steak with Milk Gravy 75
Chicken Marsala 235
Chili-Rubbed Salmon Topped with Avocado Tomato Salsa 165
Crab Fried Rice 114
Everything Seasoning-Roasted Cauliflower 232
Grilled Peanut Butter Ham 139
Jambalaya 56
Marinated Shrimp and Artichoke Hearts 194
Meatballs 149
Mushroom-Stuffed Baked Red Snapper 181
Pecan-Crusted Chicken Thighs 201

Pork Chops 51
Roast Pork with Plum
    Sauce 197
Roasted Chicken 177
Scallops Charleston 150
Stuffed Cabbage Rolls 247
Sweet-and-Spicy Ham-
    and-Turkey Sliders 248

PIES, PUDDINGS, AND TREATS

Blueberry Cream Pie 84
Caramel Custard 231
Chocolate Trifle 103
Fresh Cranberry Salad 62
Glazed Honey Bars 210
Gooey Butter Cake Bars 107
Homestyle Banana
    Pudding 36
Lemon Meringue Pie 154
Lemon Tart with Almond
    Crust 142
Rich Butterscotch Pie 25
Savannah Tiramisù 132

SAUCES, SEASONING, AND CREAM

Barbecue Sauces 22
    Earl's Barbecue
        Sauce 22
    Uncle George's
        Barbecue Sauce 22
Creamy Sweet Onion
    Potato Sauce 203
French Cream 104
House Seasoning 119

SIDES

Broccoli Soufflé 80
Buttered Rutabagas 127
Garlic Potato Salad 124
Parmesan Asparagus 58
Saturday Night Vidalia
    Onions 88
Savannah Red Rice 162
Sherry-Glazed Sweet
    Potatoes 131
Skillet Black-Eyed Peas 32
Squash Croquettes 240
Sweet Potato Chips 109
The Lady's Cheesy Mac 136
Turnip Greens with
    Cornmeal Dumplings
    128

SOUPS AND SALADS

Brunswick Stew 145
Cajun Clam Delight 59
Clam Chowder 236
Cream of Artichoke Soup 83
French Onion Soup 209
Green Pea Salad 118
Jamie's Chicken Salad 92
Michael's World-Famous
    Tuna Fish Salad 158
Pasta Salad 182
Soda Cracker Salad 174
Veggie Salad 135

ALL THE REST

Corrie's Eggnog 48
Dill Pickles 228
Benne Wafers 110
Potato Cakes 202

CREDITS

Editorial

CHAIRMAN OF THE BOARD
Phyllis Hoffman DePiano
CHIEF EXECUTIVE OFFICER
Eric Hoffman
PRESIDENT/CHIEF CREATIVE OFFICER
Brian Hart Hoffman
VP/CULINARY & CUSTOM CONTENT
Brooke Michael Bell
EDITORIAL DIRECTOR **Anna Hartzog**
ART DIRECTOR **Cailyn Haynes**
SENIOR PROJECT EDITOR
Lauren Gentry
PROJECT EDITOR **Kristi Fleetwood**
ASSISTANT PROJECT EDITOR
Savannah Donald
SENIOR COPY EDITOR
Meg Lundberg
TEST KITCHEN DIRECTOR
Laura Crandall
FOOD STYLISTS
Kathleen Kanen, Vanessa Rocchio
PROP STYLISTS **Lucy Finney,
Maggie Hill, and Mary Beth Jones**
PHOTOGRAPHERS
**Jim Bathie, Kyle Carpenter,
and Mac Jamieson**
SENIOR DIGITAL IMAGING SPECIALIST
Delisa McDaniel

Cover

PHOTOGRAPHY **Kelli Boyd**
HAIR AND MAKEUP **Emily Peterson**

Production & Marketing

EVP/OPERATIONS & MANUFACTURING
Greg Baugh
VP/DIGITAL MEDIA **Jon Adamson**
VP/MARKETING **Kristy Harrison**
MARKETING COORDINATOR
Morgan Barbay

Bob McManus and me.

Mike Styer and Eddie Zorawowicz.

ACKNOWLEDGEMENTS

There are so many people whose hard work and support helped this book come to life.

As always, I want to share my sincerest gratitude to my family, friends, fans, and supporters. Thank you for your love. Thank you for believing in me. Thank you for lifting me up time and time again.

To the president of Paula Deen Ventures, Steve Nanula, thank you for everything. We have traveled down a long road together, and we survived, buddy!

Many, many thanks to a man who willingly came into our lives at possibly the lowest point of my career, Bob McManus, CEO of Paula Deen Ventures. He has made the most incredible partner a person could ask for. Bob believed in me, and he has my total trust and confidence. We have gone on to open five fabulous Paula Deen Family Kitchen restaurants throughout Tennessee, South Carolina, Missouri, and Alabama together. Thank you, partner, for being the man you are!

I also want to thank the wonderful people at my local office, Cassie Powers, Kinzie Collett, Stephanie Peay, Theresa Feuger, and Karl Schumacher, as well as my corporate office, Monica Gotshall, Kathy Ratliff, Mark Prior, and Paul Delahunt. Your hard work and dedication mean the world to me, and I could not keep this ship running without you!

To Phyllis Hoffman DePiano and the staff at Hoffman Media and 83 Press, thank you for not only bringing *Cooking with Paula Deen* magazine to life but also this very special book. I'm so grateful for everything we've achieved together!

Thank you to my wonderful hair and makeup artist, Emily Peterson, and to Mike Styer, Jason Parrish, and Eddie Zorawowicz for helping me run my household—and my life! I am endlessly grateful for you.

Love and Best Dishes,

Paula